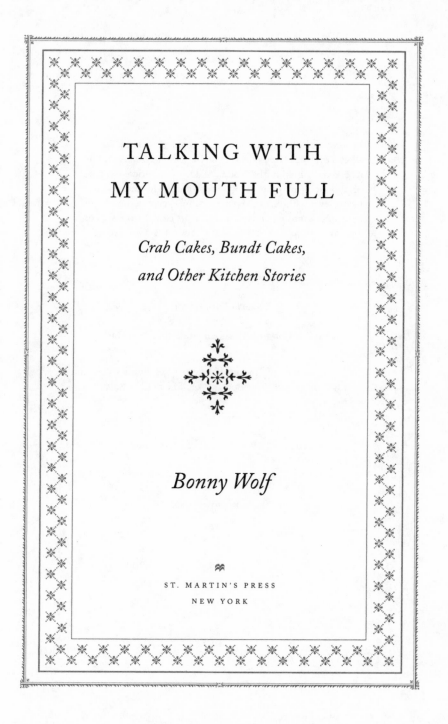

TALKING WITH
MY MOUTH FULL

Crab Cakes, Bundt Cakes,
and Other Kitchen Stories

Bonny Wolf

ST. MARTIN'S PRESS

NEW YORK

www.stmartins.com

Design by Fritz Metsch

Library of Congress Cataloging-in-Publication Data

Wolf, Bonny.
    Talking with my mouth full: crab cakes, Bundt cakes, and other kitchen stories / Bonny Wolf; foreword by Scott Turow.
      p. cm.
    ISBN-13: 978-0-312-35357-5
    ISBN-10: 0-312-35357-X
    1. Cookery.   2. Food habits—United States.   I. Title.
  TX714.W638 2006
  641—dc22   2006045580

FIRST EDITION: NOVEMBER 2006

10 9 8 7 6 5 4 3 2 1

For my parents,

FERN AND AL WOLF,

*who taught me the wonders of life at the table,
and for my husband,*

MICHAEL LEVY,

and my son,

JONATHAN LEVY,

with whom I have so enjoyed the lessons learned

※

CONTENTS

�֎   �֎   ✷

FOREIGN FOOD

ACKNOWLEDGMENTS

We should look for someone to eat and drink
with before looking for something to eat and drink,
for dining alone is leading the life of a lion or wolf.

EPICURUS

ONE OF the big attractions of cooking and eating is that it's a communal activity. I have been fortunate to share my table with a big family, kind and generous friends, and publishing professionals of the highest order.

I worked with Al McConagha years ago at a newspaper where I learned that he is not only a lyrical writer and fine reporter but also a careful editor. He wins the above-and-beyond-the-call prize for reading every word I wrote before I sent it out for anyone else to see. I could not have written this book without his gentle but honest criticism. I also thank Pam Fessler, another reporter for whom I have great respect, for her editorial and emotional support.

I especially want to thank Stu Seidel, the senior editor of National Public Radio's *Weekend Edition Sunday,* for giving me the chance to be on his terrific show and for the crash course in radio. I am also grateful to Beth Donovan, who put me in the *Kitchen Window* on NPR's Web site.

My agent, Randi Murray, is a woman of tremendous patience, kind forbearance, and enormous talent. She has walked me through every baby step of this process, holding my hand the whole time. Finding her was remarkable beginner's luck. My good fortune continued with my editor, Elizabeth Beier. She is a writer's dream: available, supportive, skilled, and smart. She also loves to cook and eat. I thank them both for making this such a pleasant undertaking.

My friends have been a source of tremendous sustenance. Kate Richardson and I have been friends since we were twelve. We've lived half a country apart for more than thirty years but are in almost daily contact. Not only did she send notes, clippings, and e-mails, but a couple of jars of huckleberry jam, too, just when I needed them.

Marcie and Bill Ferris were the first ones to look at the pieces I'd written for newspapers and radio and suggest a book. I thank them for that and for their never-flagging support.

As you'll gather in the following pages, I love my Washington, D.C., neighborhood. In addition to the location, the Victorian townhomes, and the Eastern Market, I love my neighbors. Stephanie Deutsch was the first person I met when I moved to Washington in the mid-1980s, and we have cooked and eaten together with our families ever since. She has been endlessly supportive with tasting, tea, and sympathy.

I go to the gym and Spanish class every week with a group of neighborhood women who have not only listened to me patiently, but have also shared both their stories and their recipes. Talking is exercise, right? Thank you, Elizabeth Becker, Gayle Krughoff, Carol Press, Megan Rosenfeld, and Lis Wackman. I also want to thank Carol's husband, Bill, for all the great family recipes.

But I'm not a complete parochial. Allison Beck lives in Northwest Washington and has not only been a great family recipe source but the return address on those unexpected treats in the mail, as well. She knows that a girl needs bubble bath. And Nancy Leopold of Bethesda, Maryland, has been available at the other end of the phone line for life-support needs, night or day.

Susan Lindeborg is a first-rate chef and a first-class friend. She has patiently explained many of food's mysteries to me. I also extend my heartfelt thanks to Scott and Annette Turow for their support and recipes.

There are many, many others—family and friends—who have cheerfully eaten at what my son calls "odd food events" and responded to mass e-mails looking for particular recipes. I thank you all.

I am fortunate to have a large, warm, loving family. I thank them all for their support, cheerleading, and public relations efforts.

My husband, Michael Levy, and my son, Jonathan Levy, have shown true grit through this whole experience. Every meal was an adventure and potential disaster. On the ninth or so try with one recipe, Jonathan said, "We eat more pasties than a mining family." They also do dishes, for which I am eternally grateful. Michael read innumerable drafts of every word I wrote and always said a kind word before offering constructive criticism. Jonathan, too, turned out to be an excellent editor. There are no two people I enjoy being with more.

FOREWORD

✳   ✳   ✳

EVERYBODY EATS, although there are women of the type Tom Wolfe years ago dubbed "social x-rays," who appear to make do only on the watered fruit juice they allow themselves following their daily workouts. Those ghosts aside, all of us succumb to food's temptation every day. Which means a book about food may be as close as one can come to a subject of universal interest.

Yet most writing about food somehow fails its potential unlimited audience. It's haughty or technical or arcane. This book has none of those failings—it's funny (like Bonny Wolf's paean to Thanksgiving—"pure gluttony with no religious overtones"), practical (look, even recipes!), and fully aware of food's relentless presence in our lives. Indeed, I would call *Talking with My Mouth Full* sneaky-serious, in the sense that it made me reconsider the huge space food claims within our lives. There are meditations here on the clever inventions that have added to the joy of eating and cooking, such as the Bundt pan or aprons, and on the social history embedded in distinctive foods. But what is at the heart of this book are the intimate connections that food makes in families, the politically incorrect but somewhat imperturbable links that have been forged between generations of women who take vital pride in nurturing their husbands and children. Anyone, male or female, in front of a stove joins hands with ancestors going back to Eve.

Allow me to inject one direct testimonial: The recipes contained in this book are great. I know this not because I've tried them in my kitchen but because I've enjoyed many in Bonny Wolf's home, where I've had breakfasts, brunches, lunches, and dinners, many of them still retaining a hallowed spot in the memory senses tied to my taste buds.

In my life, Bonny—and her husband, Michael Levy—were acquired by marriage. My wife, Annette (who turns up by reference now and then in these pages), and Bonny were summer students in Paris during college. They established a fond friendship, but the peregrinations of postcollegiate years—marriage, several apartments, graduate programs—had left them out of touch until a review of my first book, *One L,* appeared in *The New York Times.* Bonny took note of the itsy-bitsy credit beside the author's photograph, which identified Annette, and tracked her down through my publisher, at which point Annette dashed off to Rutgers in New Jersey to renew acquaintances. She came back talking not only about Michael, whom Bonny had married in the interval, but also about the meals they ate—at least one a celestial experience in New York's Little Italy.

Since then, Bonny and Michael have not been out of our lives, and it is a friendship that's included many great gustatory experiences. A number of years ago, when Bonny and Michael were visiting Minneapolis, where Bonny was raised, we decided to meet at the midpoint between there and our home in Chicago. That turns out to be Lisbon, Wisconsin, which, with respect, is not a resort center. The motel rooms we rented were rustic, at best, but we ate like bon vivants, savoring the elaborate meals that the two women had collaborated on long-distance. Our visits to the Wolf-Levy home always feature great eating and sometimes include food-oriented tours, such as the one to the Eastern Market, Bonny's mecca. These days my adult daughter and nephew are often guests in Bonny's dining room, and whenever I know they're going, they have my undying envy.

If you are anything like me, as you read *Talking with My Mouth Full* you will end up reflecting on the significance to you of foods that seem almost as indispensable as the blood in your veins. Reading Bonny write about the journey of the Bundt pan, I found myself thinking about the way national economics has affected the dishes I treasured growing up. Here in Chicago we have watched the odd migration of Dove Bars, which in these parts means ice cream, not soap. For years, they were a local delicacy, whose magnificence was enhanced by the long trips our fathers had to make to buy them at the South Side store where they were first concocted. Now they are a national phenomenon available to supermarket shoppers coast-to-coast, but with an outer chocolate layer thinned by commerce and no longer an eighth of an inch thick. This is good for nationhood, for residents of places more out of the way, and good for me, when it comes to buying Maine lobsters or Texas chili, but mourning is inevitable for what was a trifle better when it was only our own.

Indeed, Bonny writes often in this book about regional foods—the Maryland crab, or Virginia shad loaded with roe—the consumption of which locals regard as a trip to a sacred shrine. Of all Chicago's local fare, my favorite remains the Vienna Hot Dog, a stalwart that has endured nitrate scares or what Upton Sinclair wrote in *The Jungle*. And she also demonstrates how food can often be the emblem of a proud idiosyncrasy. Reading Bonny describe the perils of buttering toast reminded me about my aunt, a woman of strong opinions, who keeps her butter on a cupboard shelf, unrefrigerated. And there's the famous restorative power of certain meals, starting, of course, with chicken soup. Bonny's mention of cinnamon toast brought to mind a dear friend from Alabama who has a killer recipe she saves only to stave off the darkest despond.

All in all, I found myself moved and fascinated by *Talking with My Mouth Full*, thinking again and again how close food is to the heart of culture and how much it defines places, ethnicities, and, most of all, families. For virtually all of us, the foods we eat reflect a heritage as distinctive as our DNA. And this book is a funny, incisive—and, in every sense, delicious—exploration of those themes.

—SCOTT TUROW

INTRODUCTION

※   ※   ※

Food is our common ground, a universal experience.

JAMES BEARD

ONE OF the first things I did as a young bride in 1972 was to buy a blue loose-leaf, three-ring notebook to contain the recipe inflow from family, friends, newspapers, and magazines. The first month or so, I neatly and carefully glued them onto lined paper separated by category in the following order: appetizers, eggs, vegetables, meat, seafood, Chinese, Italian, soup, bread, sweets, beverages, and chicken. Some of the recipes were typed on a manual typewriter.

By my tenth anniversary, many of the recipes were neatly folded inside the front and back covers. Ten years later "neat" would no longer apply. The Internet was my undoing. Until the arrival of the World Wide Web, I could always easily find what I was looking for. But the information age was too much for my notebook. I began printing out recipes in a frenzy, and had to move the notebook and its offspring to a medium-sized sage green gift bag.

One day, I took a deep breath and decided to go through the bag, prepared to eliminate and organize. In the course of this exercise, I found the story of my life.

I ran into my great-aunts, a few cousins, old family friends, childhood friends, adult friends, and friends from whom I've been separated by decades. I followed myself from Minneapolis (fifteen recipes using wild rice) to Baltimore (crab cakes several ways) to New Jersey (Hungarian chicken paprika) to Texas (real chili) to

Washington, D.C. (the spring shad roe ritual). I revisited small and big life events—the birth of my son and subsequent birthday parties (chicken à la king and Texas sheet cake), the early years of entertaining (five different recipes for "quiche for a crowd" and the chicken divan that was my first dinner party dish), years of travel (chicken molé and sticky toffee pudding), my husband's surprise thirtieth birthday party in a log cabin on the Raritan River (six-foot-long sandwiches using lettuce from our tiny garden).

I remembered my fancy drinks period—kir royales, bellinis, strawberry fizzes, and something called guava glows. Then there were the frozen desserts—ice cream, sorbet, and granita—although the equipment needed to make them is long gone.

The food of Mexico held my interest for years. And seven years in Texas is marked by recipes for salsas, *chili con queso,* and a grease-stained recipe for something called Hot Stuff that I got from my friend Ann, whom I haven't seen or spoken to in more than twenty years. You cook onions, sugar, tomatoes, pepper, ground chilies, and salt for four hours. Then you add vinegar, bring to a boil, and serve on pinto beans or rice. I remember the first time I ate it at her house when we'd just met. After eating her Hot Stuff, I knew I wanted to be her friend. A note at the bottom of the recipe reads: Serve with salad and dessert. Dessert was probably Ann's fabulous chocolate sauce over ice cream. I have the recipe.

In my notebook, there is evidence of my son's four years as a vegetarian. The veal recipes come to an abrupt end in the early 1990s when he asked us to stop eating veal because of his outrage at the mistreatment of male calves.

Judging from the huge numbers of recipes for egg dishes—stratas, omelets, baked eggs—I have spent more than thirty years in search of dishes to serve for brunch. I still haven't found just the right one.

There are a lot of recipes for ways to cook zucchini, probably dating to the trauma of our first garden and its bottomless patch of the green summer squash. My various diets are obvious from the number of recipes for cabbage soup, turkey meat loaf, and oven "fried" chicken. In the early part of the new century, a lot of recipes using whole grains show up. I also possess an unusually large number of recipes using couscous. My friend Annette gave me a recipe for chicken and couscous when I called her twenty-five years ago looking for something to serve at a dinner party. I have it written on the back of an envelope.

My collection of Thanksgiving recipes is one of the largest. It's my favorite holiday—pure gluttony with no religious overtones. Jewish holidays are represented by potato latkes, Sis's Passover cake, my mother-in-law's spectacular chopped liver, and five different recipes for the perfect brisket.

I found the recipes Stephanie and I used for the all-rose-petal dinner we had for our friend Mary when she got married for the second time. It was shortly after the movie *Like Water for Chocolate* came out and we had learned about the aphrodisiac qualities of quail with rose petal sauce. We ordered squab (quail was unavailable) from Melvin, who runs our favorite poultry stand at Capitol Hill's Eastern Market, a block from my house. He knew we were doing something fancy with them. So when we got to Stephanie's and opened the package, the squab were looking at us. He had left the heads and feet on. We ran back for emergency surgery.

I have many, many recipes from my dear friend Eva, with whom I shared countless meals during my seven years in College Station, Texas. Eva grew up in Paris and San Francisco and was a beautiful home cook. Her house was always warm, welcoming, and smelled like freshly baked banana bread. I lit candles all over my house trying for the same effect. But a lot of it was just that she was who she was. I have her lasagna, split pea soup, and banana bread recipes, as well as instructions for some elegant European pastries I'll probably never make. Because, I realized, I'm not a baker. I'm sure some people can do both, but not me. My desserts are generally lackluster. The exceptions are homey fruit desserts, Bundt cakes, and layer cakes. I'm pretty good at those. I have Eva's

recipe for dewberry cobbler using the large black berries found
along the side of Texas roads in the summer. A newspaper recipe
for Italian prune plum torte (the plums are available for only a few
weeks in the fall) is in shreds. I have my friend's Jenifer's recipe for
her grandfather's favorite schaum torte. I make it every spring.

I have two recipes for candy: My father's microwave peanut
brittle and the toffee my mother and I used to make. Minnegasco,
the Minnesota gas company, sent recipes with the gas bill. The toffee was one of them. Both are simple and delicious. The toffee
may have been the first food I learned to cook.

The entrées I serve at dinner parties have changed through the
years. When I started out, everything I did was complicated. If it
wasn't difficult and time-consuming, it couldn't possibly be good. So
I would spend days making pasta by hand, driving miles to find some
exotic spice they didn't carry at the neighborhood A&P, going to the
seafood market for fish heads and bones for the broth necessary for
some extravagant soup. Most of these recipes came from cookbooks. Some of my copies sport handwritten notes reading, "Not
worth the effort." The only one of these I seem to have saved is for
b'stilla, a Moroccan phyllo dough pie of shredded chicken, ground
almonds, and spices. I think I made the phyllo dough by hand. My
mother had photocopied (twice) the recipe from a magazine and
sent it to me. It was worth the effort. Today I can put together a dinner for ten in a couple of hours. It took thirty years to learn how.

I have many recipes my mother cut out of the paper for me or
wrote down and mailed. For the ones she especially liked, I have
multiple copies—for emphasis. There are two photocopies of the
meat loaf in a breadbasket she made my son when he was little.
You cut the top off and hollow out a round sourdough bread loaf,
fill it with meat loaf, and bake it. Kids love it. I have her recipe for
the Spanish tongue my father loved. I will never forget seeing the
tongue in my grandmother's heavy soup pot and suddenly realizing
it was—a tongue. I have three copies—one cut out from a magazine, one photocopy of the same article, and one handwritten—
for a caramelized upside-down pear tart she liked a lot. I have two

recipes—one handwritten, one clipped from the paper—for Dump Dinner. The directions begin: "Cover the table with multiple thicknesses of newspaper." Next you put shrimp-boil spices, water, kielbasa, corn on the cob, pea pods, and shrimp in an "enormous pot." Cook until done, drain everything, and dump in the middle of the table. The directions end: "Eat with gusto."

I have three copies of the same recipe for pasties—the meat-and-vegetable turnovers that are a standard winter dinner in the Upper Midwest. They were brought by Cornish miners who came to work in the northern iron mines. A pasty is a complete meal—a crescent-shaped pie filled with chunks of meat, diced potatoes, and rutabaga.

As I went through these recipes, I realized that I remember most life events by what I ate. Every Valentine's Day on the breakfast table there was a plastic tree hung with red jelly candy hearts. Sunday nights we roasted chestnuts or made popcorn in the fireplace in the family room while watching *Bonanza*. August was the state fair, and that meant pronto pups (relatives of corn dogs).

I learned a lot in my mother's kitchen. As she cooked Aunt Ossie's borscht, Aunt Fanny's pot roast, and Aunt Esther's antipasto, she told me about her own childhood. She told me stories about dinners at her aunts' houses, my paternal grandparents' all-night diner in Chicago, and how my father fell in love with Italian food on rural farmsteads while fighting in Italy in World War II.

One of the most vivid memories I have of my wedding is that I suddenly realized I *did* like asparagus. I remember my husband's swearing-in ceremony as assistant secretary of the Treasury by the empanadas we served. My son's bar mitzvah was cold Russian chicken with walnuts. My father's ninetieth birthday was a chocolate cake with the inscription: 90 Proof, Aged to Perfection.

I went to college in Baltimore, where I met not only my husband but a whole slew of new foods, as well—crabs, snowballs, and coddies. I learned that Chinese food meant more than chow mein. My husband's grandfather was a kosher butcher, a lovely man who came to Baltimore from Poland when he was twelve. He never quite mastered English and read *The Jewish Daily Forward* in

Yiddish every day. Every time he saw me he would say, "Darling, read to me from the paper." I would explain that I could read neither Hebrew nor Yiddish. The next time he saw me he'd say: "Darling, read to me from the paper." This dance went on for a while until one day he varied the request: "Darling, can you cook a chicken?" That, I said, I can do.

My first job was as a copy girl at *The Home News*, a daily newspaper in New Brunswick, New Jersey, home to a large Hungarian community. My husband was a graduate student at Rutgers University and our first dinner parties centered around chicken paprika, a Hungarian dish it seemed appropriate to learn while we were there.

It was my responsibility to deliver corn muffins and coffee to the paper's editors. I had never heard of corn muffins, and some of the guys liked their coffee "light," which meant with cream. For a midwestern girl, this was fascinating.

I was promoted from copy girl to compiler of television listings. From there it was only a short time until I was taking obits. Finally, I was given a chance to cover a story, and it involved food.

In the winter of 1973, the Comet Kohoutek was expected in the western hemisphere. I was assigned to go to the Rutgers University observatory, where astronomers had set up shop. I got there at 3:00 A.M. to find everyone bundled up and eating "meteorite mushrooms" and "eggs Kohoutek" washed down with mugs of Irish coffee. The comet was a dud, but the party was great. And when I got back to the office at 8:00 A.M. and filed my story, my city editor was so pleased, he suggested I always drink Irish whiskey before coming to work.

We moved from there to Texas, where we were set straight about chili and barbecue and learned of the many things that can be done to a jalapeño pepper. In Mexico, we discovered that Tex-Mex food bore little resemblance to the real thing.

When we moved to Washington, D.C., we were drawn to the neighborhood of row houses behind the U.S. Capitol. It is very much like a village within the city. The neighborhood is anchored by the Eastern Market, the city's last remaining public indoor food market. On weekends, farmers set up outside with fresh produce. Our son, like many neighborhood kids, started working there when he was ten.

Our neighbors are our friends and we have had many meals together—a ritual cassoulet to recognize the first snowfall, chili for the Super Bowl, crab feasts in the alley, fund-raising dinners for the neighborhood arts workshop. After September 11, as the Pentagon still smoldered, a group of us ate together every night for a week. It seemed the natural thing to do.

We cook and eat for comfort, nurture, and companionship. We cook and eat to mark the seasons and celebrate important events. We cook and eat to connect with family and friends and with ancestors we never knew. And through this baking and breaking bread together, we come to know who we are and where we came from.

Recipes from My Blue Notebook

✳ PASTIES

Cornish miners brought pasties (pronounced PASS-tees) with them to the United States, and they transferred well to the mines of the Upper Midwest. They stayed warm for hours and could always be put on a shovel and warmed over a candle. Miners often ate the insides, then threw away the crust, ensuring that they wouldn't be poisoned by the arsenic found in some mines. The biggest problem with pasties is that they can be dry. Butter and suet give them some juiciness. Some people use broth or cream instead.

Makes 4 servings

FOR THE CRUST

3 cups unbleached,
   all-purpose flour
½ teaspoon salt
½ cup (1 stick) butter
½ cup Crisco
2 large egg yolks
½ cup cold water

You can mix the pastry by hand or in a food processor. Always looking for simplicity, I use the latter method. Mix the flour and salt and cut in the shortening (the butter *and* Crisco) until it has the texture of cornmeal. Stir in the egg yolks; then add the water, about a tablespoon at a time, and stir until it forms a soft dough. It should not be too wet. If you're using a food processor, transfer the dough to a bowl and gently press the dough together. Shape the dough into 4 balls, wrap in plastic wrap, and refrigerate for at least an hour.

FOR THE FILLING

1 pound round steak
1 small rutabaga, peeled
1 small onion
1 medium potato
2 parsnips, peeled
¼ cup chopped fresh
   parsley
3 cloves garlic, minced
1 tablespoon dried thyme
⅓ cup beef suet, ground
Salt and pepper, to taste

Butter
Milk

Roughly chop the meat in a food processor or cut into ½-inch cubes by hand. All the vegetables can be roughly chopped by hand or in the food processor into ½-inch or smaller pieces. I leave the skin on the potatoes, but they can certainly be peeled. Mix well with the parsley, garlic, thyme, and suet. Season to taste with salt and pepper.

When the dough has been refrigerated at least one hour, roll out the crusts on a lightly floured surface into oblong rather than round shapes, about six inches across. They should not be too thin. Put one-quarter of the filling on half of each crust. Dot with butter. Moisten the edges with a little water. Fold the other half over the filling and press it down along the moistened edge. Crimp the edges with a fork and poke the crust a few times, or cut a few slits so that the steam can escape. (The pasties can be frozen at this point.) Place on a lightly greased baking sheet. Brush a little milk on the top of each pasty.

Preheat the oven to 400°F.
Lightly grease a baking sheet.

Bake the pasties until they are golden brown, about 30 minutes. Serve them hot.

NOTE: Pasties freeze very well. Wrap well before freezing, defrost, and bake as above. It's an easy, quick dinner to have on hand. If you have extra filling, it can be frozen for next time.

✳ RUTH'S CHOPPED LIVER

My mother-in-law makes the best chopped liver this side of Eastern Europe. She says her secret is to sauté the onion first in oil. I told her I thought schmaltz (chicken fat) was supposed to be better. "Go ahead and add a little to the oil if you want. It can't hurt," she said. So I did. She also insists that cold chicken livers are much easier to work with so she recommends overnight refrigeration. You also want good, fresh livers. I added a little brandy. Please don't tell.

Makes 3 to 4 cups

1 large white onion, finely chopped (2 to 2½ cups)
Salt and pepper, to taste
2 tablespoons minced fresh parsley
2 tablespoons vegetable oil
2 tablespoons chicken fat
1½ pounds chicken livers
2 cloves garlic, finely minced
4 hard-boiled eggs (1 for garnish)
1 to 2 tablespoons brandy (optional)

In a large skillet, sauté the onion, salt, pepper, and parsley in the oil and fat. When translucent, remove from the oil. Sauté the livers and garlic until done but not hard. Refrigerate overnight.

Chop one of the eggs in a food processor and set aside for garnish. Then chop the onion, liver, and remaining eggs together in two batches in the food processor. Add the brandy, if using, and mix. Put in a pretty bowl and top with the chopped egg.

✳ LAYERED CHEESE TORTA

While you take your life in your hands by eating a lot of this, it may be worth it. You can buy tortas like this in a lot of specialty stores, but it's really better homemade and it's easy. You can use whatever filling you like including, of course, something you buy in a jar. I usually make it with homemade pesto.

Serves 15 to 20 as an appetizer

1 pound each cream cheese and unsalted butter, at room temperature Filling such as pesto, tapenade, salmon spread, sun-dried tomato spread Cheesecloth Crackers or bread	Mix the cream cheese and butter in an electric mixer or in a food processor until smooth and well blended.

The torta can be molded in anything you like—a loaf pan, a mold, a bowl—that holds about 6 cups. I use a deep ceramic bowl that gives the torta the shape of a beehive. Based on the size and shape of your container, cut two squares of cheesecloth, wet, wring out, and lay flat on top of each other. Use them to line your mold with enough cheesecloth to hang over the edge a little.

When I use pesto, I put a sprig of basil at the bottom of the mold. When it's unmolded, it's on the top of the torta. You can use other garnishes for other spreads.

Place about one-sixth of the cheese in the bottom of the mold over the basil or whatever you've used as a topping. Smooth the top of the layer and cover with one-fifth of the filling. Make sure the filling goes to the edge of the mold so you can see it when it's unmolded. Repeat these layers until the cheese and filling are gone. Finish with a cheese layer.

Fold the excess cheesecloth over the torta and press down to pack together. Chill for about an hour or until the torta feels firm. Don't leave it in the refrigerator too long or the filling will bleed into the cheese. Invert onto a serving plate and carefully remove the cheesecloth. Serve on crackers or bread.

❋ EVA'S BANANA BREAD

I made this banana bread every week for years. It's a perfect way to use overripe bananas and having a loaf in the freezer is useful when you have overnight guests who stay for breakfast or when someone stops by for tea. It's nice warmed in the toaster oven.

Makes 10 to 12 servings

½ cup (1 stick) butter
½ cup honey and ½ cup brown sugar (or 1 cup white sugar)
2 large eggs
2 ripe bananas
1 teaspoon orange juice
1 cup all-purpose flour
1 cup whole wheat flour
3 teaspoons baking powder
½ teaspoon salt
1 cup chopped walnuts
1 (18-ounce) package (1 cup) chopped dates

Preheat the oven to 375°F.
Grease an 8 × 4-inch loaf pan.

Blend the butter, honey, sugar, and eggs well. Add the bananas and orange juice and blend until creamy. In a large bowl, sift together both kinds of flour, the baking powder, and salt. Add to the banana mixture and blend. Add the nuts and dates and stir until just blended. Pour the batter into the loaf pan and cook about 1¼ hours or until a toothpick inserted into the bread comes out clean. Check after an hour.

❋ EVA'S DEWBERRY PIE

In Texas we used dewberries, cousins of blackberries. Any berries would be fine.

Makes 6 to 8 servings

2 cups flour
1 cup (2 sticks) softened butter
½ plus ¼ cup sugar
1 large egg
3 large egg whites

Preheat the oven to 350°F.

Beat together the flour, butter, ½ cup sugar, and egg. With your hands, press the dough into a 3- to 4-inch-deep casserole.

Continued

1 cup finely chopped walnuts or pecans	Beat together the egg whites and ¼ cup sugar. Stir in the nuts and berries. Spread
2 cups berries	this mixture over the dough. Bake for about 1 hour. Some crust will form on top. Serve with whipped cream or ice cream.

❋ GAS COMPANY CANDY

This was one of the recipes sent with our montly gas bills.

Makes ⅓ pound of candy

1 cup chopped walnuts	Spread the nuts in the bottom of a 10 × 6-inch pan.
½ cup (1 stick) butter	
¾ cup light brown sugar, loosely packed	
16-ounce package dark chocolate chips	Boil the butter and brown sugar for 7 minutes, stirring constantly. Pour over the nuts. Pour the chocolate chips on top and spread with a knife when needed. Wait until the toffee hardens and break into pieces. And, from the original recipe, "Keep in gas refrigerator."

GENERATION TO GENERATION

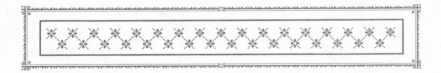

THE LITTLE CAKE PAN
THAT COULD

❋　❋　❋

Want is the mistress of invention.
SUSANNA CENTLIVRE

W HEN H. DAVID DALQUIST died in 2005, many people remembered that somewhere in the house they had one of
the classic pieces of bakeware that he'd invented—a long unused
Bundt pan.

Why did we stop making Bundt cakes? They were so easy and
so beautiful. The cakes were perfectly shaped, evenly browned,
and consistently moist. You could make anything with a Bundt
pan, a cake mix, and some instant pudding. More than 45 million
Bundt pans have been sold, making it the top-selling cake pan in
the world.

Sometime after the Bundt pan heyday in the 1970s, we became
food snobs. No more casseroles with cream of mushroom soup.
No more Bundt cakes with instant pudding mixes. We put our
Bundt pans out of reach on the top shelf.

For my mother's ninetieth birthday party, I took mine down. I
had made plum tarts and pear tatins, and I decided to throw in the
chocolate-pistachio Bundt cake she used to make to rave reviews.
It calls for cake mix, instant pistachio pudding mix, and chocolate
syrup. After the party, that was the recipe all my guests wanted.

Mr. Dalquist's death definitely touched a culinary nerve. Newspapers published stories about the Bundt pan phenomenon and the
Internet was lit up with Bundt pan exchanges. I did an essay for National Public Radio on the Bundt pan, and the people who track these
things told me 1,125 people e-mailed the piece to someone else.

NPR also got a number of letters such as the one from Jan Frank in Bloomfield, Minnesota. The recipe for the chocolate-pistachio cake mentioned in the radio essay was the same one Jan had eaten as a child. It had appeared in the 1975 Leonhard Elementary School's PTA cookbook. "It remains the most worn, most ingredient-soaked page of that cookbook," she wrote. "That cake never failed to satisfy. Sunday afternoon, my twelve-year-old son and I dragged out the cookbook and the Bundt pan and started a new generation of pistachio cake lovers."

That recipe was a particular favorite of my mother and her best friend, Leah. You could be pretty sure if you ate at their houses, there would be a chocolate-pistachio Bundt cake for dessert. It was the dessert I made when I was newly married. Our friend Wayne would come from New York to our New Jersey apartment—what he called a trip to the country—just for a piece of that Bundt cake.

The existence of the Bundt pan is the happy result of a fortuitous Judeo-Scandinavian cultural exchange.

Dave Dalquist and his wife, Dotty, invested five hundred dollars in a basement business in their Minneapolis home in 1946. They produced rosette irons, ebelskiver pans, krumkake irons, and other Scandinavian bakeware. Nordic Ware has been in business ever since.

After they had been open for four years, the Dalquists received a visit from the ladies of the local chapter of Hadassah, the national women's Zionist organization. The chapter president had a ceramic kugelhopf pan in which her German grandmother had made a dense cake filled with raisins, fruits, and nuts. She wanted one in metal. So Mr. Dalquist, a metallurgical engineer, made his first Bundt pan in cast aluminum, with fluted sides and a center tube, like a kugelhopf pan.

The pan's name comes from the German word *bund* for "gathering," a cake suitable for a gathering. Mr. Dalquist added a *t*, trademarked the name, and the Bundt pan was born.

Things were pretty slow in the Bundt pan business until 1966, when Ella Helfrich of Texas won second place in the seventeenth annual Pillsbury Bake-Off for her Tunnel of Fudge cake, made in a Bundt pan. (First place went to a Nevada woman for a recipe for snack bread using processed cheese spread and dry onion soup mix.)

Bakers went nuts. Pillsbury got more than two hundred thousand letters from people wanting to know where they could get a Bundt pan. The Dalquist factory ramped up production and the Bundt-cake era began. Home cooks had found a way to bake the perfect cake—simple, sculpted, and evenly cooked. As a bonus, frosting was optional. Bundt cakes are so pretty, they don't need more than a sift of powdered sugar or a drizzle of simple syrup.

For a while, everyone made Bundt cakes—blueberry cream cheese, walnut rum, even one with 7-Up. The Harvey Wallbanger Bundt cake—the first fancy dessert I learned to make—used yellow cake mix, vanilla pudding mix, eggs, oil, orange juice, vodka, and Galliano liqueur, just like its namesake cocktail. The margarita cake involved margarita mix, orange liqueur, and tequila.

In 1971, Pillsbury launched a line of Bundt cake mixes, and Dorothy Dalquist wrote a cookbook called *Over 300 Delicious Ways to Use Your Bundt Brand Fluted Tube Pan*. It includes recipes for cakes and other desserts, breads, entrées, and salads. The Bundt pan was originally used for pound cakes so there are many of those in Mrs. Dalquist's book. There are cakes made from scratch and cakes made from mixes. Bread recipes call for ingredients such as beer, cheese, and saffron. A recipe for Bean Bread uses a can of pork and beans and a package of hot roll mix. Entrées include Elegant Pressed Chicken (in aspic), Frosty Lime Seafood Salad (with lime and apple gelatin; a can of tuna or crab, and French dressing), and various meat rings with mushroom soup, peanut butter, or canned pineapple.

In 2004, Nordic Ware published a new book called *Bundt Entertaining* with one hundred recipes "for all meals of the day and for all times of the year," a sign that the Bundt pan was back.

I have gone to five weddings recently for which the bride and groom have registered for Bundt pans as gifts. Besides the classic original, Bundt pans now come in more than thirty shapes and sizes. There are flower pans wrought as daisies, roses, sunflowers, wildflowers, and chrysanthemums. Others come in the form of hearts, stars, fleur-de-lis, and Christmas trees. There's even one shaped like a Gothic cathedral. Bundtlette pans make six muffins and mini-Bundts make tiny individual Bundt cakes. Cupcake, loaf, pound cake, popover, and shortbread pans have all joined the classic Bundt pan, available in two sizes.

I hadn't thought about a Bundt pan in years until I saw the movie *My Big Fat Greek Wedding* in 2002. In one hilarious scene, the groom's mother brings a Bundt cake to a party given by the bride's mother. The Greek woman stares in bewilderment at the "cake with a hole in it." She solves the problem by putting a potted geranium in the center. With a Bundt, you can do anything.

※ CHOCOLATE PISTACHIO CAKE

Makes 12 to 14 servings

1 (18¼-ounce) box white or yellow cake mix
1 (3½-ounce) box pistachio instant pudding mix
½ cup orange juice
½ cup water
4 large eggs
½ cup oil
1 teaspoon almond extract
¾ cup chocolate syrup
Confectioners' sugar (optional)

Preheat the oven to 350°F.

Grease and flour a 12-cup Bundt pan (or a 10-inch tube pan).

In a mixing bowl, combine the cake mix, pudding mix, orange juice, water, eggs, oil, and almond extract. With an electric mixer, blend at low speed until moist. Beat for an additional 3 minutes at medium speed, scraping the bowl occasionally, until well blended.

Pour about two-thirds of the batter into the pan. Add the chocolate syrup to the remaining one-third of the batter. Mix well. Pour over the batter in the pan. Run a knife through the batter to marble it.

Bake for 1 hour. Allow the cake to cool in the pan for 15 minutes. Loosen cake with a blunt knife and turn onto a cake plate. Sprinkle with confectioners' sugar, if desired.

❊ AUNT GEORGIE'S POUND CAKE

This recipe comes from my friend Bill's aunt Georgie. His family thought so highly of the cake, they served it at Aunt Georgie's funeral. It's a classic pound cake using no leavening agents. The first pound cakes were made with a pound of butter, a pound of sugar, and a pound of flour, hence the name. While slightly modified from pound cakes of the 1700s, this one is still plenty rich. It works very well in a Bundt pan. Cake flour produces a lighter cake. Have the butter, eggs, and milk at room temperature.

Pound cakes are easily flavored. Substitute a little lemon zest and lemon juice for the vanilla for a lemon pound cake. Add some cinnamon, allspice, and nutmeg for a spice pound cake. The combinations are limitless. Pound cake is good toasted for tea, covered with fruit and whipped cream, used in a trifle, or just eaten plain.

Makes 14 to 16 servings

3 cups sugar
1 cup (2 sticks) softened
   butter
5 large eggs, room
   temperature
½ teaspoon salt
3 cups cake flour, sifted
1 cup milk, room
   temperature
1½ teaspoons vanilla extract
Confectioners' sugar

Preheat the oven to 325°F.

Cream the sugar and butter well. Add the eggs, one at a time. Add the dry ingredients, alternating with the milk. Add the vanilla. Mix well. Pour into a 12-cup Bundt pan and bake for 1 hour, or until a skewer inserted into the center of the cake comes out clean.

When the cake has cooled, put it on a serving plate and sift confectioners' sugar over the cake.

❋ OLIVE AND GRUYÈRE SODA BREAD

This bread is adapted from a recipe in *Bundt Entertaining,* and is printed by permission of Nordic Ware. It's made in a sunflower-shaped pan (which has no tube), giving it a pretty pattern.

Makes 16 servings

4 plus 1¾ cups unbleached, all-purpose flour
4 teaspoons baking powder
1¼ teaspoons baking soda
1 teaspoon salt
⅓ cup butter, cut into pieces
1 cup shredded Gruyère cheese
¾ cup pitted, chopped Kalamata olives or other ripe olives
1 large egg, lightly beaten
2¼ cups buttermilk

Preheat the oven to 350°F.

Grease and flour a sunflower or other 10-cup Bundt pan.

In a large bowl, mix 4 cups of the flour, the baking powder, baking soda, and salt. Add the butter. Mix until crumbly. Stir in the cheese and olives.

Mix the egg with the buttermilk. Slowly add the egg mixture to the flour mixture. Mix until blended and a soft dough forms, adding the remaining flour one-quarter cup at a time.

On a lightly floured surface, knead the dough 3 to 4 minutes. Pat the dough into a 9½-inch circle; place in the prepared pan.

Bake for 45 to 50 minutes or until dark golden brown. Remove from the pan and cool on a rack.

AUNT ESTHER'S ANTIPASTO

✳ ✳ ✳

Education is a progressive discovery of our own ignorance.
WILL DURANT

I WAS married and living in the East before I found out that antipasto did not originate on the Minnesota Iron Range.

The epiphany came after my husband ordered antipasto at an
Italian restaurant in central New Jersey and asked the waiter if it
was big enough to share. This should have been my first clue. But
I was still struck dumb when we were served a large platter filled
with smoked meats, cheese, olives, and marinated vegetables.
"This is not antipasto," I announced with smug superiority.

Antipasto, I explained, was an "it" not a "they." It came in a jar
and was eaten on a cracker.

My husband looked at me like I was from Pluto. I was, in fact,
from Minnesota—famous for lutefisk, not lasagna.

I grew up in Minneapolis in the 1950s in what was called a
double bungalow. My maternal grandparents lived in one attached ranch house and we lived in the other. A basement con-
necting the two houses contained cabinets full of the strawberry
jam my grandma preserved every spring, the huge quantities of
maple syrup my grandfather brought back from business deal-
ings in Canada, and the antipasto my mother canned at the end
of the summer. Cocktail parties at my parents' house involved
gin martinis, bone-dry Manhattans, and some of that antipasto
on crackers.

The antipasto was a mixture of cooked cauliflower, green

beans, mushrooms, peppers, celery, tomatoes, onions, olives, and cucumbers mixed with canned tuna and anchovies in a peppery vinegar and oil sauce. It had a sweet, pickled taste and I could easily have eaten a jar at one sitting. As far as I knew, the provenance of antipasto was Eveleth, Minnesota, a small town in the northern Mesabi Iron Range, now best known as the home of the U.S. Hockey Hall of Fame and the world's largest hockey stick.

When my mother was married in the 1930s, her aunt Esther gave her a jar of antipasto made by my aunt's Sicilian neighbor in Eveleth, a place we called "up north." A Jewish matchmaker in Minneapolis had found a husband for Aunt Esther there in the early 1900s. So at nineteen, she left her family and moved north to her arranged marriage to a fireman—Abe Levant. Uncle Abe had left the mines to fight the big forest fires that swept the Range.

There was an orthodox synagogue in Eveleth, and Aunt Esther kept a kosher home. They had very modest means, but my elegant aunt used her sterling silver every day at lunch when they had their meat meal. She arrived in the mining community with rudimentary cooking knowledge, based on the Eastern European meals of her Russian mother. But Aunt Esther was a sophisticated and meticulous cook. She kneaded her fudge. "Everything she made was perfect," my mother says. Moreover, she was open to the surprising culinary influences of Eveleth.

By the time iron mining had replaced logging as the area's main industry, immigrants from about forty countries had come to dig out the ore and seek economic opportunity. After they came, the Range became a place of astonishing gastronomic diversity.

Now the mines are still, but many of the Old World dishes are still thriving: porketta, an Italian-inspired boneless rolled pork roast seasoned with fresh fennel and spices; potica (po-TEET-sah) a sweet Slovenian walnut bread; and the pasties, introduced by Cornish miners.

Jews who settled in the Upper Midwest also learned to adapt traditional recipes to local products. So instead of making gefilte fish with carp as they would have in the old country, they used trout from Lake Superior.

Her Sicilian neighbor made the antipasto Aunt Esther sent my parents every year. They liked it so much, my mother wrote for the recipe. There was no recipe, Aunt Esther wrote back. Her neighbor just made it.

The Sicilian neighbor spoke no English, but her daughter did. She and my aunt watched her mother put together her jars of antipasto and worked out a recipe. For years, my mother made batches of it, adding shrimp and other fresh foods when she served it as a first course.

This Sicilian dish was apparently not restricted to the Minnesota Iron Range. My mother had a friend who grew up on the Range and knew the recipe. She had gotten a no-cook version from someone in California. It calls for cocktail onions, sweet pickles, a jar of pimiento, two jars of artichoke hearts, and a bottle of chili sauce.

Then in the summer of 2002, more than sixty years after my mother got her first jar of antipasto, I had dinner at Nick's Italian Café in McMinnville, Oregon. One of the appetizer choices on the five-course dinner was "Sicilian-Style Antipasto." My husband, now clear on what true antipasto was, said, "Let's see if it's like Aunt Esther's."

Almost exactly. I asked to talk to the chef.

Nick Peirano grew up in Pittsburg, California, which has a large Sicilian community. It was also a mining town. He said a lot of Sicilian families there made this antipasto in quantity for weddings and other big family occasions. The only addition he's made is to add more hot red pepper. He said that a friend had found the antipasto on a restaurant menu in Palermo.

So I called my friend Jenifer, the archaeologist. She has spent an enviable amount of time in Sicily digging for shards of Greek pottery and eating Sicilian food. She's also from Minneapolis, so was not surprised by the Iron Range connection. "Sounds like

caponata," she said. But caponata always includes eggplant in addition to onion, celery, olives, capers, and an antipasto-style sauce.
Jenifer referred me to Mary Taylor Simeti's *Pomp and Sustenance:
Twenty-five Centuries of Sicilian Food*, in which the author quotes
from another source:

> *According to one book, the chefs of the aristocracy would also
> serve caponata "sprinkled with bottarga, tuna roe, hard-boiled egg
> yolk, all reduced to a powder, crumbled hard-boiled egg whites,
> tiny octopus boiled and chopped, small shrimps, boned sardines in
> oil, and all the shellfish you wish."*

So apparently, there is room for invention.

Okay, I thought, it's not just some weird Minnesota interpretation of an Italian staple. It's esoteric and little known, but not con-
fined to the Range.

Then, one fine day, I found 26.4-ounce jars of my aunt Esther's
antipasto at Costco.

This is not a boutique gourmet food shop. We're talking cav-
ernous warehouses with birds flying through the rafters and shoppers lined up with their carts at opening time for bargain olive oil
and television sets.

The Costco antipasto—described on the jar as "tangy vegetables with tuna"—is manufactured by Something Special Deli-
Foods Ltd. in Alberta, Canada.

Something Special began life in 1986 as a small delicatessen that
sold soups, sandwiches, and what they called gourmet antipasto.
The antipasto was so popular that the deli was sold in 1988 and a
manufacturing plant was built to produce large enough quantities
of antipasto to can and sell to small grocery chains throughout Alberta. Then they began to sell it to Costco stores in Canada and the
United States.

In addition to putting it on a cracker or a piece of crusty
bread, Something Special suggested using the antipasto in pasta
casseroles, in sandwiches, as a pizza topping, as spaghetti sauce,

and on bruschetta with mozzarella cheese sprinkled on top and baked at 350°F. until the cheese melts.

Gail Hiller, Something Special's comptroller, said they use an Italian family recipe. Alberta, too, had a lot of Italian immigrants. Most stores, she said, think of the antipasto as a seasonal product and stock it from Thanksgiving through the Super Bowl. "We do send out a case here and there because people say they can't live without it, and they get kind of cranky," she said.

Something Special gets hundreds of calls from Canada and the United States from people saying that the antipasto tastes just like their grandmother's.

The antipasto is made in small batches in their commercial kitchen. Gail said they have six kettles running at once, and prepare about twenty-five hundred cases a day, twelve jars to a case.

"We're not making it in huge piles," she said. "That's what makes it good."

After I told my adventures-with-antipasto story in the *Minneapolis Star-Tribune*'s "Taste" section, I was flooded with e-mails. Several were from people who knew my aunt Esther; one was from the niece of Aunt Esther's husband, Uncle Abe; another's mother went to high school with my mother; and one e-mail was from a woman from Minneapolis now living in Jerusalem who thought we'd grown up together. Three people wrote that they had been to my aunt Esther's for a Passover seder.

One woman who had grown up on the Range "and, of course, knew all the Levants" still has a jar of antipasto her mother made with Bede Zimmerman, Bob Dylan's mother. Dylan—formerly Zimmerman—grew up on the Range. "I have poison signs all over it, but its historical connections may someday make it a great sell on eBay," she wrote.

Many writers were nostalgic about not only antipasto but also the Iron Range of a different time. "Eveleth and the Range was such a multiethnic place, that we were exposed to foods from across the world—antipasto, pasties, strudel, potica, and on and on," wrote one woman. "I have an Irish and Slovenian heritage, but all of us on the Range had entry into a world market of treats from friends and neighbors."

Another woman remembered an antipasto-like mixture her Slovenian grandmother made. "I can still picture the rows of jars simply labeled 'End of Garden,'" she wrote.

When my mother was a little girl, she and her brother would visit Aunt Esther and Uncle Abe every summer. She remembers that they had a beautiful garden full of flowers and vegetables. Many of the vegetables went into Aunt Esther's antipasto. I still believe antipasto comes from those northern gardens.

✳ AUNT ESTHER'S ANTIPASTO

Aunt Esther's recipe was, like many recipes of that time, a little vague—"a can" of this, "a handful" of that. I have updated with more specific measurements, but encourage cooks to use it as a guide rather than Scripture. Make changes based on preferences and what's at the market or in the garden. Cooking times remain general because they will depend on the size of the vegetables and the vagaries of the stove. The following recipe makes an awful lot. Aunt Esther's neighbor canned her antipasto after making it, but refrigeration has improved since then and it will keep for a couple of months in the refrigerator. Or cut the recipe in half. But it's great to can and give as holiday gifts. Sealed, it will keep for years.

Makes 12 quarts

---

2 large heads cauliflower
1 pound small onions
2 bunches celery, without leaves
4 cups fresh green beans
8 cups fresh white mushrooms, sliced

Coarsely chop the cauliflower, onions, celery, green beans, and mushrooms and cook separately in salted water until about half cooked (they will cook more later). This will take 2 to 5 minutes, depending on the vegetable. They should be just tender but not fully cooked. Drain and run under cold water. Set aside.

1 pint cider vinegar
2 quarts olive oil
48 ounces canned tuna
  packed in water, drained
2 pounds anchovies
Handful of chopped Italian
  flat-leaf parsley
3 pounds green tomatoes,
  coarsely chopped
3 pounds red tomatoes,
  coarsely chopped
2 pounds green peppers,
  coarsely chopped
5 pickling cucumbers,
  unpeeled, coarsely
  chopped
2 (6-ounce) cans tomato
  paste
1 quart canned navy beans,
  drained
4 (6-ounce) cans olives
  (2 black, 2 green), whole
2 hot peppers, chopped
Salt, to taste

Place the vinegar, oil, tuna, anchovies (with most of the oil drained), and chopped parsley in a large soup pot and bring to a boil. Lower the heat and simmer for 15 minutes. Add the coarsely chopped tomatoes, peppers, and cucumbers and cook over medium-low heat for 10 minutes. Add the rest of the ingredients and cook for another 10 minutes. Cool and refrigerate or can in hot jars.

✳ SALLY'S NO-COOKING ANTIPASTO

Sally grew up on the Range and found this no-cook version of antipasto in California. It's pretty good.

Makes 3 quarts

2 (6-ounce) cans white
  tuna, packed in water
¼ cup olive oil
2 tablespoons cider vinegar
8 ounces tomatoes
1 jar cocktail onions, drained
3 ounces pickles (sweet
  gherkins)
1 (2-ounce) jar pimientos
1 cup black pitted olives,
  drained
1 cup green olives stuffed
  with pimientos, drained
2 (6-ounce) jars artichoke
  hearts, drained
8 ounces fresh mushrooms,
  sliced
1 (12-ounce) bottle chili
  sauce

Mix all the ingredients together in a large bowl and let sit for 24 hours in the refrigerator.

AN ODE TO TOAST

※ ※ ※

When the girl returned, some hours later, she carried a tray, with a cup
of fragrant tea steaming on it; and a plate piled up with very hot
buttered toast, cut thick, very brown on both sides, with the butter run-
ning through the holes in it in great golden drops, like honey from the
honeycomb. The smell of that buttered toast simply talked to Toad, and
with no uncertain voice; talked of warm kitchens, of breakfasts on bright
frosty mornings, of cosy parlour firesides on winter evenings, when one's
ramble was over and slippered feet were propped on the fender, of the
purring of contented cats, and the twitter of sleepy canaries.

KENNETH GRAHAME,
The Wind in the Willows

M Y SON had to get a college education for me to fully understand toast.

He was a theater student at New York University, studying
method acting. His first assignment was to get to know a teacup.
Every day for a week, he was to spend thirty minutes with his
cup—learning its shape, feeling its grooves, measuring its
temperature—so he could go to class and re-create holding a
teacup through "sense memory."

My first reaction was: For this we're paying the price of our
first home every year? But my second was: toast.

Sense memory is when you reach into a dark closet and can
pull out the sweater you want because you remember how it feels.
You bite into an ear of sweet corn and remember every summer
barbecue. You smell toast and you're transported to warm
kitchens, breakfasts on cold mornings, and cozy times by the fire.

There's even a scientific explanation for eau de toast. The smell, taste, and color of toast comes from something called the Maillard reaction, a chemical change that happens when bread is heated to a certain point and the sugars and starches begin to caramelize. This turns the bread brown and makes it smell like a cozy kitchen.

Toast may be the most multitalented of all foods. It can be dead simple on its own or used as a vehicle for wild extravagance. Anything can go on toast, from Cheddar cheese to Beluga caviar. Bruschetta is simply toast with garlic, olive oil, and tomatoes. I read somewhere about melting dark bitter chocolate topped with Camembert on toasted panettone and running it under the broiler. Whoa.

Toast is the ultimate comfort food. It is one of the first solids a baby tastes. If you're sick in bed, all you can eat is maybe a little toast. Whenever I need a quick hit of comfort, I make toast. Parents use toast tricks to get their children to eat eggs. My mother cut a hole with a shot glass in the middle of a piece of bread, fried it in butter on one side, then turned it over, cracked an egg into the hole, and cooked it until done. It was called egg in a frame. I could have eaten it every day. British children eat eggs and soldiers. Pieces of toast are cut into strips (soldiers), that are dipped into soft-boiled eggs.

People have decided opinions about how toast should be made, what should go on it, and how it should be served.

The English, for example, eat toast cold. I think this is a mistake. While silver English toast racks are very Jane Austen (and, therefore, desirable), they promote cold toast. They do keep the pieces of toast from touching each other and, therefore, steaming each other soggy. While they are charming, the racks are better used for sorting mail.

Some people, however, like cold toast. Why? Butter. A piece of cold toast is a perfect surface on which to spread a thick layer of butter. The butter, however, must be softened. There's nothing worse than trying to spread cold butter on toast. It tears, it bruises, you say bad words. You need to hear just the right sandpapery sound to know that the toast temperature and consistency are ready for butter. Honey and peanut butter should only be spread on hot toast. Peanut butter—which must be chunky—is a particularly good thing to spread on hot toast. It melts into a peanut cream with chips sticking above the surface. It is best to apply jam when toast is slightly cooled but not cold. The hazelnut spread Nutella, of course, can go on cardboard.

Toast that's buttered for you by someone else is unacceptable. My husband loves the diagonally cut, white bread toast with melted butter you get at a diner. The bread is often packaged and limp and is never toasted enough. I find it grossly overbuttered and soggy.

Proper toasting is a critical problem for toast lovers. The bread never seems to toast evenly. In our toaster oven, the corners are burnt while the center remains untanned. One side gets toasted and the other doesn't. Some people make toast in a cast-iron pan. Others recommend state-of-the-art toasters that cost three hundred dollars. I have heard that you get the crispiest result from putting bread on a toasting fork and holding it over an open fire. I'm sure we did this at camp, but I can't remember the results. It's unlikely I'll be near a campfire with a loaf of bread anytime soon.

"One of the most difficult things in cooking is to get toast just right," James Beard wrote in *James Beard's Delights and Prejudices*. "The toast must be firm enough to hold the food without drooping, but not so dry and brittle that when you bite into it, the toast shatters all over your hand, your clothes, and the floor," he writes.

My friend Susan, the chef, says toast is her favorite food. When interviewing prospective cooks, her first question is, "How do you make toast?" She says, "I ask that because toast is so complicated. Every kind of bread toasts differently and you toast bread for different reasons. Brioche toast points are difficult because they have sugar and a high fat content. French bread has no fat so you need to eat it right away or it will be a hockey puck. You grill bread for crunch and its smoky flavor. Some bread you're going to eat right away. Some you're keeping for later. Toast should be crunchy on the sides and soft in the interior. You really have to think about it." She finds the toast test a good way to learn a lot about how someone cooks. "No one else will ask them that question," she says. "It takes them off guard and tells me how thoughtful they are about this kind of work."

Like many other things, America probably got toast from England, where it is part of any proper breakfast and a popular teatime snack. The Brits have eaten toast since they discovered fire. Friends of mine moved to a flat in London with a tiny oven and a huge toaster. The English have their priorities. In the United States, almost every kitchen, no matter how small, has something in which to make toast.

People are clearly still buying toasters. The Williams-Sonoma catalog features nine styles priced from $20 to $379.95. The top-of-the-line model is a variation of one Chuck Williams saw in a store window on the Left Bank in Paris. Two removable chrome-plated baskets can hold whole sandwiches in place. It is hand assembled in England so you know it's the real thing. There even exists a portable toaster you can plug into a car cigarette lighter. So while you're sitting in rush-hour traffic, you can make yourself a piece of toast.

However we make it, toast has long been part of the American experience. *The Settlement Cookbook,* first published in Milwaukee in 1901, includes recipes for dry toast (toasted on a fork over the heat), water toast (dipped in boiling salt water, then buttered), melba toast (thin toast), cinnamon toast, French toast, and cream or milk toast (with a sauce poured over dry toast). Milquetoast has come to mean someone who is bland and unassertive. But to food writer M. F. K. Fisher, milk toast was romantic. She wrote that toasted bread in a bowl with milk, butter, salt, and pepper "is a warm, mild, soothing thing, full of innocent strength . . . a small modern miracle of gastronomy."

Cinnamon toast was one of my main reasons for living as a

child. We had a white ceramic shaker filled with a mixture of cinnamon and sugar to sprinkle over buttered toast on winter mornings. The toast must be buttered hot and the cinnamon sugar
sprinkled on immediately so it all melts together. In the seventeenth century, a paste of cinnamon and sugar moistened with
wine was spread on toast—cinnamon toast for grown-ups.

There is an innocence and purity about toast that you turn to in
times of need. You smell toast and you feel better. Let it snow. Let
it get dark at 4:30. You're in a warm house, wearing fuzzy slippers
and a flannel nightgown, and you're making toast. If you're really
lucky, you have a shaker filled with cinnamon and sugar.

✳ TOAST

Makes 1 serving

1 slice bread	Place the bread in the toaster. Turn to ON.
Softened butter, to taste	
(cold butter can tear	Adjust the setting from light to dark, ac-
toast)	cording to your preference. Toast should be
	crisp but not burned.

When the toast pops, remove from the toaster. The toast will be hot, so
pull quickly from the heat source and in the same motion put it on a real
plate. Do not use a paper plate—the toast will sweat, the plate will become
soggy and fall apart, you will have to throw it away and clean the counter,
and your toast will end up cold.

Spread softened butter across the hot, toasted bread. Immediately take a
big bite, chew well, and sigh deeply.

VARIATIONS Sprinkle a 1-to-1 mixture of cinnamon and sugar over buttered toast; or spread with jam, jelly, or honey; or coat with peanut butter,
which will then melt; or top with poached eggs.

✳ FRENCH TOAST

Challah makes delicious French Toast. This recipe is assembled the night before and baked in the oven rather than fried. It has a texture a bit more like bread pudding than traditional French Toast but gets puffy and crispy and is easier for a brunch than standing at the stove.

Makes 12 servings

12 slices challah,
(each 1 inch thick), cut in
half diagonally
Butter
6 large eggs
2 tablespoons Grand
Marnier or other orange-
flavored liqueur
½ cup heavy cream
½ cup milk (any kind)
1 tablespoon grated orange
peel
3 tablespoons orange juice
½ teaspoon ground
cinnamon
½ teaspoon cardamom
Confectioners' sugar
Syrup
Jam

Butter well a 15 × 10 × 2-inch baking dish.

Slice the challah, discarding the ends.

Arrange the bread in the prepared dish. (You may need more than one.)

Whisk together the eggs, liqueur, cream, milk, orange peel, orange juice, cinnamon, and cardamom. Pour over the bread. Let the bread sit for at least 1 hour, or overnight in the refrigerator.

Bring bread to room temperature. Preheat oven to 375°F and bake toast for 20 to 30 minutes, or until puffed and golden brown. Don't overcook.

Sprinkle with confectioners' sugar and serve immediately with syrup and jam.

KITCHEN TOOLS

✳   ✳   ✳

*I don't know whether to throw all these tools away
or put them back in the kitchen drawers. I mean, you never know
when you're going to need one of these things.*

ANDY ROONEY

(In a 60 Minutes *television commentary on kitchen tools,
behind a desk covered with gadgets.)*

R EUSABLE NONSTICK silicone baking mats are considered a must
for any serious cook these days. They rinse off quickly, store
easily, are made in France, and are certified kosher. No more
charred crumbs or discolored pans. You can use them three thousand times before they give out. Yet I don't own a single one.

What I do have is a cabinet full of old, bent, ratty-looking
cookie sheets. They are truly disgusting. Until this minute, it has
never occurred to me to employ either high-tech silicone or old-
fashioned cleanliness. The only one worth saving is an extra-large
rimmed sheet that my mother saved from my grandfather's brief
stint as a restaurant owner.

While I can't explain the state of my cookie sheets, there *are*
other odd bits of ware in my kitchen for which I have some excuse.
I freely admit the justification is usually sentimental.

I never knew my father's parents. However, I have my grandfather's name (modified) and my grandmother's rolling pin. My
Aunt Ruthie had given her daughter Barbara our grandmother's
rolling pin and red-handled hand eggbeater (labeled "high speed
super center driver beater made in the United States of America").
Barbara and her sister Tina gave them to me. I was already fanati-

cally attached to this grandmother's heavy soup pot that I had in-
herited thirty years earlier.

The eggbeater came just in time. The electric hand mixer I had
gotten as a bride had finally moved beyond the considerable pow-
ers of duct tape.

The rolling pin looked more iffy. I already owned two beautiful
wooden rolling pins—one with and one without ball bearings.
Grandma Tillie's rolling pin is a slim, French tapered pin bearing
scars from a century of use. Then I touched it. It was as soft as silk,
as butter, as a baby's bottom. It felt incredibly good in the hand.
Then I used it. All of a sudden, I could make a piecrust. One of
these days, I'll get rid of the other two rolling pins.

I have a small round copper tray in the kitchen that my maternal grandmother bought for five cents fifty years ago. I like having
both my grandmothers in the kitchen with me.

My mother had a furniture store and sold beautiful handmade
round cutting boards with slim handles that could be hung on the
wall. I've had one for more than thirty years and am so devoted to
it I've had it repaired twice.

I picked up a little copper box that reminded me of one my
mother had in her kitchen filled with salt. I had a wooden cover
made (like she had), filled it with salt, and keep it next to the stove.
I use my silver baby spoon for sugar and the silver porridge dish
with my initials and date of birth for chocolates to pass around after dinner.

I'm not as softhearted about my electrical appliances. Now that
the electric hand mixer is gone, it might be time to reconsider the
blender I got for a wedding present. It's broken and encrusted with
decades of smoothies and margaritas. It still works, though.

My Kitchen-Aid mixer, 14-cup Cuisinart, and thermal cof-
feemaker are wonderful kitchen tools. But I'm not emotionally attached to them. If they break, I won't hold them and gaze out the
window as I did when my beloved wooden salad bowl sighed its
last.

One electrical appliance I'll never have to even think about is a can opener. My husband has taken few positions on kitchenware over the years but has firmly stood his ground on the electric can opener. This, he claims, is technology run amok. It does seem to be an awful lot of space to give up to something so simply done by hand.

I have, however, mourned and never replaced the French mini-processor Louis gave me years ago. I watched as it lost its feet and, finally, its will to live. The name of the company has worn off the body, and neither Louis nor I can remember what it was. No other machine works as well, so I do without.

I have felt less deprived since my friend Barbara gave me an Alaskan ulu. The Inupiat Indians have used this incredible cutting tool (known as a *mezzaluna* in Italy) for about five thousand years for hunting, fishing, skinning, and filleting. I use it to chop parsley.

I do have an electric juicer, but prefer my chipped porcelain hand juicer. I don't use it often, but I like owning a waffle iron. I find making waffles very satisfying. You pour the batter over a hot griddle, shut the lid, and open it to find heart-shaped waffles. (It was a Valentine's Day gift.)

My measuring cups and spoons are in pretty sorry shape, but I'm strangely fond of them. I got a set of glass liquid measuring cups in various sizes at a yard sale. They're all chipped, but they still hold liquids in whole cups and their increments. My ¼ cup stainless-steel dry measuring cup is battered out of shape. The plastic equivalent is half melted. But they're always there for me.

Someday, I would like really good knives. I went for about twenty-five years with a whole rack of knives that barely cut. Then my son's college roommate sold Cutco knives one year for a summer job and to stop him from showing me, again, how they can cut a penny so it will function as a corkscrew, I bought a bunch. They're fine. But I still yearn for the perfect knife. I don't know what it is, but I've been doing research.

My friend Susan, the chef, favors Sabatier carbon steel–bladed knives. She says carbon steel blades are lighter weight than the stainless–carbon mix, sharpen more easily, and stay sharp longer. They do, however, stain easily and, if not sharpened properly, can wear unevenly. Razor-sharp Japanese knives have become popular but are very expensive.

Susan says if you can have only a few knives, go for a paring knife, an all-purpose boning knife, a 10-inch chef's knife, and a ser-rated bread knife. "These four could carry anyone from cradle to grave," she says.

Whatever I do or don't get, I will always keep EA's boning knife. My husband's grandfather was a kosher butcher and a charming man. When he died, my mother-in-law gave us several of his knives. The cleaver's in the basement wrapped in three beach tow-els, but the boning knife is always close at hand.

I keep my knives—the good and the bad—on a rack screwed to the side of my butcher block. My husband's and my first apartment was in a duplex in New Brunswick, New Jersey. Our landlords—two Italian brothers—lived upstairs. I was in the laundry room one day and noticed what I was sure was a real butcher block painted the green of park benches. One of the brothers worked for the city recreation department. I asked them about it and they said, "Oh, that's Pop's old cutting block." Pop had been an Italian butcher and this was his butcher's block. I said I'd like to buy it. They said I could have it. It was my first and last refinishing project. I stripped it, pol-ished the brass hardware, and put it on casters. The top has a curved hollow from years of chopping and scrubbing.

Then there are the many things in my kitchen drawers I can't explain. Why, for example, do I have nine loaf pans? I use the same one, maybe two, over and over. I just know, though, that the minute I give them to Goodwill I'll need them.

I try to keep an open mind. For example, I used to adore my zester and have now transferred my affections to my microplane.

I've never used the plastic squeeze bottle I bought a few years ago for some forgotten reason. I use one of my five peelers and one of my two pastry cutters. I actually do use my kitchen scale. When the recipe calls for a pound of apples, I know I'm using a pound of apples.

But what do I do with the pretty wooden spoons friends bring from their trips to Africa, Malaysia, New Zealand?

Kitchens are idiosyncratic places, reflecting the cooking style and personality of their inhabitants. Louis is wild about the simple, metal garlic press he got thirty years ago. I don't use a garlic press. I prefer to mince. He uses the same little, old frying pan for virtually everything he makes despite the fancy French pots and pans he has hanging from the wall. I use all the pots on my pot rack. He has dozens of wooden spoons but uses for practically everything the one his mother gave him forty years ago. I'm indiscrimate and unsentimental about the wooden spoons.

I still, however, don't know what to make of silicone.

✳ PERFECT PIECRUST

This piecrust is from Lola Nebel of Cambridge, Minnesota. She has won the pie sweepstakes at the Minnesota State Fair nine times. It comes out perfectly. My grandmother's rolling pin is instrumental to my success.

Makes 2 piecrusts (9 inches each)

2 cups all-purpose flour
1¼ teaspoons sugar
½ teaspoon salt
¾ cup vegetable shortening
1 large egg, separated
1¼ teaspoons distilled
    white vinegar
¼ cup cold water

Combine the flour, sugar, and salt in a mixing bowl. Cut in the shortening (I use Crisco) with a pastry blender until crumbly. Lightly beat the egg white and reserve 1 tablespoon for brushing on the bottom crust before filling.

Beat together the remaining egg white, yolk, vinegar, and water. Stir into the dough with a fork until the dough sticks together. Divide in half. Flatten each half into a disk. Wrap in plastic and chill for at least 1 hour.

MOTHERS' DAYS

❋　❋　❋

I refuse to believe that trading recipes is silly. Tuna fish casserole
is at least as real as corporate stock.
BARBARA GRIZZUTI HARRISON

JONI VISITED her dying friend and offered to do anything to help. Referring to a manila folder holding every recipe she loved, Alana responded, "I want to leave these to my girls."

So Joni took the folder filled with recipes ripped out of magazines and newspapers or written on scraps of paper and Alana's old cookbooks held together by rubber bands. After a month typing up these favorites, Joni made each girl a copy of the recipe book with a picture of that daughter and her mother on the cover. Alana saw a copy of the book just days before she died. She told Joni: "This is the best gift you could ever give me."

Shortly after I heard Joni's story, my own mother became ill. I spent a lot of time in Minneapolis, where she was in the hospital. I went back to my parents' home at night and looked through the burlap-covered notebook in which she began collecting family recipes for me when I got married in 1972. It is still a work in progress. As I turned the pages, I realized that handing down recipes from one generation to the next is an intimate, simple act of love and connection.

I asked my friends and neighbors to go through their handed-down recipes and to give me the ones that evoked the best memories.

Without a pause, Bill across the street said, "Mom's War Cake. I love it. I make it. And it's all about Mom." He said what the Madeleine was to Proust, war cake is to him. His mother had learned to make it during World War II because it didn't call for any expensive or rationed ingredients such as eggs, milk, or butter. Sugar, however, was an exception. During the war, everyone was allowed small amounts of basic staples. War Cake uses ingredients available to most households at the time—raisins, lard, cinnamon, salt, baking soda, sugar, and flour. It's a testament to the human spirit that even during a time of war and privation, homes were filled with the smell of cake baking.

Bill's sister put together a family cookbook that opens with Mom's War Cake and goes on to document other family favorites: To-Die-For Sweet Potatoes, Dot's Taco Salad, Aunt Sis's Bread Pudding, Mom-Mom Bessie's Fudge, and Nancy's Just Tastes Good.

A lot of people have family cookbooks.

Allison's is spiral-bound and has a photograph of her large extended family on the cover. It has a preface describing how everyone met, fell in love, got married, and had children and features a brisket recipe including these instructions: "No matter what anyone tells you, NEVER, NEVER buy a first cut; it'll come out dry . . . there just isn't enough fat. Remember, FAT = JEWISH = GOOD."

I know a number of Allison's family recipes personally. Every year to break the fast after Yom Kippur, the Jewish Day of Atonement, Allison invites approximately a million family members and friends over for, among other things, the Garfinkle Family Noodle Pudding. This is the Platonic form of noodle kugel. It has 8 ounces of cream cheese, 16 ounces of sour cream, ½ pound of butter, and a cup of sugar. And when you've been fasting for twenty-four hours, it's hard to apply the principles of portion control.

The Hilken Family Cookbook is dedicated to Lis's mother "for lovingly preparing tasty, nutritious meals for us, night after night, year after year." Like all family cookbooks, the recipes are personal: Grandy's cheese ball, Ruthie's potato soufflé, Laura's chicken feta burritos, Claire's pasta, Mom's lemon pie. Lis's sister Mary put the book together, and writes in her introduction: "This is supposed to be a cookbook, but I find the memories of the food are intimately entwined with memories of the whole experience. I picture the six of us around that solid oak table."

Family cookbooks have recipes for Jell-O salads and Christmas cookies. No recipes call for foie gras or truffle oil.

Stephanie's mother was food editor of a major metropolitan newspaper. Despite such sophistication in the family kitchen, the dish Stephanie remembers most fondly was one she and her three sisters called "glop." There's no recipe. Her mom would poke around in the refrigerator and make something with whatever she found. A classic glop would be hamburger meat broken up and sautéed with various vegetables in a tomato sauce. Stephanie reported that she made "a very good glop" recently. She found some wild rice in the pantry, did some exploration in the freezer where she came up with one weiswurst, discovered a cooked capon wing and some fresh mushrooms in the refrigerator, and knew it was all coming together. She sautéed the mushrooms with onions, cooked the wild rice and the weiswurst, cut the capon meat off the bone, and mixed it all together. She served it with a salad and some cranberry relish from Thanksgiving, a month earlier. "It was," she said, "a sensational dinner."

When he was growing up, my son called his favorite meal "scraps." The classic scraps dinner was a platter of any cooked meats we had lying around—salami, chicken cut off the bone, lunch meats—served alongside a cutting board full of bits of cheese left in the cheese bin. This was rounded out nicely by a green vegetable, a role played by a jar of Italian peppers. I remember one night putting out leftover corn bread and olive bread, barbecue, flank steak, hummus, baby carrots, pickles, coleslaw, and canned corn.

Recipes for sweets are common hand-me-downs. Louis is an excellent cook, even though he's a vegetarian. Fortunately, the special family recipe in Louis's repertoire is a dessert using no meat. It is called Millie's Mother's. The formal name is Millie's Mother's Maid's Chocolate Torte. Millie was Louis's mother's aunt, a robust, energetic, and intellectual giant of a woman, he says. She had the foresight to pack her maid's chocolate torte recipe before fleeing Nazi Germany.

Millie's Mother's is made with hazelnuts rather than flour, and red currant jam is slathered between the layers. It is extremely dense, and young children are given only small slices.

When Annette was married, she asked her octogenarian grand-mother for her mandel bread recipe. Mandel bread is a traditional Jewish hard cookie, similar to biscotti. *Mandel* is Yiddish/German for "almond." Some people use the full Yiddish name, *mandel brot* (bread). Annette's grandmother called it "hardtack," which usually refers to a big, hard biscuit that sailors take on long voyages. Her grandmother wrote: "I understand you want my recipe for the hardtack. It was really given to me by a friend but I never wrote it down. I shall do my best with it." A recipe follows with an end-note: "After reading all this, go out to a bakery and buy something ready-made. It's much easier."

Important family recipes sometimes surface when children go to college. Pam found the only homemade thing she consistently sent her son freshman year was the Irish raisin soda bread her grand-mother used to bake for family holidays. It was what he wanted. My mother sent my son her fabulous chocolate chip cookies, which he adores. The postage cost more than the ingredients. She denies any secret ingredients and claims to follow the standard Toll House recipe. Then why are her cookies so much better than everyone else's?

After Megan graduated from college and moved into an apart-ment, her mother gave her a recipe called "Pot Roast to Last for a Week." It begins, "Sear biggest pot roast that will fit in your biggest pot. Sear means get pan hot and brown meat on one side, then the other." You fill the pot with as many vegetables as you can fit, add some broth, cook for three hours, then heat up every day until it's gone.

In my family, the great-aunts were the great cooks. Their style in the kitchen had a strong effect on my mother. The aunts taught her to cook, and she taught me.

Many of my mother's collected recipes are from Aunt Ossie, the most influential of the great-aunts. She was a legendary cook and hostess. My mother says when she was growing up, it was al-ways an open house at Aunt Ossie's.

I have recipes for Aunt Ossie's summer borscht and gefilte fish, Aunt Tessa's poppy seed cake, Aunt Debbie's chopped herring, Aunt Esther's fudge and lemon filling, and Aunt Fanny's pot roast, bake-in-the-oven fryers, and kuchen. Aunt Fanny was not, technically, a relative. She was Aunt Ossie's best friend and considered one of the family. She was a great cook.

My mom's notebook also includes her favorite recipes from friends, collected over the last fifty years. There is Ann's braised celery, Terry's Roquefort dressing, and Patti's Jell-O salad. There are a great number of recipes from my mother's friends Sis and Mary, whom she regarded as very good cooks. "Sis's chicken" and "Mary's lamb" recall a time when home cooks had signature recipes.

I was back in Minneapolis for the funeral of my friend Kate's mother. After her death, Kate went through her mother's heavy, locked jewelry box. In the top tray were the pearls and dinner rings she rarely wore. Beneath was a locked drawer where Kate assumed her mom kept her most important possessions. She unlocked the drawer, pulled out the tray, and found her mother's handwritten recipe for Huckleberry Dessert. That meant more to Kate than jewels.

✳ BILL'S MOM'S WAR CAKE

Makes 10 to 12 servings

1 pound raisins (any kind)	Preheat the oven to 325°F.
2 cups water plus 1 cup cold water	
½ cup Crisco or lard (Bill uses 1 stick of butter)	Butter a Pyrex deep-dish casserole 3-4 inches deep.
3 teaspoons ground cinnamon	Stew the raisins for 15 minutes in 2 cups of water. Add the 1 cup of cold water. Stir and
1 teaspoon salt	drain, reserving the water. Add the rest of
1 tablespoon baking soda	the ingredients, using the water from the

2 cups sugar
4 cups all-purpose flour

raisins to moisten the batter. Bake for 1 hour, or until a toothpick inserted into the cake comes out clean.

❈ AUNT OSSIE'S SUMMER BORSCHT

My great-aunt Ossie was a legendary hostess and cook. She never served fewer than ten for dinner—and usually more. She always used linen napkins. She probably devised this cold sweet-and-sour soup in the 1920s. It's very easy and very pretty.

Makes 6 to 8 servings

1 pound spinach, chopped
1 can beets or bunch of
   fresh beets, shredded
½ pound rhubarb, diced
1 (20-ounce) can tomatoes
1 medium onion or 1 bunch
   green onions, coarsely
   chopped
3 to 4 new potatoes, diced
1 to 1½ quarts water
6 large egg yolks or 3 large
   whole eggs
1 pint sour cream
Brown sugar and lemon
   juice, if needed
Salt and pepper to taste

Put all the vegetables in a soup pot and cover with the water. (Not too much or the soup will be thin.) Bring to a boil and cook until the vegetables are soft, about 10 minutes. Beat the yolks or eggs very well. Add the sour cream to the yolks or eggs. Beat the egg mixture into the vegetables while they are hot, but not boiling. Add the brown sugar or lemon juice (or both) to taste for more sweet-and-sour flavor. Add salt and pepper to taste. Chill. This keeps well.

❋ GARFINKLE FAMILY NOODLE PUDDING

Makes 10 to 12 servings

1 (8-ounce) package thin egg noodles	Preheat the oven to 350°F.
1 (8-ounce) package cream cheese	Butter a 13 × 9-inch baking pan.
1 (16-ounce) container sour cream	Cook the noodles. Beat the next 7 ingredients with a mixer until smooth.
1 cup (2 sticks) melted butter	
8 large eggs	
1 cup sugar	
1 teaspoon salt	
1 teaspoon vanilla extract	
½ (15-ounce) box or less golden raisins	
Ground cinnamon to taste	

Spread half of the cooked noodles over the bottom of the pan. Add the raisins and sprinkle with cinnamon. Cover with the remaining noodles. Pour the egg mixture over the noodles. Sprinkle with cinnamon again. Bake for about 1 hour. Cut into squares and serve.

❋ AUNT TESSA'S POPPY SEED CAKE

My great-aunt Tessa was the youngest of my grandfather's eight siblings. She lived in Regina, Saskatchewan, so she seemed somewhat exotic. My mother says she was "an elegant cook." This cake is loaded with poppy seeds, filled with custard, and frosted with chocolate.

Makes 10 to 12 servings

FOR THE CAKE

¾ cup poppy seeds

1½ cups milk

½ cup (1 stick) butter

1½ cups sugar

2 cups cake flour

2 teaspoons baking powder

4 large egg whites (save
   2 yolks for filling), stiffly
   beaten

1 teaspoon vanilla extract

Preheat the oven to 350°F.

Butter two 9-inch cake pans.

Heat ¾ cup of the milk. Pour over the poppy seeds. Let stand overnight

Cream the butter and the sugar. Add the remaining ¾ cup of milk, alternating with the flour mixed with baking powder. Fold in the poppy seeds, then the beaten egg whites and vanilla.

Pour half the batter into each cake pan. Bake for about a half hour or until browned and a skewer stuck into the cake comes out dry. Cool. Place one layer on a serving plate and cover with the filling. Top with the second layer.

FOR THE FILLING

1 cup milk

¼ cup sugar

2 large egg yolks

1 tablespoon cornstarch

½ teaspoon vanilla extract

Mix all the ingredients and cook in a small saucepan over medium heat until the mixture is thick and custardy. Cool. Spread the filling between the cake layers.

FOR THE CHOCOLATE

FROSTING

2 cups powdered sugar

2 large eggs, slightly beaten

¼ teaspoon salt

½ teaspoon vanilla extract

½ cup milk

4 squares bitter chocolate

6 tablespoons butter

Place the sugar, eggs, salt, vanilla extract, and milk in a bowl over another bowl of ice water and stir to mix. Melt the chocolate and butter together and, while warm, add to the milk mixture. Beat and beat and beat until thick and creamy. Frost the cake.

❆ PAM'S GRANDMOTHER'S IRISH RAISIN SODA BREAD

Elizabeth Dunn came to the United States from Tullamore, Ireland, in 1904 at the age of twenty. She brought this recipe with her. "The bread is pretty plain," Pam says. "But it always makes me feel good to eat a thick slice with butter on it, just like I did as a kid, sitting on the kitchen stool next to the oven."

Makes 1 loaf

4 cups flour
4 teaspoons baking powder
1 teaspoon salt
1 cup sugar
2 cups raisins (any kind)
2 tablespoons butter
1–1½ cups milk

Preheat the oven to 350°F.

Combine the flour, baking powder, salt, and sugar. Mix in the raisins until all are coated. Melt the butter in a baking pan. (Note from Pam: "I use a 10-inch cast-iron frying pan. I've tried other things, but it just doesn't taste the same.") After coating the bottom and sides of the pan, drain the remaining butter into the dry ingredients and mix. Gradually add the milk until you get a moist but stiff dough. Spread the dough in the pan into a round loaf. Cook at 350°F for 45 minutes to 1 hour, until golden brown.

Cool. Remove from the pan. Slice. Enjoy with lots of butter and a nice cup of Irish breakfast tea with milk.

COLD COMFORT

※   ※   ※

*I doubt whether the world holds for anyone a more
soul-stirring surprise than the first adventure with ice-cream.*
HEYWOOD BROUN

I N AN episode of *The West Wing*, President Jed Bartlet and Senator Arnold Vinick, the Republican candidate who hopes to suc-
ceed him, go down to the White House kitchen together after a
meeting. Bartlet takes six tubs of ice cream from the freezer and
the two men sit there on stools and eat right from the carton. "The
hardest thing about this job," Bartlet says, "is knowing this stash is
down here twenty-four hours a day." Whatever else you think
about them as politicians, you now know they're both good guys.

Ignoring the bar in the president's residence, they go down to
the basement like two little boys and eat ice cream, unsanitarily
double-dipping their spoons into buckets of vanilla fudge swirl. In
the middle of a serious discussion of religion and prayer, Bartlet
says, "Try the pistachio."

People decompress, celebrate, or cheer up with a bowl of ice
cream. I once worked at a magazine with a guy who dealt with
heavy pressure by eating a whole pint of ice cream at his desk
while he worked. He remained remarkably thin.

Our inner children are ready to drop everything, even TV matters of state, for ice cream. It's a happy food. It takes us back to
peak childhood memories—birthday parties, lightning bugs, the
beach. Which may be why the best ice cream in the world is wherever you grew up. Many neighborhood ice cream parlors are gone

and we eat plenty of high-quality nationally produced chocolate fudge mocha. But our hearts belong to the hometown brand.

Rory is from Cincinnati, which, he says, means "Graeter's ice cream runs through my veins like life's blood." Rory's an actor, but I don't think he's being overly dramatic in this case. Too many people agree with him. The Graeter family has been making traditional French pot ice cream by hand, two gallons at a time, since 1870. The good people of Cincinnati wait patiently.

Rory's pulse begins to race when he thinks about Graeter's chocolate chip ice cream. Liquid chocolate is poured into the ice cream while it is spinning in the French pot machine. When the ice cream is frozen, a paddle is used to break up the frozen chocolate layer into huge chunks. One ninety-year-old Cincinnati grandmother packs Graeter's ice cream in dry ice and sends it to deprived relatives in Florida.

Like other small companies, Graeter's offers seasonal flavors. In fall, they have pumpkin spice and cinnamon ice creams and apple cider sorbet. In summer, watermelon sorbet is made along with peach ice cream and a chocolate coconut almond fudge ice cream that Rory's aunt stockpiles for the year.

In Sacramento, summer nights mean Gunther's ice cream. Ryan's dad was in a softball league, and every Thursday after the game they'd go to Gunther's. On his own, Ryan went to Vic's, a little black-and-white-checkered neighborhood place where his mom still gets her hot fudge sundaes. His aunt from San Diego always carries a pint of Vic's hot fudge back with her on the plane.

People in San Francisco practically weep when talking about Mitchell's. Another family-owned place, Mitchell's has been making exotic handmade ice creams in San Francisco's Mission District since 1953. There are the usual seasonal flavors such as cantaloupe and white peach, the unusual tastes such as Thai tea and cinnamony Mexican chocolate, and the totally unexpected—purple yam and avocado. When I stopped in one summer afternoon, the line snaked out the door and down the block.

In Minneapolis where I grew up, summer was a swim in the lake, a painful sunburn, and a bike ride to Bridgeman's for peppermint bonbon ice cream. It was pink with little bits of peppermint candy that stuck to your fingers. Bridgeman's was a hangout. You went after swimming, after dancing school, after Sunday school. It was the home of the Turtle Sundae and the Lalapalooza—eight scoops of ice cream smothered in butterscotch, pineapple, and strawberry toppings with nuts, cherries, and a sliced banana. My friend Mike once ate a whole one.

In Texas, Blue Bell ice cream is almost a religion. With characteristic Texas understatement, the Brenham Creamery Co., which makes Blue Bell in little Brenham, Texas, claims Blue Bell is the best ice cream in the country. "We eat all we can, and we sell the rest," they say. It is very good ice cream. Texans' strong feelings for Blue Bell almost caused an international incident. In 1987, at the height of tensions between the United States and Japan over trade issues, an article came out in the Texas papers saying a Japanese company was making a knockoff ice cream called Blue Bell. Texas was furious, and its senior senator, Lloyd Bentsen, sent a scathing letter to the U.S. trade representative. It was all over the news. A panicky Japanese embassy let the folks in Tokyo know that they were in danger of a meltdown, and the government shut down the phony Blue Bell operation.

More passion-stirring hometown ice cream makers: Mayfield Dairy in Athens, Tennessee, started in 1923 with a few Jersey cows, is now one of the largest milk and ice cream companies in the South. Chicagoans from the North Shore are loyal to Homer's, which opened in Wilmette in 1935, and supposedly was a favorite of gangster Al Capone. Downtown Chicagoans still go to Margie's, where scoops of homemade ice cream are heaped into clamshell-shaped bowls.

Others swear by ice cream from the Creamery at Penn State, where they've been churning it out since 1896. There's Amy's in Austin; Carl's in Fredericksburg, Virginia; and Gray's in Rhode Island. Every one of them makes the best ice cream on the planet. Just ask people who grew up anywhere near where they're made.

But if we can't be with the one we love, we love the one we're with. Since Ben and Jerry met in seventh-grade gym class, high-quality, premium ice cream has become big business. Something like 95 percent of Americans eat ice cream—about 22 quarts per person per year.

Even a diet-crazed nation won't give up its ice cream. There are low-fat, low-sugar, low-carb versions. But let's be clear. What makes ice cream really good is butterfat. A lot of butterfat. And this is the ice cream that sells. Premium ice creams—the ones that taste like you got them at the little ice cream parlor in your hometown—outsell both regular ice cream and any of the diet ice creams. We just don't want a USDA-authorized portion of low-fat ice cream. We're looking for serious indulgence and that means a big bowl of high-fat ice cream.

The FDA won't let you call yourself ice cream unless you contain at least 10 percent butterfat. "Premium" ice cream has to have at least 16 percent butterfat and often packs in far more. Throw in some eggs and you can call it French ice cream. The fat is what makes the ice cream rich and smooth. It is also what makes ice cream fattening and expensive. We don't mind paying four dollars for a cup of coffee with some fluffy milk, so we gladly shell out the same for a scoop of really good ice cream.

Today's flavors have gone way beyond vanilla, chocolate, and strawberry. Chocolate chip cookie dough and dulce de leche seem old hat compared to ice creams flavored with beer, bacon, and barbecue available at some seashore shops. I experienced the outer limits of flavor weirdness in Dolores Hidalgo, Mexico. It's a pretty, colonial town in the high plains famous as the birthplace of Mexico's fight for independence, colorful Talavera pottery, and really wacky ice cream. In each corner of the town's central square, vendors sell locally made ice cream in these flavors: tequila, cilantro, avocado, corn, cheese, shrimp, and fried pork rind. I thought the tequila was pretty good.

Despite all the choices available, the most consistently popular ice cream flavor is simple, plain old vanilla. Especially if it tastes like the rich, handmade, comforting ice cream of childhood.

✳ ANN'S CHOCOLATE SAUCE

A friend in Texas gave me this recipe; it's sinfully good.

Makes 1½ cups sauce

¼ cup (½ stick) butter ¼ cup shaved unsweetened chocolate (about 1 square)	Stir the butter and chocolate together over low heat until smooth.
¼ cup unsweetened cocoa ¾ cup sugar ½ cup heavy cream ⅛ teaspoon salt 1 teaspoon vanilla extract	Add the remaining ingredients. Bring the mixture to a boil. Remove from the heat. Add the vanilla.

Serve over "the world's best" ice cream of your choice. Refrigerate and reheat what's left over in hot water.

KITCHEN MAGIC

✳   ✳   ✳

Cuisine is both an art and a science.
LUCIEN TENDRET

E VEN IF they'd been invented last week, popovers would seem old-fashioned. They're the peonies of the muffin world—something your grandmother would have had on a table covered with a damask cloth, lace doilies, and the good china.

Popovers mean tea on country estates and meals in the formal dining rooms of elegant department stores. A big treat in 1950s Minneapolis was to go to the Oak Grill at Dayton's. It was a very grown-up restaurant with formal table service in a clubby, oak-paneled room. After you were seated in comfortable armchairs, the hot popovers arrived. Dayton's, like many local department stores, is gone. But the original Neiman Marcus in Dallas is still serving the huge, warm popovers with strawberry butter and a cup of chicken broth—that they've offered since the 1950s.

The Jordan Pond House in Maine is a classic popover kind of place. They have been serving popovers with strawberry jam for afternoon tea on the lawn since the 1800s when fashionable visitors dropped by in horse-drawn carriages.

My friend Nancy's parents camped in Acadia every summer for twenty years. "The high point of the whole trip," she says, "was going to the Jordan Pond House for popovers. My dad could hardly wait for teatime at four. Killing time before popovers was a major activity." On the first anniversary of her father's death, her mother, family, and some old friends made a pilgrimage to Jordan Pond for tea and popovers.

Popovers even have the Good Housekeeping seal of approval. They've been the stars of lunches at the magazine for at least the last sixty years.

In what many young people probably think of as prehistory, home economics classes (now called family and consumer science classes) taught girls how to make popovers while the boys were in shop class learning how to make wooden cutting boards.

All I remember about my eighth grade home ec course is that I got an F on my sundress and an A on my popover.

Actually, I remember something else. I learned from my popover that cooking is magic. You can pour a soupy mixture of eggs, milk, flour, and salt into muffin tins and 40 minutes later take a tray full of puffy golden little chefs' hats out of the oven. No baking soda, no baking powder, no yeast.

Popovers, of course, have more to do with chemistry than magic. Given the right conditions, batter with a lot of liquid produces enough steam to act as a leavening agent. As the batter bakes, it rises and "pops over" the sides of the tin, producing a hollow muffin with a crisp brown crust and moist insides.

After learning the technique from Mrs. Johnson in home ec, I successfully prepared popovers at home for several days. But in the years between then and now, I left popovers behind.

Then I took my son, who was a student at New York University, to lunch at the Popover Café on the Upper West Side. He was thrilled. He said he's always loved popovers and remembers my making them "all the time" when he was little. That's not the way I remember it, but I love the idea that he thinks of me as the kind of mother who always made popovers.

I realized then, there is absolutely no reason not to make popovers all the time. They're good for breakfast with jam, at a luncheon with salad, or for dinner served under chicken à la king. Popovers make such a dramatic entrance wearing their big, poofed hats, you will be deemed a cook of tremendous skill. Plus, they've been out of general circulation for years, putting you on the cutting edge of retro food.

Americans have been making popovers—once inexplicably called Laplanders—for a couple of centuries. Our popovers are probably offspring of English Yorkshire pudding which, of course, is nothing like pudding. What it is like is a giant popover. In Mrs. Glasse's *Art of Cookery Made Plain and Easy*, America's most popular cookbook in 1776, she instructs Yorkshire pudding cooks to make a mixture like pancake batter, add it to some boiling meat drippings in a pan on the fire, and serve with roast beef. "It is an excellent good pudding; the gravy of the meat eats well with it," Mrs. Glasse writes. It is a popover.

Many cultures have popoverish concoctions. In France, *choux* pastry—used to make éclairs and gougères—is, basically, a popover recipe. The English toad-in-a-hole is a sausage cooked in a popover. One of my mother's special Sunday brunch recipes is a German apple pancake, a huge popover filled with apples sautéed in butter and sugar. She makes the pancake/popover in a skillet in the oven, fills it with the apple mixture, and rolls it into a showstopping package.

One Passover, my mom brought popovers to the breakfast table. She had found a recipe that conformed to the holiday's restriction on using grains other than matzo by using matzo cake meal.

However you make popovers, wherever you make them, the chemistry remains the same.

Because popovers follow a formula to produce a chemical reaction, you can't change the proportions. The ratio of flour to liquid is 1 to 1. Added fat is not necessary, but many people like a little melted butter in the batter. The only other ingredient is salt.

When the popover batter hits the oven heat, the liquid sends off steam and the popovers balloon into hollow shells. Normally in baking, flour forms gluten, a chain of protein that gives the bread its shape. In popovers, the flour is so diluted, the egg proteins make the shell hold its shape. These proteins allow the batter to stretch, hold the steam, and form crusty sides. I wish Mrs. Hill, my lovely high school chemistry teacher, could see how far I've come.

There are a few things on which most (but certainly not all) cooks agree:

- The batter (which can be made ahead) should be at room temperature.
- Use large eggs, not small, medium, or jumbo.
- Don't overmix.
- Generously grease the popover pan or muffin tin with melted butter or a neutral oil, such as canola
- Start with a hot oven (400°F to 450°F) for the first 20 minutes to make them pop, and then lower to 350°F to set the batter.
- Don't peek. Ever. If you open the oven door, the heat escapes, the oven cools, the steam condenses, and the popovers collapse.

Some people start with a cold oven. Others prefer to keep the batter in the refrigerator until ready to use. Some cooks sift the flour. Others add melted butter to the batter.

Then there's the question of the pan. Popovers can be made in custard cups or muffin tins, although most popover mavens agree that a popover pan should be deeper than it is wide. There are special popover pans of aluminum, tin, cast iron, glass, and ceramic. I have an aluminum one that looks like something from the space shuttle, with the cups separated by rods to allow hot air to circulate around each popover. It makes huge, light popovers.

I also have a cast-iron popover pan from Lodge Manufacturing in Tennessee. The Lodge family has been making cast-iron cookware for more than one hundred years. Lodge is the only domestic cast-iron cookware foundry and America's oldest family-owned cookware manufacturer. I figured they knew what they were doing by now, so I bought one of their popover pans. "It won't make those big poufy ones," the woman at the store said. You need a deeper bowl to make a popover that's as big as your head. The Lodge pan popovers are the small, dense kind.

I know someone who makes Yorkshire pudding at Christmas in

her cast-iron popover pan. She preheats the pan, pours the fat from the roast into the cups and tops with the batter. That way, guests get individual puddings. Not a bad idea.

Popovers are best when they're hot and steaming, but I'm told they can even be made in advance and frozen. If you're not serving them right away, remove from the pan and puncture the sides to let the steam out quickly before the interior gets soggy. Place on a cookie sheet and put back in the turned-off oven for up to 30 minutes before serving. Or, put them in a Ziploc bag and freeze. Full disclosure: I've never served popovers any way but hot and straight from the oven, but the experts swear it can be done.

This is chemistry, but it's not rocket science. Four ingredients and fairly simple directions.

Still, sometimes popovers don't work. It could be anything— humidity, the oven, a draft, bad karma. But if the conditions are just right and the popovers pop, they'll take you back to your grandmother's for tea.

✳ POPOVERS

Makes 12 small popovers, 6 large

1¼ cups all-purpose flour
¼ teaspoon salt
3 large eggs, at room
   temperature
1¼ cups milk, at room
   temperature

Preheat the oven to 450°F and set the rack in the middle.

Spray a popover pan with vegetable oil.

In a bowl, mix the flour and salt. Whisk the eggs and milk together and add to the dry ingredients. Mix until it reaches the consistency of heavy cream, but don't overbeat. Pour the batter into a 2- to 4-cup liquid measuring cup for easy pouring. Let the batter sit at room temperature for at least ½ hour.

The batter can be made in advance and refrigerated in a sealed container for up to 4 days. Bring back to room temperature before using.

Preheat the greased pan in the oven for 2 to 3 minutes, until hot. Fill the cups half full with batter. Many cooks pour the batter in every other cup so the popovers don't touch. I'm too greedy for that. If they touch, I just gently pull them apart.

Bake for 20 minutes; then lower the heat to 350°F and bake for 15 to 20 minutes more. They should be golden brown and crisp. *Do not open the oven during baking.*

NOTE: Popovers make a wonderful bed for chicken à la king. See page 104.

✳ PASSOVER POPOVERS

Makes 20 small popovers, 12 large

½ cup vegetable oil
1⅓ cups water
½ teaspoon salt
1½ cups matzo meal
½ cup matzo cake meal
1 tablespoon sugar
7 large eggs

Preheat the oven to 400°F.

Grease the muffin tins or popover pans well.

Place the oil, water, and salt in a large saucepan and bring to a boil. Add the matzo meal, cake meal, and sugar. Stir until the mixture comes away from the sides of the pan. Cool.

Place the mixture in a food processor. Add the eggs, one at a time, turning the processor on and off after each addition. Beat together for 4 to 5 minutes.

Pour the batter into the muffin tins or a popover pan. Bake for 15 minutes; then turn the oven down to 375°F and bake for another 40 minutes. *Do not open the oven door.*

❊ MOM'S GERMAN PANCAKE

This is a wonderful, dramatic breakfast or brunch dish for company. I don't know why it's called a German pancake, but my mother always referred to it that way.

Makes 4 to 6 servings

3 large eggs, at room temperature	Preheat the oven to 425°F.
1 cup milk at room temperature	In a medium bowl, combine all the ingredients except the butter and filling. Beat for 2 to 3 minutes by hand or with an electric mixer until the batter is smooth.
1 cup unbleached, all-purpose flour, sifted	
½ teaspoon salt	
1 tablespoon unsalted butter	
Apple Filling (recipe follows)	

Put the butter in a 12-inch heavy skillet and place in the preheated oven. When the butter has melted and is very hot, remove the skillet from the oven and turn it so the butter coats the bottom of the pan. Pour in the batter and bake 15 minutes. The pancake will puff up during the first 15 minutes of baking. Lower the temperature to 350°F and bake for about 10 minutes more, until the pancake is crisp and golden brown. Puncture it with a fork.

Remove the pancake from the oven, loosen it from the pan, and place it on a serving platter. Spoon most of the filling over the pancake and roll it up. (Save a little filling for the top.) Cut the pancake into serving pieces crosswise. Serve immediately.

FOR THE APPLE FILLING

3 tablespoons butter	Melt the butter in a sauté pan large enough to hold the apples. Sauté the apples for several minutes. Add the brown sugar and cook about 10 minutes more, turning often, until the apples can be easily pierced with a sharp knife. If the apples seem too firm, cover the
4 large, firm, apples of any kind, peeled and thinly sliced	
2 tablespoons brown sugar	
1 tablespoon lemon juice	

½ teaspoon ground
  cinnamon

pan and steam for another few minutes.
Watch carefully. The apples should retain
some crispness and not be mushy. Take the
pan off the stove, mix in the lemon and cinnamon, and let the apples cool slightly. The
filling can be made ahead of time and reheated.

LET THEM EAT CAKE

❋   ❋   ❋

There are three hundred and sixty-four days when you might get
un–birthday presents . . . and only one for birthday presents, you know.
LEWIS CARROLL

FOR ONE day every year, you are the center of the universe. On that day, you can have your cake and eat it too.

Birthday cake rituals often are established at an early age and for some people never deviate. Others, as they get older, opt for more grown-up confections. No one, however, outgrows the expectation that on the date of his or her birth there will be a cake. What kind of cake depends on whether you're a traditionalist or a risk taker.

Every year for her children's birthdays, Gayle made an angel food cake with the white seven-minute frosting from *The Joy of Cooking*. When her son turned thirty, Gayle suggested trying a different kind of cake. Nothing doing. Message: Do not tamper with my sacred childhood memories. At least not quite yet. The white cake is back.

Sarah's mother always made her a carrot cake. Now Sarah makes the same cake for every family birthday, for most of her friends' birthdays, for dinners in the neighborhood, school functions, and office parties. She's upped the number of carrots and cut back on the sugar. Still, her cake won a prize at the office summer picnic bake-off.

Jen, too, always made a carrot cake for her three daughters' birthdays. She's an artist, so it was the same recipe but the form shifted. "I made it in various shapes and sizes," she says. "One was the hedgehog, where you cut a round cake in half, glue it together with cream cheese icing, and put toasted sliced almonds all over it for its prickles. That's a big hit for the two- to seven-year-old crowd. But it's good enough to serve adults, and can be made very beautiful sliced in thick cubes, decorated with half a walnut in the middle, with a little sugar silver ball in each corner."

Cakes don't have to be elaborate to be good. Ann's mother saw a beautiful cake at a catered party and knew she could get the same effect with far less effort. She bought an angel food cake and sliced it in half horizontally. A pint of sweetened whipped cream was the filling between the cake layers. (Only use a third of the cream.) Then she unwrapped a bunch of little Heath bars, put them in a bag, and smashed them with a hammer. She folded them into the remaining whipping cream, frosted the cake, and refrigerated it for a couple of hours. "It was incredibly light and looked really special," Ann says. This has been the family birthday cake ever since.

Jen remembers her mother often made a plain sponge cake and topped it with hot melted chocolate and a dollop of whipped cream for birthdays. "Quite yummy," she says. She remembers less fondly, however, the fruit salad sometimes served as birthday dessert. Really not in the spirit of the day.

Bunny's family chocolate cake is on its third generation. "My mother made it. I make it. My sister makes it. My cousin Marilyn up the street makes it, and now my daughter Alexa makes it," she says. Her mother always served it with a piece missing. She tasted it first to make sure it was okay. Bunny says it always was.

Annette in Chicago and Beth in Washington, D.C., do not know each other. Yet, they use almost exactly the same recipe with different frostings for their children's birthday cakes. They were undoubtedly both drawn to its simplicity. Annette has three children (now grown) and Beth has four (still young). This cake uses a cake mix and a pudding mix. Beth and Annette are both excellent cooks and say this cake is not only foolproof but delicious, as well.

Annette made it as a layer cake and cut it in the shape of the number of years of the birthday child. When they became teenagers, she made two layer cakes to accommodate the double digits. Beth makes hers as a Bundt cake.

The only big-deal cake I ever had for my son was for his first birthday. I ordered a train cake from a local bakery and it was spectacular. It had a colorful cake engine and caboose and cake cars carrying licorice logs. Sadly, of course, he doesn't remember it. For his childhood birthday parties, I made a Texas sheet cake, the fallback of many people I know. It is a thin chocolate sheet cake made with sour cream and cocoa with fudgy chocolate frosting. It's simple, delicious, and easy to decorate. I have no idea where the name came from. It's big; maybe that's why it has a Texas association.

Some cakes have a seasonal theme. Mary Susan was born in May, and her mother always made her a Maypole cake. It was baked in a round pan and had a large pastel candy stick in the center. From the top of the candy stick she hung multicolored pastel ribbons that attached to the cupcakes that were satellites around the larger cake. Now that's cool. My son's birthday is in the fall so I've always made an apple tart for the *family* birthday dinner.

I remember only one birthday cake from my childhood, but it was a thing of beauty. For my fifth birthday, my mother baked a many-layered cake with a doll coming out of the top. The cake tiers looked like the doll was wearing something from Scarlett O'Hara's closet.

Birthday cakes go from the sublime to the ridiculous.

Megan's parents lived in Ethiopia in the 1960s and her mother spent years writing a book called *Empress Taytu and Menelik II*. The Ethiopians believed their royal family, headed by Menelik I, was directly descended from the Queen of Sheba. So when her mom heard about a Queen of Sheba cake, that became Megan's birthday cake. It is a flourless chocolate cake served with a custard sauce. Megan's mother's instructions begin, "Whack up ½ cup of blanched almonds." Megan has done a translation.

On the other end of the spectrum is the Twinkies' cake. Margaret's cousin had a cake made of Twinkies when they were little and she never got over her envy. So she made one for her son when he was in grade school. He was shocked that he was getting something so utterly forbidden.

Plain or fancy, silly or serious, there has to be a cake. Everyone wants—everyone expects—a birthday cake. A birthday without a cake is like a wedding without a bride.

✳ ANNETTE/BETH BIRTHDAY CAKE

Makes 10 to 12 servings

1 (18¼-ounce) box devil's food or fudge cake mix
1 (3.4-ounce) box chocolate fudge pudding mix
1 cup sour cream
4 large eggs, beaten
½ cup water
½ cup canola oil
1 (12-ounce) package Nestle chocolate chunks (not chips, according to Beth)
Annette's Frosting (recipe follows)

Preheat the oven to 350°F.

Place all the ingredients except the chocolate chunks and frosting in the bowl of an electric mixer and beat until fairly smooth. Stir in the chocolate. Pour into buttered cake pans (2 round pans for layer cake or a Bundt pan). Bake for 50 minutes. Frost when cooled.

ANNETTE'S FROSTING
¼ cup heavy cream
1 tablespoon instant coffee
24 ounces semisweet chocolate chips

Heat the cream in a small saucepan until it bubbles around the edges. Add the instant coffee and stir. Add the chocolate chips and cook, stirring, until melted. Annette: "This is the best icing in the world." Beth's frosting is just cream and chips with a little corn syrup. She melts the whole thing in the microwave and tops with sprinkles.

✳ BUNNY'S FAMILY SOUR MILK DEVIL'S FOOD CAKE

Makes 10 to 12 servings

3 squares baking chocolate (unsweetened)

½ cup shortening (use ¼ cup butter and ¼ cup margarine, softened to room temperature)

1½ cups dark brown sugar, loosely packed

2 large eggs

2 cups cake flour

1½ teaspoons baking soda

¼ teaspoon salt

1½ cups buttermilk

1 teaspoon vanilla extract

Frosting (recipe follows)

Preheat the oven to 350°F. Grease two 8-inch cake pans.

Melt the chocolate in a double boiler or in the microwave. Set aside to cool slightly.

Meanwhile, cream the shortening in a mixer. Add the brown sugar a little at a time. Mix thoroughly. Add the eggs one at a time. Mix until well blended. Add the melted chocolate and blend well.

Sift the flour, baking soda, and salt. Then add the flour mixture and buttermilk to the chocolate mixture, alternating, beginning and ending with the flour. Add the vanilla. Pour into the cake pans and bake for 25 to 30 minutes. The cake is done when a toothpick comes out clean, about 30 minutes.

Frost the cake. Serve whole or with a slice missing.

FROSTING

½ cup (1 stick) butter or margarine (or mixture), softened to room temperature

1½ cups confectioners' sugar, sifted

1-ounce square unsweetened chocolate, melted in double boiler or microwave

1 tablespoon instant coffee, dissolved in a little hot water

¼ teaspoon vanilla extract

In a food processor, cream the butter or margarine. Gradually add the sugar; beat until smooth. Add the melted chocolate, coffee, and vanilla. Beat until blended. (If the frosting is too thin, add more confectioners' sugar; if it's too thick, add more coffee).

※ TEXAS SHEET CAKE

Makes 20 to 24 servings

1 cup (2 sticks) butter
1 cup water
¼ cup cocoa
2 cups flour
2 cups sugar
⅛ teaspoon salt
1 teaspoon baking soda
½ cup sour cream
2 large eggs
1 teaspoon vanilla extract
Frosting (recipe follows)
1 cup chopped pecans
   (optional)

Preheat the oven to 375°F.
Butter a 15½ × 10½ × 1-inch jelly-roll pan.

Combine the butter, water, and cocoa in a saucepan. Heat to boiling, stirring occasionally.

In the bowl of an electric mixer, mix together the flour, sugar, salt, and baking soda. Remove the butter mixture from the heat and add to the dry ingredients. (Don't clean the pot. You'll use it for the frosting.) Blend well. Add the sour cream, eggs, and vanilla. Blend again. Pour into the pan and bake for 20 minutes, or until a toothpick inserted into the cake comes out clean.

While the cake is baking, make the frosting. Pour the frosting on the hot cake and spread. Sprinkle with chopped nuts, if desired.

FOR THE FROSTING
½ cup (1 stick) butter
1 box (1 pound)
   Confectioners' sugar,
   sifted
¼ cup cocoa
6 tablespoons milk
1 teaspoon vanilla extract

Combine all the ingredients in a saucepan and heat, stirring until smooth. The frosting will be thick because it softens on the hot cake.

❊ SARAH'S FOURTEEN-CARAT CAKE

Makes 14 to 16 servings

2 cups flour
2 teaspoons baking powder
1½ teaspoons baking soda
1 teaspoon salt
2 teaspoons ground
cinnamon
1¼ cups sugar
¾ cup vegetable oil
4 large eggs
½ cup applesauce
1 pound carrots, grated
½ cup chopped nuts

FOR THE FROSTING
½ cup (1 stick) butter
8 ounces cream cheese
¾ cup powdered sugar
1 teaspoon vanilla extract

Preheat the oven to 350°F.
Butter two 9-inch cake pans.

Sift together the flour, baking powder, baking soda, salt, and cinnamon. Mix in the sugar, oil, and eggs.

Using an electric mixer, blend the cake ingredients and pour into the cake pans. Bake for 30 to 40 minutes.

Cream all the frosting ingredients in a food processor. Allow cake to cool. Frost.

❊ QUEEN OF SHEBA CAKE

Makes 8 to 10 servings

½ cup blanched almonds
(or preground almonds)
3 tablespoons cornstarch
11 tablespoons sugar
4 ounces semisweet
chocolate
2 tablespoons water
1 teaspoon instant coffee
½ cup applesauce

Preheat the oven to 350°F.
Grease and lightly flour a cake pan or springform pan.

Pulverize the almonds, cornstarch, and 7 tablespoons of the sugar in a food processor.

Melt the chocolate, water, coffee, and butter in the top of a double boiler. Let cool

Continued

¼ cup (½ stick) butter
4 large eggs, separated
Confectioners' sugar
Custard sauce

slightly and stir in the almond mixture.
Turn the mixture into a medium bowl.

Stir the yolks, one at a time, into the chocolate mixture. Beat the whites with the remaining 4 tablespoons of sugar and fold
into the chocolate mixture.

Pour into the prepared cake pan and bake for 25 minutes, or until a toothpick inserted into the cake comes out clean. Cool for 10 minutes and then
remove from the pan. Let cool on a rack.

Sprinkle some confectioners' sugar on top. (Megan sprinkles the sugar
through a doily. It makes a pretty design.) Serve with a custard sauce.

Make a custard sauce (Megan uses the *Joy of Cooking* recipe) with enough
time to chill it before serving.

TIED TO MY APRON STRINGS

❋   ❋   ❋

I thought, as I wiped my eyes on the corner of my apron:
Penelope did this too . . . This is an ancient gesture, authentic, antique. . . .
EDNA ST. VINCENT MILLAY

WHEN SHE was a toddler, my neighbor Phoebe would visit me every day, go straight to the kitchen, pull my apron down from its hook, and hand it to me. She seemed to think I was incomplete without it. She was right.

Phoebe couldn't go to bed without a large, flop-eared rabbit in a gingham dress. I can't go into the kitchen without my apron.

I don't remember when I started wearing an apron. It was probably when I got married in the 1970s to emulate my mother—in much the same way that I served my new husband cocktails before a dinner of meat, potatoes, and two vegetables. After gaining ten pounds in three weeks, we concluded that we could cut the cocktails and eat lighter. But I stuck with the apron. I may be one of the few women to still have a kitchen drawer dedicated solely to aprons.

The dictionary defines an apron as a garment fastened in the back, worn to protect clothing. True. But I like the second meaning, which is that an apron is a "protective shield."

Aprons may be as old as man. In Genesis, after they ate the forbidden fruit, "Adam and Eve sewed fig leaves together, and made themselves aprons." Even George Washington wore an apron. It was made of white lambskin, the symbol of a master mason. Many loyal lodge members wear their aprons into the grave.

There actually was a time when people did not have closets full of clothes. A woman might have one or two dresses that she washed by hand and hung to dry. Her apron protected the dress. She could wash the apron every few days and keep the dress clean for quite a while. Cooks, blacksmiths, butchers, carpenters, and bakers still wear aprons to protect their clothes.

Aprons even can be used for sex education. As a girl, my first clue that babies didn't come from the supermarket was in the lyrics of the folk song "Careless Love":

Once I wore my apron low,
You'd follow me through rain and snow.
Now I wear my apron high,
You'll see my door and pass it by.

The first thing girls learned in home ec class was how to make an apron with a waistband. Then, for gender reinforcement, we put on our aprons and cooked at the stove. When I was growing up, kids were in the yard, dads were at the office, and moms were in the kitchen wearing aprons.

A friend said that when she got married in the mid-seventies, the woman next door made her seven gingham, cross-stitched half aprons, one for each day of the week. Another friend of the same vintage says when she got married her West Texas grandmother made her an orange, ruffled hostess apron. It came with a matching pot holder.

Form did not always follow function in the apron world. My mother and her contemporaries made so-called hostess aprons out of things such as organdy and sequins for fancy parties. I remember seeing someone else's mother in a turquoise blue taffeta number.

I haven't seen a hostess apron lately. Although, when I moved into my new house, my friend Stephanie gave me a starched, cream-colored linen-and-lace French apron as a housewarming gift and I wear it on very special occasions such as the evening I served dinner to my son and his friends on his sixteenth birthday.

I may have a genetic predisposition to aprons. My mother says my great-grandmother always wore an apron—a yard of fabric with a piece of string run through a hem at the top. My mother has finally given up her apron, and now wears a cotton T-shirt dress in the kitchen. But she still has one hanging on a hook in the pantry. I wear it when I visit.

During World War II, my grandfather had a factory in Chicago that made pillows for soldiers that spelled out MOTHER and "the many things she means." He gave my very creative mother the leftover satin—tons of it—and told her to "design something." While my father was fighting in Italy, she took the leftover material, hemmed it, gathered it and put a ruffle on it. It was an apron. Then she had "To my love from Camp Landing, Fla."—or some other military post—silkscreened on the front, and they were sold at the PX. Mom used the proceeds from her apron business to buy the handmade, sterling silver flatware she still sets her table with.

Aprons fell out of fashion with the rise of the women's movement. When women began to spend less time at home and more time at the office, the kitchen apron became an emotionally charged symbol, a reminder of female drudgery.

There has been, however, something of an apron revival—modern chefwear catalogs feature clogs, chef's pants, and serious aprons. I have seen ads for aprons with Velcro closures to "avoid the frustration of trying to tie a conventional apron behind your back."

La Cuisine, a fine kitchenware store in Alexandria, Virginia, reports that sales of full-length French bistro-style and bib aprons are up dramatically. These are no-nonsense aprons in a heavy cotton canvas weave in denim, white, or black. Nancy Pollard, the owner, says people are buying aprons for the same reason they are buying Jeeps and Land Rovers. We've gone back to the land and back to the kitchen.

There are hundreds of vintage aprons for sale on eBay—handpainted and crocheted, in silk and in gingham. You can wear them while making martinis in an art deco cocktail shaker.

Aprons also are used as a communications tool. Fabrics are emblazoned with bright chili peppers, schools of fish, and coffee cups.

Restaurants and specialty shops sell aprons bearing their slogans.

There are joke aprons: "If bowling is a sport, I'm an athlete" or "Martha Stewart doesn't live here." Stephanie's son brought her an apron from his cross-country trip. It pictures the naked behinds of four men and reads, "I'm somewhere behind Mount Rushmore." It's one of her most treasured possessions.

With the return of the apron, I feel as if I can finally come out of the pantry. I remember putting on my apron after a long day of work and feeling politically incorrect. But for me, an apron has always been empowering.

Every morning, I dress in my workout clothes and go into the dark kitchen where I put on my apron—before I have coffee, before I look at the paper, before I quiet the barking dog. Sometimes I wear it over my bathrobe. I've come home cold and late from a long, harried day at work and put an apron on over my winter coat. A friend recalls that when her mother got home from work she would be tired and dragging. She'd put down her briefcase, walk into the kitchen, and it was as if the act of putting on her apron energized her. Wearing her armor, she was ready for anything.

✳ STEPHANIE'S FRIED CHICKEN

Frying anything requires at least one apron. The more fastidious cook may even change aprons in the middle of frying. Every Fourth of July, Stephanie fries chicken for just about anyone who walks past her house on his or her way to watch the fireworks at the U.S. Capitol. I often help her. This takes the better part of a day, several aprons, and a shampoo. A heavy pan such as cast iron is essential to distribute the heat evenly. Peanut oil is good to use because it has a high smoking point. How much you season the buttermilk and the flour is up to you.

Makes 6 to 8 servings unless you have a lot of growing boys

1 quart buttermilk

Kosher salt, to taste

Black pepper (or cayenne if you like it spicy), to taste

5 pounds chicken pieces

Flour

Salt and pepper

Peanut oil

Mix the buttermilk, salt, and pepper.

Place the chicken pieces in shallow pans (or large Ziploc bags) and cover with the seasoned buttermilk. Refrigerate for several hours or overnight.

Pour the flour into a bowl, shallow pan, or big piece of waxed paper, and season with salt and pepper. You can also put the flour and chicken in a brown paper bag and shake.

In a large cast-iron skillet, heat about 2½ inches of oil over medium-high heat until just beginning to smoke.

Take the chicken pieces out of the buttermilk, shake off the excess, and dredge through the flour. Fry until golden brown, about 10 minutes a side, and turn. Turn only once. Cut into the chicken and make sure it's cooked before turning. White meat cooks more quickly than dark. Use long tongs. Place the chicken on paper towel–lined trays to absorb some of the grease.

The chicken may be served hot or at room temperature.

FAMILY DINNER

✳ ✳ ✳

The dinner table is the center for the teaching and practicing
not just of table manners but of conversation, consideration, tolerance,
family feeling, and just about all the other accomplishments of
polite society except the minuet.

MISS MANNERS

J UNE CLEAVER has left the building.

And she's taken Ward's slippers, her good pearls, and the illusion of the perfect family sitting down to dinner together every night with her. (Didn't Wally and the Beav ever whine?)

Most parents absolutely, firmly believe that the family dinner is important. Far fewer are actually able to put it together most nights. It's just not as easy as it was before life went to warp speed. In households where both parents work, or a single parent runs the household, there's often no one home to make dinner. Everyone's on a cell phone or IMing their friends. Then, there are the soccer games, the play rehearsals, SAT prep, the board meetings, and, of course, the demon TV. (Although there are still those who remember *The Shadow* and *Jack Benny* being played on the radio during dinner in the dark ages.)

I grew up before the child-centered home had been invented. Both my parents worked and were tired when they got home. We always ate together as a family, but not until after my parents relaxed and had a martini or two. At 7:30 or so it seemed like a late dinner to a child. We ate in the dining room, used cloth napkins, and had no bottles or jars on the table. After my grandfather died, my grandma came from next door to join us. My dad told jokes;

we talked, in turn, and my brother and I kicked each other under the table. We had to help clear and do the dishes.

My friends with big families had a children's dinner hour, usually with a parent at the table or in the kitchen, and their parents ate later. They all ate together at a big sit-down dinner on the weekend—Friday night in Jewish homes (not mine) and Sunday everywhere else. These meals featured a roast, buttered vegetables, dinner rolls, and animated conversation. Everyone was cleaned and pressed. There was often Jell-O.

I first experienced a Friday night dinner when I started dating my husband and he took me to his parents' house in Baltimore. The table was laid with pretty linens, fresh flowers, and silver candlesticks. It was set for twelve—a slow night. Every Friday night, my mother-in-law cooked for her four children and various friends and neighbors. The food would be set out on the sideboard and often included several main-course options: crab imperial and roast beef, or corned beef and roast chicken. There was usually a platter of marinated, canned vegetables and seasoned rice or twice-baked potatoes.

By the middle of dinner, there would often be twenty people of all ages in the dining room. Newcomers just pulled up a chair and either joined in the meal or the conversation. At some point during this particular evening, my husband and his aunt Rita got into such a heated political argument that they both ended up standing and shouting at each other at opposite ends of the table. There was bad language. No one paid any attention to them. The whole scene had a certain appeal.

I have been having regular Friday night dinners since my elderly parents moved to Washington, D.C. I invite friends, neighbors, and relatives, and the children of friends, neighbors, and relatives. It's lively and festive and something my parents can look forward to.

The golden age of the family dinner was in the innocent years before it was discovered that all food is bad for you. We didn't know from lean meats, whole grains, and seven to nine servings of fruits and vegetables at every meal. McDonald's had sold only a few million hamburgers when I was in grade school, and we were not allowed to eat there because it was "junk." Our parents—those who could afford it—had red meat for dinner almost every night. My husband's grandfather was a butcher and brought his family a weekly supply of meat. Each weekday night was assigned a different cut: Monday, steak; Tuesday, hamburgers or spaghetti with meat sauce; Wednesday, lamb chops; and Thursday, roast beef. Friday night was always roast chicken. There was the occasional veal chop or slab of liver, cold cuts, and rye bread for Saturday sandwiches, and lox and bagels for Sunday brunch. Sunday night was loose—Chinese carryout, sloppy joes, or hot dog casserole with mashed potatoes. You always knew what to expect.

While both my mother and mother-in-law worked outside their homes, they had more regular and shorter hours than today's parents. The nine-to-five workday went out with the parental cocktail hour. They also didn't have cell phones, BlackBerries, the Internet, or cable television. I'm not making excuses. My generation tried and often succeeded. Sometimes, though, a family dinner was just impossible. When I worked for a magazine, I didn't get home until after 10:00 P.M. twice a week—too late for a six-year-old to eat dinner. Pam and I would meet in the bathroom to discuss who was the worst mother. "I called the babysitter and told her to take hot dogs out of the freezer and put them in the microwave," I'd say. "Toss-up," she'd say. "My boys are having mac 'n,' cheese from a package." I can't remember where our husbands were.

Everyone from Harvard University to the National Pork Board has done studies on what Pam and I did wrong. What they've found is that kids who have regular family meals do better in school, have better vocabularies, are better behaved, more courteous, and less likely to smoke, drink, do drugs, have eating disorders, become depressed, and have sex. Oh, and they also get better nutrition.

Family dinners are where we give our kids meals, manners, and the meaning of life. The dinner table is like a finishing school, the place where children are civilized. They learn not to talk with their mouths full, to say please and thank you, to keep their elbows off the table, to serve from the left, and remove from the right. They learn to participate in a conversation and, sometimes, they learn to listen to other people talk. They see how adults reason, or don't.

The idea is to make it so much fun, kids want to come to dinner. My friend Marguerite writes a syndicated column on parenting and raised four children who became productive members of society. I therefore consider her the expert. She says there aren't many things we can give our children other than "good schools, good values, good times, and good memories." A lot of this is served with dinner. "We didn't fuss at our kids at dinner," she says. "It was a pleasant time." This is not the time to tell your children how disappointed you are in their grades, choice of friends, or body piercings and tattoos.

Things come up when you sit down together and there are fewer distractions. I'm glad I was at the table the night our seven-year-old son asked, "If they found the lost city of Atlantis, how many electoral votes would it have?" When he was even younger, he looked up from the peas he was pushing around the plate and said, "Mommy, don't use drugs. If someone comes up to you and says, 'Here are some drugs' just say 'No.'" If you don't eat together, you don't hear this stuff.

Sarah and her husband, who both work full-time, sit down to dinner with their two young sons almost every night. When everyone's seated, Will, a second grader, says, "So, how was your day, Mom?" Sarah says dinner table conversations have covered everything from what happened on the playground to a discussion about the finer points of *Star Wars* and the Senate filibuster.

When my son was in college, he wrote an essay for an urban studies class and sent it to me to proofread. It read, in part:

In my childhood home my mother spent many hours in her kitchen creating brilliant culinary sleights of hand. While most of my

*friends ate prepackaged, chemically enhanced "family style" din-
ners, my mother stealthily hid a well-rounded meal beneath the
covering of gourmet taste. These meals were always the high point
of home life for me. Both of my parents, being hardworking professionals, spent a great deal of time at their jobs. I had sports or a
play to occupy my time after school. But in the evening, we would
sit around the kitchen table and talk about our day, current events,
or the neighbors. My mother would run back and forth from the
table to the stove, checking on that evening's fare. Those dinners
helped hold our family together at the seams.*

I have not lived in vain.

Family meals don't have to be every night, and they don't have
to be dinner. My friend Kathryn, her husband, and children ate
breakfast together every day until the kids graduated from high
school.

We do the best we can, but even stressed, overworked, over-
programmed twenty-first-century families can probably do better.
We have microwaves, food processors, slow cookers, and rotisserie
chickens. The television can be turned off. We have voice mail.

The marketplace has felt our pain and responded. Supermarkets
from the mundane to the elite now function as sous chefs. You can
buy prewashed salad mix, cut-up vegetables, preseasoned chicken
strips, marinades, simmer sauces, seafood stock, and twenty-seven
different fresh and dried pastas. You can buy ready-made entrées to
just pop in the oven or meats already marinated. The industry calls
them "meal solutions." I call them a gift from God.

For those of us who want to be a bit more hands-on, planning
is key. Stock the pantry with ingredients you can turn to in an
emergency. Potatoes, carrots, and onions last a long time. A stock-
pile of dried pasta, varieties of rice, lentils, and couscous are always useful. Canned tomatoes, corn, and other vegetables can be
thrown into last-minute pasta sauces and soups. Canned beans can
be turned into soups and salads. Make sure you have plenty of

spices, oil, and vinegars for dressings and marinades. Nuts can be tossed into salads, pasta, and stir-fries for some extra protein.

Remember that the freezer is your friend. There are lots of good frozen vegetables, and grated cheese and nuts freeze well. Buy meat and bread in bulk at your neighborhood wholesale warehouse and freeze in meal-sized portions. Whenever you cook pasta sauce, soup, or casseroles make twice as much as you need and freeze the extra.

There are an infinite number of books and television shows on how to make meals in under thirty minutes. Companies called things such as Let's Dish, Dream Dinners, and My Girlfriend's Kitchen bring home cooks to commercial kitchens where they can put together twelve meals in two hours. The shopping has been done, the ingredients have been sliced and diced, the cleanup happens after you leave. You get step-by-step recipes and freezer bags. There's wine, music, and conversation. It's a party. All you need to bring is a cooler to take your meals home. It gives new meaning to the concept of homemade.

Family dinners don't have to be up to June Cleaver's standards. Women don't have to wear shirtdresses and children don't have to shine their shoes. A carryout pizza and tossed salad are fine. It doesn't matter if moms come to the table in jeans and kids in flip-flops as long as they all get there together.

✳ WEEKNIGHT TACOS/PIZZA

Anything children can put together themselves works. It gives them choice and control. Both tacos and pizza can be put out quickly and easily. They can even be nutritious. Many of the ingredients can be kept on hand in the refrigerator, freezer, or pantry for last-minute needs.

TACOS

Hard taco shells or soft
  corn or flour tortillas
Ground beef sautéed with
  packaged taco spices or
  your own (cumin,
  coriander, ground chili,
  salt, pepper, canned
  chiles, etc.)
Shredded iceberg (or other)
  lettuce
Grated Monterey Jack
  cheese
Prepared guacamole
Sour cream
Canned black beans,
  drained
Salsa

Put the taco shells or tortillas in a basket
and everything else in bowls.

PIZZA

Prepared spaghetti sauce,
  pizza sauce, tomato paste
Ready-made pizza dough
  (freezes well) or Boboli
Grated cheeses
Olives
Mushrooms
Chopped onions
Sliced peppers
Sliced meats (salami,
  pepperoni, sausage,
  chicken, turkey)

Preheat the oven to 375°F.

Spread the sauce on the pizza dough or shell.
Put everything else (the possibilities are limitless) in bowls and let everyone assemble
their own pizza or section. Place on pizza
pans or cookie sheets and bake until the ingredients are cooked, the cheese is bub-
bling, and the crust is golden brown, about
15 to 20 minutes.

✳ BROILED FLANK STEAK

Flank steaks are sold in packages of three at membership-only warehouse food clubs. I always keep a few in the freezer. They're thin and defrost quickly. Both Stephanie and I make flank steak, potatoes, and green salad for the first dinner home for our adult children. It's their favorite. Stephanie marinates hers for an hour in a cup of soy sauce, ½ cup red wine, lots of crushed garlic, some grated gingerroot, salt, and pepper. I often use a prepared mixture of about the same ingredients. Amounts depend on the size of the steak. Cook under the broiler or on the grill for 10 minutes or so on each side and slice against the grain.

✳ GARY'S SHEPHERD'S PIE

My British friend Gary, a landscape architect, cooks for his wife and two daughters every night. He often cooks Thai and Indian dishes, but makes shepherd's pie every Thursday night. It's his daughter Emily's favorite dinner. Even his shepherd's pie has an East Asian accent. Gary never makes it the same twice and doesn't measure, but he's done his best to write it all down. You can buy prepared garam masala but it often doesn't include cardamom, which has a strong flavor and is an acquired taste. I think it adds to this dish.

Makes 4 to 6 servings

FOR THE FILLING
2 tablespoons olive oil
1 medium onion, peeled
  and finely chopped
1 clove garlic, peeled and
  minced
¼ teaspoon ground cayenne
  pepper

Heat the oil in a medium frying pan. When hot, add the onion. Stir the onion until it is soft and very lightly browned, about 10 minutes. Add the garlic and cayenne pepper. Stir for another minute.

1 pound lean ground beef
½ cup red wine
½ cup ketchup
1 tablespoon
  Worcestershire sauce
1 bay leaf
¼ cup chopped fresh
  cilantro
½ teaspoon salt
Garam masala (½ teaspoon
  cardamom seeds,
  ¼ teaspoon allspice
  seeds, ½ teaspoon cumin
  seeds, 3 whole cloves,
  ⅛ teaspoon black
  peppercorns—all finely
  ground together)
¼ cup water

Add the ground beef to the mixture. Stir and fry the meat for 10 minutes, breaking up any lumps as you do so.

Add the wine, ketchup, Worcestershire sauce, and bay leaf. Bring to a boil, cover, turn the heat down, and simmer for 15 minutes.

Add the chopped cilantro, salt, garam masala, and water. Mix and bring back to a simmer. Cover and cook on low heat for 5 minutes more. Discard the bay leaf.

While you are simmering the filling mixture, prepare the potato topping.

FOR THE TOPPING
1½ pounds Idaho potatoes
  (4 to 6 medium)
1 small rutabaga
½ teaspoon turmeric
¼ cup milk
¼ cup (½ stick) butter
½ teaspoon salt

Peel the potatoes and rutabaga. Cut into 1½-inch cubes and boil for 20 minutes in water with the salt and turmeric. Drain. Add the milk, butter, and salt and mash until smooth.

ASSEMBLY
2 tablespoons butter
  Freshly ground black
  pepper
Seeds of 2 green cardamom
  pods, ground

Place the cooked ground beef filling into a 3-pint oval deep dish. Level the top. Place the cooked mashed potato mixture on top. Level and finish with a large fork to produce small ridges on top. Add knobs of butter on the surface. Sprinkle with the freshly ground black pepper and the ground cardamom seeds. Place under a hot broiler and brown the surface. Watch carefully so the top doesn't burn. It should only take a minute or two.

❈ BUCATINI

Stephanie is a bit like the little old lady who lived in a shoe. She has three children and a husband, three sisters and a slew of nieces and nephews, and a lot of friends and neighbors. Hordes of them eat at her house. Every night. So she has recipes she can whip up quickly on short notice for however many there are at her table. Her children—and their friends—have called from college for this recipe. Her son once called from work and asked if she could possibly have a pot of it ready for him to pick up on his way home. Her daughter makes it for her ten closest friends when they come to her apartment for dinner. So this has been well tested at the family dinner table. They call it simply "bucatini," after the hollow spaghetti used in the dish. Other tubular pastas would also work. It is traditionally made with pancetta, unsmoked Italian bacon. You can substitute lean bacon. Blanch it for a minute in boiling water, then drain. That will take away the smoked flavor but won't cook the bacon.

Makes 4 to 6 servings

3 tablespoons olive oil
1 medium onion, finely
   chopped
4 ounces pancetta, finely
   chopped
1 can (28 ounces) whole
   Italian tomatoes, drained
   and roughly chopped
½ teaspoon red pepper
   flakes, or to taste
1 teaspoon salt
1 pound fresh bucatini
¼ cup freshly grated
   Pecorino or Parmesan
   cheese

In a sauté pan, heat the oil and add the onion. Cook until it wilts and begins to color, 2 to 3 minutes. Add the pancetta and sauté until crisp, about 2 to 3 minutes. (If you want a sauce with less fat, cook the pancetta separately and drain on paper towels before adding to the sauce.) Add the tomatoes, pepper flakes, and salt. Simmer gently until the tomatoes and fat separate, about ½ hour. Remove the sauce from the heat and taste for seasoning.

Heat a large pot of boiling salted water. Add the fresh pasta and cook, stirring often, until al dente—tender yet firm to the bite. Drain the pasta well
and mix with the sauce and cheese over low heat until the pasta is coated.
Adjust the seasonings and serve immediately.

JELL-O REDUX

※　　※　　※

Always dial J-E-L-L-O, and if the "lime" is busy,
you can still get strawberry, raspberry, cherry, orange, and lemon.
THE JACK BENNY RADIO SHOW

J ELL-O HAS jiggled its way back into fashion. I know this because I
heard it in New York, at my yoga class, and on the Food Network.

Of course, many Americans get rather snippy at the suggestion
that Jell-O is the Model T of the American table. I did an NPR
piece in which I called Jell-O a "retro" food, to the annoyance of an
Illinois listener. "Retro? Retro?" he asked. "How can Jell-O be retro
when it never went away? My eighty-three-year-old dad still makes
lime Jell-O with lettuce in it and a dollop of mayonnaise on top. Go
ahead. Try telling my dad he's retro." That listener and his dad
make an excellent point.

Jell-O never left many homes, cafeterias, diners, and church
basements, where it still regularly appears as salad, entrée, and
dessert. Probably no school or hospital cafeteria has ever been
without a Jell-O option.

This gelatin dessert has a Norman Rockwell–esque history.
First it's very in; then it's very out. Then, it's in again.

Gelatin, now a fast food, began life as a labor-intensive undertaking. In her interesting, fun book *Jell-O: A Biography*, Carolyn
Wyman describes the old way to make it:

> *First you had to get two calves' feet, scald them, take off the hair,*
> *slit them in two, and extract the fat. . . . Then you had to boil*
> *them, remove the scum, and boil again for as long as six or seven*
> *hours before straining, letting the product cool, skimming the fat,*

boiling once more, adding the shells and whites of five eggs (to pick
up impurities), skimming again and straining twice through a
jelly bag that you will have had to make yourself. . . . Then you
would add flavoring, sugar and spices; pour into a jelly mold; pack
with ice and go to bed while it set—it now being midnight.
(Gelatin was also sometimes—no more easily—made from deer
antlers or from the air bladders of sturgeon.)

In 1845, according to Wyman, the first gelatin dessert was patented but not marketed. It wasn't until 1897 when a cough medicine manufacturer developed a fruit-flavored version of gelatin that the thing took off. His wife named it Jell-O.

By 1902, an ad proclaimed Jell-O "America's Most Famous Dessert." Immigrants at Ellis Island were welcomed to the country with Jell-O. By the 1920s, congealed salads and aspics had become so popular that a third of the salad recipes in many cookbooks were gelatin-based. During the Depression, Jell-O helped families stretch whatever they had in the refrigerator or pantry. Then convenience foods became integral to cooking. Recipes from the 1950s through the 1970s used cake mixes, canned soups, and Spam, as well as Jell-O. Of course, in those days, 7-Up was used to baste meat.

Jell-O is there for us in good times and bad. Steve wrote me about growing up in Charleston, West Virginia, where a Mrs. Ruben was called the Jell-O Mold Queen. "If there was any kind of event in anyone's life," he wrote, "she made a Jell-O mold."

She had a car accident and the woman she ran into was so nice that Mrs. Ruben made her a Jell-O mold. The nice woman still sued her. When Steve's aunt died, Mrs. Ruben brought over a Jell-O mold. His mother called to thank her and tell her how good it was and that she thought Mrs. Ruben had made it for her before. The Jell-O queen said that was impossible because she had a happiness mold and a sadness mold and she had never made the sadness mold for Steve's mother. "You may have been sick and I could have made you a Jell-O mold," she said. "But it would have been a happiness mold. You weren't dead." So-called funeral molds remain part of the culture. My friend Bill has a family recipe for Bootsie's Funeral Mold. Same idea.

By the 1970s, highbrow cooks cleared the creamed soups and boxes of Jell-O from their pantry shelves. People traveled more widely and expanded their cooking repertoires. We began to worry about chemicals, freshness, and purity. We didn't want to eat foods out of season or out of state. Salads of mesclun and arugula replaced neon green gelatin. Cuisine became minceur, nouvelle, and some other French things. They do not eat Jell-O in France. Jell-O was out.

But sometime in the 1990s, things began to change. I went to my book club one night and someone suggested we all bring a "good casserole recipe" the next month. There was a stunned silence. We were serious women, serious cooks. We didn't do casseroles.

There were more signs. Bell bottoms, surely one of the more ill-advised fashion trends, were everywhere. Frye boots and tie-dyed clothing were in store windows. I began looking for cars with fins. The 1950s and 1960s were back in style, not only at the mall but in the kitchen, as well. Yes, people were making casseroles and deviled eggs again. Hip and trendy restaurants started serving a wedge of iceberg lettuce with blue cheese dressing. Jell-O's time had come again.

With apologies to the man in Illinois, this trend is called retro food. It has been especially popular with people who were too young to remember such 1950s standbys as canned green bean casserole made with canned cream of mushroom soup topped with canned fried onions. Fashionable thirty- and forty-something New Yorkers began taking Jell-O salads to potluck dinners or, gasp, serving them in their own homes.

Nouveau Jell-O salads look little like their forebears. Gone are the mini-marshmallows. Fresh strawberries and cranberries have replaced canned fruit cocktail and Cool Whip has given way to crème fraîche. These creations are served in elegant glasses or cut crystal bowls.

A sophisticated Manhattanite reports attending a party where dessert was a Canadian flag made of Jell-O. I heard about a New York business luncheon that included ramekins of layered Jell-O and fruit—fresh fruit, of course. A note of caution: You cannot use fresh or frozen pineapple, kiwi, gingerroot, papaya, figs, or guava in Jell-O. These fruits contain an enzyme that inhibits jelling. Cooking deactivates the enzyme.

Not all Jell-O has gone uptown, however. Plenty of old favorites linger. Andy Oakland, aka Chef Andy, is the cyberworld's Jell-O king. The most common request he gets on his Jell-O Pages Web site is from people trying to find a childhood recipe. Andy himself makes a strawberry pretzel gelatin dessert that he says gets raves. "Whenever I bring it to a gathering, guests eat up every crumb," he says. "They can't believe they're doing it, but they can't stop themselves."

In addition to the retro food movement, there are several reasons for the Jell-O revival.

The vilification of the carbohydrate gave Jell-O a big boost. For a special treat, low-carb diets recommend sugar-free Jell-O. So people who had been packing away the pounds in the twenty years since they last saw their reflection in a bowl of Jell-O now have a shelf in the pantry for the little boxes.

Then Jell-O shots came out of the frat house and into the mainstream. Vodka and other booze congealed into brightly colored gelatin cubes began appearing at grown-up parties at the beach house.

Finally, Jell-O got the imprimatur of the tastemeisters. Martha Stewart ran a recipe for blackberry–red wine gelatin in her magazine. The Food Network offered pomegranate gelatin. And *Bon Appétit* contributed cranberry-port gelatin with crystallized ginger and celery.

There's no way of knowing how long the Jell-O renaissance will hold its shape. Like all culinary trends, it may dissolve at any time. It will, however, probably come back. Whether it's nouveau or retro, there's always room for Jell-O.

※ CHERRY-WINE JELL-O

This is a refreshing dessert to serve after a heavy meal.

Makes 6 to 8 servings

1 can (15 ounces) pitted
  black cherries
6 ounces cherry gelatin
2 cups red wine
2 tablespoons lemon juice
1 cup heavy cream,
  whipped with a
  tablespoon of kirsch

Drain the cherries and reserve the liquid. Add enough water to the cherry liquid to make 2 cups, and bring to a boil. Pour the boiling liquid over the gelatin and stir for 2 minutes, until the gelatin dissolves. Add the wine and lemon juice and then the cherries. Pour the mixture into a 1-quart, nonreactive mold and refrigerate until firm, about 4 hours. Unmold and serve with the whipped cream.

※ HUDDY COHEN'S RASPBERRY JELL-O MOLD

This traditional Jell-O mold is from my friend Marcie's mother. It's delicious.

Makes 10 to 12 servings

6 ounces raspberry gelatin
2 cups hot water
10 ounces frozen
  raspberries
3 bananas, mashed
½ cup finely chopped
  pecans
1 cup sour cream
Sprigs of mint, for garnish

Dissolve gelatin in hot water in a bowl and let cool. Do not chill.

In another bowl, thaw the raspberries. Stir them and add mashed bananas and nuts. Pour this mixture into the cooled gelatin and stir well.

Pour half of this mixture (about 2½ cups) into a mold and refrigerate until firm. When firm, spread with half a cup of sour cream. Pour the rest of the gelatin mixture on top of the sour cream and chill.

When ready to serve, cut into squares and top each with a dollop of sour cream and a sprig of mint.

NOTE: This can also be made with strawberry gelatin and frozen straw-berries.

✳ CRANBERRY-ORANGE MOLD

This spiced gelatin mold is nice at Thanksgiving or any time in the fall and winter.

Makes 10 to 12 servings

1½ cups boiling water
6 ounces cranberry gelatin
1 can (16 ounces) cranberry
  sauce with whole berries
1 cup cold water
1 tablespoon lemon juice
¼ teaspoon ground
  cinnamon
⅛ teaspoon ground nutmeg
⅛ teaspoon ground cloves
2 clementines, sectioned
  (cut each section in half)
½ cup chopped walnuts or
  pecans

Pour the boiling water over the gelatin and stir for 2 minutes or until dissolved. Add the cranberry sauce, cold water, lemon juice, and spices and mix well. Refrigerate until thickened, 1 to 2 hours.

Stir in the clementine pieces and nuts. Pour the mixture into a mold. Refrigerate until firm, about 4 hours.

A DAY AT THE FAIR

⁂

(Between Minneapolis and St. Paul) . . . lay, every fall, the State Fair. . . . The fair was one of the most magnificent in America.

F. SCOTT FITZGERALD,
A Night at the Fair

WHEN I was ten, my grandfather would leave me with two dimes and my five-year-old brother at the all-the-milk-you-can-drink tent at the Minnesota State Fair. We were settled on chairs and told not to move, while he went to the deli stand for a card game. The server poured milk into our glasses from five-gallon cans. For twenty cents we drank until our bellies bulged.

The state's dairy farmers built a permanent red barn in 2005 for the fiftieth anniversary of their milk stand. The milk now is stored in three-hundred-gallon containers in a second-story refrigerated loft and flows down through two hundred feet of stainless-steel pipes into the customer's cup. The price has gone up to a dollar. All the milk served is low fat, and chocolate milk has been added to the menu.

Things can change at the fair, but the fundamentals remain the same. Since 1859, one year after Minnesota became a state, the fair has been about food—growing it, cooking it, and eating it. This is where farm families come for twelve days at the end of August to show their prized bull, their biggest squash, and their best pickles and pies. About 1.5 million visitors come to look at the livestock exhibits, the dahlia show, new farm equipment, and the blue-ribbon cakes. Others come for the Tilt-A-Whirl and the carnival games on the Midway. Politicians come for the votes. Everyone comes for the food.

If you get to the fair early in the morning, you can start the day with deep-fried cheese curds. Breakfast should always include a dairy product, right? Cheese curds are fresh, young Cheddar before it has been made into blocks and aged. If you don't eat curds within twenty-four hours, they don't taste fresh anymore. They just taste like fairly bland, rubbery cheese. Cheese curds look like chubby Cheetos, feel like silly putty, and squeak when you eat them. Dipped in batter and fried, they're amazing.

After that nutritious start, you could head over to the Tom Thumb mini-donut stand for a bagful of tiny donuts hot from the fryer and sprinkled with powdered sugar. Take them over to the Salem Lutheran Church dining hall to have with Swedish egg coffee. They mix an egg with the grounds to take away the bitterness. It's better in concept than reality. Or go to the Hamline Church Dining Hall, the oldest site at the fair, for pancakes and eggs, ham loaf, or meatballs. Lutheran church dining halls are very Minnesota State Fair.

So are politicians, many from the DFL, the Democratic-*Farmer*-Labor Party. An obvious food connection. And there is a persuasive case to be made that Teddy Roosevelt had a big effect on fair food. In 1901, he stopped at the fair to give a speech on foreign policy. For the first time, he said these words: "Speak softly and carry a big stick." The Minnesota State Fair is known for its foods on a stick. Coincidence? I think not.

There are forty-nine foods on a stick at the fair. They represent the good, the bad, and the truly gross. The good—the *best*, the original—is the Pronto Pup. Several people have claimed they invented the Pronto Pup. I'm going with the story that it was invented at an Oregon lumber camp and brought to the Minnesota State Fair in 1947. It's been there ever since. By 10:00 A.M., the line is a block long for the "weiner dun in a bun," as the sign reads. One of those big life questions that always comes up at the fair is:

"What is the difference between a Pronto Pup and a corn dog?" A corn dog is a hot dog on a stick dipped in a cornmeal batter and deep fried. The Pronto Pup is dipped in a wheat flour batter. It is on a stick. It is eaten with a lot of yellow mustard. It *is* the fair.

The Pronto Pup, however, is just the beginning.

There are the classics: pork chop on a stick, corn on a stick, and deep-fried cheese on a stick. Pickles are represented by a plain pickle on a stick, a batter-fried pickle on a stick, and something called a pickle dog on a stick—pastrami and cream cheese wrapped around a pickle spear. The Asian influence is seen in egg rolls on a stick, chicken fried rice on a stick, shrimp toast on a stick, and teriyaki ostrich on a stick.

Every year, new foods are stuck. Recent additions are spaghetti and meatballs (yes, battered and deep-fried) on a stick, cheese-burger calzone on a stick, and low-carb, bacon-wrapped turkey tenderloin on a stick.

One summer, the new kid on the stick was the Reuben dog—corned beef, sauerkraut, and Swiss cheese, battered and fried. I asked a woman who was eating one how it was and she said, "It's kinda different," which is Minnesotan for "get me to the Pronto Pups."

Dessert options include: fried Snickers on a stick, key lime pie on a stick, and battered, deep-fried Bananas Foster bits on a stick. Deep-fried Twinkies on a stick are sold across from a health fair display. You can wash it all down with chai frozen mocha on a stick.

There are plenty of nonstick options: a foot-long walleye sand-wich, wild rice burgers, and lefse (Norwegian griddle cakes) as a reminder that you're in Scandinavian territory. I sometimes grab a milk shake made by University of Minnesota students at the Gopher Dairy Bar to coat my stomach.

Food on and off the stick is crucial to the fair experience, but it is all the by-product of what is in the animal barns, the agriculture buildings, and the creative activities (read "women's") buildings. This can be a somewhat startling experience for city dwellers, who on some subconscious level think food grows at the supermarket or the fast food restaurant.

Minnesota is still one of the country's leading agricultural producers, and nearly 30 percent of its citizens live in rural areas. The Great Minnesota Get-Together, as the fair is called, is just the place for a refresher course on agriculture: Food grows in the ground and grazes in the pasture.

For a more visceral understanding, get to the fairgrounds early and walk through the animal buildings as the incredibly fresh-faced farm kids start their day. After a night in the straw or on a cot near their animals, they're mucking out the stalls, walking and grooming the livestock, playing cards, or just hanging out. The chickens come in every shape, size, and color. The sheep sit serenely in their stalls wearing brightly colored handmade wool sweaters. The goats and rabbits look healthy and well cared for.

I find the pigs (formally called swine) particularly fascinating. They're really big. Pigs weigh about three pounds at birth and 255 a few months later when they're ready for market. One summer I was transfixed by Terry, the 1,220-pounder who won the largest boar contest.

I usually go from pigs and cows to apples and honey. You can, of course, stop for a bite along the way if you get hungry. The fairgrounds have paved streets where, among the fair vehicles, a farmer walks his sheep to an exhibition, a horse with a ribbon-braided mane is ridden to the coliseum for a show, Smoky Bear waves from a float, and high school flag twirlers and marching bands twirl and march.

The bee and honey pavilion displays rows and rows of those little plastic bear bottles filled with honey ranging in color from light gold to dark brown. At a beekeeping demonstration you'll learn that bees use 327 flowers to make honey. You can also get honey sunflower ice cream and honey lemonade. I swing by the apples and sometimes get a cider freeze—pure apple cider pressed from Minnesota-grown apples, frozen into plastic push-up sleeves. Very refreshing. While you're digesting, check out the crop art. This is

Minnesota's version of primitive art. Untrained artists paste seeds on a board to make a picture. Entries depict cartoon characters, Barbra Streisand, even Jesus Christ. It's food as art.

I make all these stops on my way to see Princess Kay of the Milky Way, the state dairy industry's goodwill ambassador. Her first official duty is to sit in a thirty-eight-degree rotating glass cooler, wearing her crown and a down parka as her likeness is sculpted in a ninety-pound block of butter while fairgoers in shorts and tank tops watch from outside. The princess, from one of Minnesota's twenty-four thousand dairy farms, is given her butter head after the fair to keep in her freezer, serve at a community corn roast, or use for Christmas cookies.

After a rest stop—and possibly a quick bite—I head for the Creative Activities Building. This is where it all comes together, where both the city mouse and the country mouse find true happiness. Here, in addition to handmade quilts, sweaters, and weavings are handmade foods: jams and jellies made from strawberries, raspberries, apples, and rhubarb and mint jelly in every possible color of green; dill pickles, watermelon pickles, beet pickles, and pickled peppers; maple syrup in many hues; canned cherries, plums, peaches, blueberries, apricots, corn, tomatoes, and beets; and breads, muffins, fruit cakes, pies, and more Bundt cakes than I've seen since the 1970s. This is not fancy food: It reflects home cooking instead of food fashion. The foods displayed on these shelves follow seasons, not trends, and are the products of the state's farms, gardens, and recipe boxes. It's a beautiful sight.

Lois Thielen grew up on a top-producing dairy farm in Stearns County, Minnesota, and began entering the fair's baking competition in the mid-1990s. Her recipes, she says, were typical of what she calls the "down to earth" recipes found in the cookbooks compiled by the editors of the *Farm Journal*.

"On a farm," she says, "one cooks constantly—using garden produce, feeding the family and any hired help or drop-in visitors, bringing food to social functions, or preparing it for fund-raisers. I believe farm cooks are the best, both because they get so much practice and because time and money limitations force them to be creative in using what they have on hand."

Karen Cope hadn't entered baking competitions since she was a child and then started again when she moved to the Minneapolis–St. Paul metropolitan area. "The first year I didn't win anything," she says, "but the second year I won two blue ribbons. That's when I really got hooked on entering." She now submits up to thirty entries, usually the limit. Her sister enters photography and crop art contests and they both go to the fair on opening day to see how they did.

Both Judy Olson and her mother are pie bakers. They live in Braham, Minnesota, population 1,276, fifty miles north of the Twin Cities. In the middle of their town is a huge mural of a pie, a tribute to Braham's status as the Homemade Pie Capital of Minnesota. On the first Friday of every August, Braham has a one-day pie festival with a pie race that involves running with coffee and pie, eating pie, mixing dough, and rolling out a piecrust; a pie eating contest and, of course, a pie baking competition that now draws more than six hundred pies.

Judy started making pies in 4-H and said she didn't think she was "much of a pie baker" until she won a contest in Braham two years in a row. She went on to win awards and sweepstakes at the state fair, a contest her eighty-three-year-old mother also still enters.

Lola Nebel of nearby Cambridge, Minnesota, is a regular at Braham's pie day and the state fair, where she has won the pie sweepstakes nine times. Her mother was "a great baker of bread, cake, and cookies," she says, but not pie. Lola learned to bake pies in a community education class. Her granddaughters are interested in pie baking so the family pies have a good chance of remaining competitive.

The winners are happy to share the recipe for their pie fillings. Their crusts, however, are another matter. Because the crust is worth 60 percent of the total score in competition, the recipes are closely held secrets.

After Creative Activities, it's hard to do much more in a day at the fair unless you're young. In that case, you could probably still take a ride on the avalanche roller coaster and catch Lynyrd Skynyrd at the Grandstand before stopping at Kirschner's Beer Stube in the Agriculture Building for a Grain Belt to go with alligator meat on a stick.

For all the fun and games, there is a slightly frenzied atmosphere at the fair. This is summer's last hurrah and a bittersweet ritual leave-taking for Minnesotans who face a short fall and long winter. Dads with sleepy children in their arms walk to their cars, geese fly south overhead, and you swear you can see the leaves beginning to turn. Before you leave, stop at the gift shop for Pepto-Bismol on a stick. And I'm not making that up.

✳ CHOCOLATE PECAN COOKIES

Karen Cope won her first blue ribbon at the Steele County Free Fair in Owatonna, Minnesota, when she was nine. She didn't bake competitively again until about fifteen years ago. She was living in Minneapolis and says she got hooked. "I baked my way through thirty pounds of butter" one year, she says. These meringue-like cookies were a sweepstakes winner in the cookies and bars category and beat five hundred other entries to take the top honors.

Makes about 2 dozen cookies

3 cups confectioners' sugar	Preheat the oven to 350°F.
7 tablespoons unsweetened cocoa	Line baking pans with parchment paper.
2 tablespoons all-purpose flour	Combine the confectioners' sugar, cocoa, and flour in a mixing bowl. Add the egg whites and salt and beat at high speed for 1 minute. Stir in the pecans.
3 large egg whites	
Dash of salt	
1 cup toasted pecans, chopped	

Using about 1½ tablespoons of batter for each cookie, drop about 2 inches apart on the prepared pans. Press the tops lightly to flatten. Bake 15 minutes. Let the cookies cool completely on the pans before removing.

✳ ZUCCHINI BREAD

Lois Thielen of Grey Eagle, Minnesota, won a first-place blue ribbon at the state fair with her zucchini bread recipe. "When zucchini first became common in midwestern home gardens in the late 1970s," she says, "we looked for ways to use it up because it was so prolific." She says it was important to make something people were willing to eat "since zucchini was new and people were leery of anything too strange." This is a particularly light, moist version of this common recipe of the 1970s. I made a similar zucchini bread at that time and added raisins. I think zucchini is like tofu—it takes on the flavor of whatever it's cooked with. But the flecks of green are pretty and the vegetable adds moisture. This is nice with a cup of tea.

Makes 2 loaves

3 cups sifted, unbleached, all-purpose flour plus 1 teaspoon
1½ teaspoons ground cinnamon
1 teaspoon baking soda
½ teaspoon salt
¼ teaspoon baking powder
3 large eggs
2 cups sugar
1 cup cooking oil
1 tablespoon vanilla extract
2 cups grated zucchini (squeeze out the excess moisture before measuring)
½ cup chopped walnuts

Preheat the oven to 350°F.
Grease and flour two 8½ × 4½-inch loaf-pans.

Sift together three cups of flour, the cinnamon, baking soda, salt, and baking powder.

Break the eggs into the bowl of an electric mixer and beat well. Gradually add the sugar and oil, mixing well. Add the vanilla and the dry ingredients; blend well. Stir in the zucchini.

Combine the walnuts with the teaspoon of flour and stir into the batter. Pour into the loaf pans.

Bake 1 hour or until the bread tests done. Cool in the pans on a rack for 10 minutes. Remove the breads from the pans and cool on racks.

THE COMFORTS OF FOOD

✳   ✳   ✳

On days when warmth is the most important need
of the human heart, the kitchen is the place you can find it;
it dries the wet sock, it cools the hot little brain.

E. B. WHITE

My MOTHER came to stay with us for three weeks after my son was born. Every night I asked her to make the same soothing dish for dinner. Somewhere along my road from childhood to childbirth, chicken à la king became for me the most comforting of foods.

This dish has many of comfort foods' requisite features. It's rich, white, creamy, and served over a starch: rice, toast, or, at my house, popovers. It seems like the right thing in times of need. When they were in their nineties, my parents moved to Washington and into an assisted-living facility, a difficult move for independent, high-spirited people. One of the first nights they were there, the dining room served chicken à la king. With the first forkful, it seemed things might actually work out okay.

To truly comfort, a food must function like a hug from your mother. It makes you feel all better. We ate creamy puddings, roast chicken, and cookies hot from the oven long before we learned the word *stress*. Maybe if we eat them again the stress will go away. As the world becomes an ever-more-anxious place, we need our chicken à la king, mac and cheese, or bowl of oatmeal just as a child needs a security blanket. Foods that made us feel safe as children make us feel safe as grown-ups.

So it's no surprise that after September 11, restaurants served more stewed chicken and chocolate pudding than ever before. Home cooks started mashing potatoes and serving pancakes and syrup for dinner. One woman I know heard the news, left work, and went to a market in New York's Chelsea neighborhood to stock up on turkey, bread, fruit, and cheese. She got home to find that her husband had bought the same foods. As natural and human-wrought disasters become commonplace, we find ourselves in the market or the kitchen looking for solace.

I saw a show on the Food Network enumerating the top comfort foods: hot chocolate, fried chicken, ice cream, chicken soup, and the number one comfort dish, meat loaf. My friend Lis says meat loaf has always been her comfort food of choice. Her mother made it with ground beef, pork, and veal, onion dip mix, and a whole bottle of Heinz chili sauce on top. It was always served with mashed potatoes and frozen peas. "And then," Lis says, "everything was right with the world again."

Like other plain, simple foods, meat loaf didn't get much respect once food became stylish. Then meat loaf was reinvented with buffalo and pancetta, turkey and zucchini, venison and sage. I'm not sure nouveau meat loaf has the same comfort quotient as mom's meat loaf or the blue plate special at the diner, but at least once meat loaf went trendy, saying you felt like making a meat loaf was no longer greeted with a raised eyebrow. If calling pudding *mousse au chocolat* or macaroni and cheese *fettuccine Alfredo* makes you less embarrassed to eat old favorites, why not?

It turns out the consolation we get from certain foods is not just in our heads.

Anthropologists tell us that our predecessors would chow down on high-calorie, fatty foods because some brain wave told them to grab a leg of deep-fried woolly mammoth whenever possible to store up fat for leaner times.

Stress Age *Homo sapiens* have not evolved that much from Stone Age man. University of California physiologists say nervous tension causes the adrenal glands to release so-called stress hormones.

Lab rats respond by seeking pleasure, including eating high-energy food. For rodents, this is usually sucrose and lard. For humans, it's more likely a pint of Cherry Garcia. Indulgence sends a message to the brain to relax.

A University of Illinois study has found that men find comfort in the foods their mothers made for them (mashed potatoes, pasta, meat, and soup). The study says that women, "are not generally accustomed to having hot food prepared for them" so look to less labor-intensive sweets for comfort. Ice cream is gender neutral. When stressed out, we all scream for ice cream.

Starch is not mentioned in these studies, but seems to me essential. Everything involving the potato, for example, is comforting. My friend Scott is a writer and credits the humble spud with consoling him many times on his way to success. "Comfort food in our house has only one meaning," he says. "French fries." His wife took him to the college snack bar for French fries each time he got a rejection letter. "French fries have been our way of cushioning life's little blows," he says. French fries are a favorite of the college-aged. Grease and starch appeal both to those seeking comfort and those seeking hangover relief.

Many people turn to mashed potatoes in anxious times. Gayle says they must be eaten "with loads of whole milk and butter" and mashed with a wooden-handled masher. Kathryn's mom always made potato soup. "If there is time between needing comfort and total meltdown," says my friend Susan the chef, "an Idaho baked potato done just right in the oven with a no-holds-barred attitude toward butter has to be near heaven."

Kate says "real comfort food is a Thomas' English muffin with the edges crisped and tons of butter in every hole and then peanut butter (preferably chunky) on top of that." Of course, peanut butter eaten directly from the jar with either a spoon or a knife can make you feel a whole lot better, too.

For most of my adult life, I thought my mother had invented the iconic comfort food meal when I was in elementary school: a grilled cheese sandwich and a bowl of cream of tomato soup. I'm instantly transported to a cold winter morning, trudging through deep snow the three blocks between my grade school and my mother's kitchen, where the windows would be steamed up and the smells of tomato and toasting cheese wrapped me up like a warm sweater. Just as the scientists say, it's a perfect childhood memory: good grease. It turns out that millions of other mothers invented the same lunch to soothe and nourish their children. There are many good recipes for tomato soup. I am, however, happy to eat it from a can. Note: A slice of tomato on the grilled cheese sandwich makes it even that much better. Some people up the fat quotient further with a strip of bacon.

Many comfort foods are regional. Southerners want grits and pimiento cheese spread. Native Americans mention fry bread. New Englanders are soothed by chowder.

Then there are the personal, idiosyncratic choices. In addition to chicken à la king, my mother and I both head for egg salad in a crisis. My friend Megan has levels of need: "When highest degree of comfort is needed: Hostess cupcake and a glass of cold milk. Medium: pasta with garlic, salt, and butter. Minor: corned beef hash and an egg."

Jenifer's family had a live-in nurse for her brother for a couple of years because he had suffered severe burns. "Gran" made them soft-boiled eggs mixed with butter, salt, and pepper in a bowl. This apparently eased the pain for the whole family.

Comfort often is about cooking as much as eating. It's the process: wiping off the countertops, taking things out of the cupboard, chopping, mixing, and chopping some more. It's like gardening; it requires mindless concentration and produces results. I'm not much of a baker, but when the world overwhelms me I make a cake. It's so orderly. Measuring and sifting flour is somehow satisfying and the whir of the electric mixer is a calming sound. As a bonus, your house has the comfy smell of warm vanilla.

Such comforting perfumes are often as important as taste. Beth has four children at home. "For my kids," she says, "the smell of caramelized onions is the ultimate comfort scent. It means Mom's home, in the kitchen, and happy. It's my all-purpose starter, so the kids know all is right when the house smells of sweet, gently browned onions."

It also matters where you take your comfort. There is a coziness factor to most comfort foods. Avoid a formal dining room or a fancy restaurant. Main course comfort foods such as chicken à la king or meat loaf belong at the kitchen table. Ice cream and rice pudding are best when you're curled up on a soft sofa with a handmade afghan over your lap watching *Casablanca*. A fire in the fireplace doesn't hurt.

Our mothers cooked to comfort us, and we often cook the same foods to comfort others. When friends of ours suffered a loss, I made them chicken à la king, the same food I wanted when I became a mother. They said they hadn't eaten it since they were kids. For all of us, it was a dish associated with childhood, with simpler times, and simpler places—a dish just right for grown-up life.

✳ CHICKEN À LA KING

I usually make this with leftover cooked chicken. If you don't have leftovers, either broil or poach about 1½ pounds of chicken. I use both white and dark meat.

Serves 4 to 6

---

4 tablespoons butter
¼ cup flour
3 cups chicken broth, at
  room temperature
3 cups cooked chicken,
  skinned, boned, and cut
  into 1½-inch pieces

In a large saucepan, melt the butter, stir in the flour, and blend. Add the chicken broth slowly. When the sauce is boiling, smooth, and thickened, add the chicken, mushrooms, and pimientos. Reduce the heat to medium-low.

1 cup fresh mushrooms,
  sliced and sautéed in
  butter until golden
  brown
¼ cup pimientos, drained
  and chopped
2 large egg yolks, slightly
  beaten
¼ cup blanched, slivered
  almonds, sautéed or
  toasted
2 tablespoons dry sherry
1 cup frozen peas, thawed
Salt and pepper, to taste

Put the egg yolks in a small bowl and pour a little sauce over them. Mix together and return to the pan. Add the almonds, sherry, and peas and heat through. Season with salt and pepper.

Serve over rice, toast, or popovers.

The sauce may be made ahead and reheated in the top of a double boiler. You may have to add a little broth to thin it.

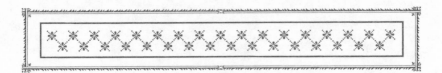

FEEDING THE
MULTITUDES

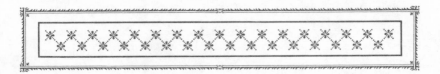

CROWD PLEASERS

✳ ✳ ✳

One cannot have too large a party.
A large party secures its own amusement.
JANE AUSTEN,
Emma

I LIKE A small, intimate dinner party as well as the next person. It's an opportunity to bone quail, drink expensive wine, and make individual soufflés. What I really love, though, is cooking huge amounts of food for hordes of people.

Everyone likes a good feast. It has it all: lots of good food and lots of good company. Feasting has been popular in every culture since the ancient Greeks, and the enthusiasm for it shows no signs of dimming.

Thanksgiving is the big American blowout, but we also have backyard barbecues, clambakes at the beach, and ice cream socials. I am a big supporter of any occasion for prolonged merrymaking and celebrate foreign as well as domestic occasions. I do a lot of foreign travel through my cookbook library and have found three prototypes easily adaptable to the American backyard and dining room.

Couscous, grand aïoli, and paella have all the requisite attributes of food for the many. They're easy to put together, delicious to eat, and have a high ooh-and-aah factor. They also feature the ice-breaking benefit of audience participation.

I made couscous for the first big party I had when I was in my early twenties. I invited fifteen people for dinner, then realized I had no idea how to feed that many people other than to make a Thanksgiving meal. I called Annette in San Francisco. She was a couple of years older and I considered her very sophisticated. She said, "Make couscous."

Annette and I had met at summer school in Paris a few years earlier. It was there we ate North African couscous at bohemian Left Bank dives thick with the smoke from Gauloise cigarettes. It had never occurred to me that you could cook something that exotic in a duplex in New Jersey.

It was a great party and a revelatory moment. I saw that you could have a big, fun, delicious dinner that was easy. I learned about simplicity, quality ingredients, and thoughtful presentation. I was hooked on entertaining.

Craig Claiborne called couscous, the Moroccan national dish, one of the dozen greatest dishes in the world. In his obituary, he was quoted as saying that it was a serving of couscous in Casablanca during his navy service in World War II that gave him his "unquenchable interest in food."

Couscous is usually made from semolina. We probably had the Algerian millet couscous in Paris that, according to food writer Paula Wolfert, is "undeniably robust but about as delicate as a fiery curry." Wolfert is largely responsible for the popularity of couscous in the United States. Her definitive book *Couscous and Other Good Food from Morocco* has introduced many to the great cuisine of North Africa, where couscous is such a staple that some of the local names for it are the same word used for *food*.

Purists steam couscous in what the French call a *couscoussière,* a kind of double boiler. You take the granules out and sprinkle them in the water and oil as many as seven times during cooking to make sure the grains remain separate.

Or, you buy the precooked couscous in a box. It takes five minutes to cook. You just boil chicken broth, pour in the couscous, add butter, and cover it for five minutes. Fluff with a fork. The results can be a bit lumpy so some people steam even the supermarket version, break it up with a fork or by hand, sprinkle with a little salted water, and steam again.

While there are many ways to use couscous, it is traditionally served under a meat or vegetable stew. Wolfert offers more than twenty different recipes in her book. Annette told me to make a curried chicken to serve with the couscous. Guests then added whatever they wanted from condiment bowls filled with raisins, shredded coconut, peanuts, sliced bananas, and chutney.

Couscous, hearty and warming, is the perfect winter party. When the snow melted and the days got longer though, I needed a new banquet style. Leafing through a French cookbook, I saw a grand aïoli and it was love at first sight.

My choral group was having a Sunday afternoon concert in March and my ticket-selling strategy is to invite people for dinner after the performance. I decided to try this Provençal communal feast on the music lovers.

Aïoli is ideal for a meal that needs to be prepared in advance. The whole thing can be made ahead over several days. The ingredients are chosen, washed, blanched, poached, cut up, and refrigerated until the day of the party, when all that's left is assembly.

A grand aïoli (also called an *aïoli monstre*) is a magnificent way to celebrate just about anything. It is not, however, a meal for the timid. The whole point is garlic. Lots and lots of garlic. Aïoli—a composite of French and Latin words words for "garlic" and "oil"— is a garlic mayonnaise that forms the centerpiece of a grand feast. It is served with platters of meats, fish (traditionally poached salt cod), hard-boiled eggs, and as many raw and cooked vegetables as you can think of. Guests take a plate, fill it with vegetables, meat, and fish and add a few dollops of aïoli in which to dip it all.

The sauce so captures the essence of the area that Nobel Prize–winning poet Frédéric Mistral called his Provençal journal *L'Aïoli*. "Aïoli epitomizes the heat, the power, and the joy of the Provençal sun, but it has another virtue—it drives away flies," he wrote in 1891.

The word *aïoli* refers to both the pungent, fly-chasing mayonnaise itself and the meal that revolves around it. What you serve at a grand aïoli is limited only by your imagination and what's available at the market. The aïoli is the star, so the other foods are prepared simply.

I fill a large, round stainless-steel platter with colorful vegetables arranged like spokes in a wheel and set a bowl of aïoli in the middle. (For extra presentation points, you can hollow out an artichoke or a small red cabbage and scoop the aïoli in there.)

Poach a cod fillet or try salmon, which adds color to the spread. Put boiled potatoes in a bowl and hard-boiled eggs, peeled and halved, on their own colorful plate.

In France, tiny snails are often part of a grand aïoli. I've used snails and also have substituted frozen, cooked squid rings sautéed in a little oil.

If you want to save even more time, use canned chickpeas, canned artichoke hearts, and canned beets and buy a rotisserie chicken or two, cut them up, and put on a platter with some parsley. Set the whole spread out with plenty of dishes of aïoli.

It is colorful, bountiful, and festive. With the work all done in advance, you can relax and have fun at your own party.

In the summer, Spanish paella is a natural for a large group. The dish was born in Valencia, a rice-producing area on Spain's eastern coastline, and early paellas were cooked outdoors over wood-burning fires for farmworkers. They were made with rabbit, snails, and beans, and traditionally eaten straight from the pan. This is very appealing to me, but I haven't yet worked up the nerve to suggest it to germ-phobic Americans.

I wrote about paella for National Public Radio and got a letter from Nancy Colon, who was an American exchange student in Valencia in the mid-1980s. She says that her first paella there was made with rabbit, blood sausage, and wide flat green beans. "The head of the rabbit, skull bones and all, was placed in the middle of the pan. The family had made the paella on their small farm outside of Puerto de Sagunto on the Valencian coast and brought it back to their apartment to have for lunch. We were all given a spoon and told to dig in. The rabbit head was offered to me first as the guest. However, I politely declined it and watched my Spanish mother eat it by sucking out the inside of the skull," she says.

We may not be quite there yet.

Paella can, of course, be made on top of the stove or in the oven. But in Spain, families and friends gather outdoors to cook paella over an open fire or a specially designed paella grill, available at U.S. cookware stores. Your backyard barbecue will work just fine, though.

The pan used to make paella gives the dish its name and the modest investment in authenticity pays off in taste. A paellera is shallow, wide, and round with slightly sloping sides. This shape ensures that the rice cooks evenly in one layer.

In Spain, you can find a dish called *paella turista* that loosely translates as "strictly for tourists." It approximates the kind of paella many Americans know—a mixture of ingredients from land and sea served over rice that is often overcooked and sometimes artificially colored. I made it that way for years and enjoyed it. It turned out I was doing everything wrong.

Real paella, I learned, is all about the rice. And, you can't use just any rice. The best paella rice, of course, is from Spain. And the best of the Spanish rice is called bomba. This short-grained rice can absorb about three times more liquid than regular rice, meaning three times more flavor for your paella. Despite all the liquid, the rice remains firm. It's available at some cookware stores and through the mail. Arborio—the rice used to make risotto—also can be used. Just stay away from long-grained rice, which is less absorbent and doesn't have the right taste or texture..

The next misconception I had to toss out was that paella is loaded with ingredients—chicken, sausage, peas, peppers, onion, whitefish, shellfish, the kitchen sink. Real paellas focus on meat, fish, or vegetables, but not all mixed together. If you do that, the experts say, you can't appreciate each ingredient.

When my friend Luis was growing up in Galicia in the northwest corner of Spain he never ate paella. It was a southern dish, he says, and he was a northerner. But when he went back to his village as an adult he visited a cousin who served paella, now common throughout the country.

Where Luis comes from, they eat a lot of mussels. So his cousin cooked a big pot of mussels and used the resulting liquid for the rice. He added squid, shrimp, and clams to make a seafood paella. The only non-seafood ingredient addition was Spanish chorizo to further flavor the rice. Luis warns that only Spanish chorizo should be used. Mexican chorizo, he says, is full of chili and will overwhelm the delicate flavor of paella.

Both making and eating paella is a very social production. While you're cooking, guests can sit outside sipping sangria or cava (Spanish champagne) and eating marconas (Spanish almonds) and manchego (Spanish cheese). They can help ferry ingredients from the kitchen and take turns stirring. It feels like a summer evening in Spain and you haven't even left your zip code.

✳ SEAFOOD PAELLA

Don't panic. This recipe, prepared under Luis's guidance, looks a lot more complicated than it is. Like a stir-fry, everything can be prepared ahead so you just have to do assembly at the grill. And don't shy away from the grill. As a controlled experiment on this dish, I made a smaller version inside on the stove. There was no comparison. Head outdoors.

All the fish, shellfish, sausage, and vegetables can be cleaned, cut up, and refrigerated hours in advance. Substitute whatever seafood you like. There is a debate among paella makers about whether to use onion; I thought it added to the dish.

I have a 17-inch paellera that serves at least ten. It's probably the biggest that can fit into most ovens. It fits comfortably in a Weber kettle. The pans go up to 52 inches if you're serving up to two hundred.

Makes 10 servings

3 dozen mussels, cleaned
and debearded
½ cup water
6 to 8 cups clam juice mixed
with mussel broth (have
extra clam juice on hand
in case you need more
liquid)
½ teaspoon crumbled
saffron (Luis
recommends using only
saffron from Spain to
ensure it's the real
thing)
1½ pounds firm-fleshed
fish, cut into bite-sized
pieces (I use cod)
2 dozen medium shrimp, in
their shells
Salt, to taste
3 tablespoons minced
parsley
8 to 10 cloves garlic, minced
2 tablespoons fresh thyme
leaves
2 teaspoons paprika
8 tablespoons olive oil
1 pound Spanish chorizo,
cut into ½-inch rounds
1 cup onion, finely chopped
8 small scallions, finely
chopped
3 cups Spanish or other
short-grain rice
2 dozen small clams,
thoroughly cleaned
Lemon wedges for garnish
1 (2-ounce) jar of pimientos

When you're ready to put the paella to-gether, build a fire. The fire just needs to be hot enough to bring the liquid to a boil when the rice is added. Everything is cooked sequentially in the *paellera* or skillet over the grill. (I do sauté the fish, shrimp, and the chorizo in advance in the kitchen.) The grill is never covered. I've read that throwing fresh herbs or grapevines on the coals would further flavor the paella. Having no grape-vines, I used sprigs of rosemary and thyme. I don't know if they added flavor, but the yard sure smelled good.

Place half the mussels in a saucepan with ½ cup water. Cover and bring to a boil. When the mussels open, take the meat out and set aside. Throw out the shells, but *save the liquid*. Combine it with enough clam juice to make at least 6 cups. Pour the liquid into a large pot. Have extra clam juice on hand in case you need more liquid. Stir in the saffron. (Cool and refrigerate the mussel meat and the broth if you are doing it ahead. If you make the dish straight through, keep the broth hot on the stove over a low heat.)

Use paper towels to dry the fish and shrimp well. Sprinkle generously with salt and let sit 10 minutes at room temperature. Next you want to mash the parsley, garlic, thyme, and a little more salt together. This should probably be done with a mortar and pestle, but I've never mastered that. I use an ulu or my big food processor. Mix in the paprika and a little water if you need it to make a paste. (This can be done up to a day in advance. Refrigerate and bring to room temperature before using.)

Continued

Heat 6 tablespoons of the oil in a skillet and quickly sauté the fish and shrimp for 1 to 2 minutes. They should not be fully cooked. Put the seafood on a warm platter. In the same pan, sauté the chorizo until cooked through. Set aside. Both seafood and sausage can be cooked over the fire. I just find it easier on the stove. (This can be done an hour or so in advance.)

When you're ready to prepare the paella, bring the broth to a boil.

When you have a good, hot bed of coals, put the remaining 2 tablespoons of oil, the onion and scallions in the paella pan and cook over the grill until the vegetables are slightly softened. (The paella pan sits on top of the grill.)

Stir in the rice and coat well. Pour in enough boiling broth to cover the rice. Stir the rice and turn the pan occasionally. Add the reserved mussels, fish, chorizo, and parsley mixture. Keep the shrimp aside. Boil until the mixture is not soupy but there's still enough liquid to cook the rice. Add liquid as needed, a quarter of a cup at a time, as you would with risotto.

Place the shrimp, the uncooked mussels, and the clams on top of the rice. Arrange so that the mussels and clams will open faceup. Cook, uncovered, for 15 to 20 minutes until the rice is almost al dente. (If the mussels and clams aren't opening, they may be removed and steamed in a separate pan on the stove, then added to the paella.) Remove the pan from the fire and cover with foil. Let sit for 5 to 10 minutes. Garnish with lemon wedges. Sprinkle pimiento slices on top for color.

I serve a simple gazpacho for a first course and plenty of Luis's sangria.

✳ LUIS'S SANGRIA

If you like sangria sweet, use a light red wine. If you prefer it drier, use a hearty red. If the wine is very dry, you may want to add another tablespoon or two of sugar. Substitute other fruits if you like.

Makes 18 to 20 servings

1 apple
1 orange
1 peach
2 quarts red wine (light for sweet, hearty for drier)
½ cup brandy
½ cup sugar, plus more as needed
½ quart club soda

Cut the fruit into ¼- to ½-inch chunks.

Mix the wine, brandy, and sugar and add the fruit. Stir well and refrigerate for 3 to 5 hours. Just before serving, add the club soda. Stir to mix and serve over ice. Make sure everyone gets some fruit.

✳ GRAND AÏOLI

You don't really need hors d'oeuvres to accompany this meal, although a bowl of almonds is nice with a drink. A dry rosé in the style of Provence or the Rhône Valley is especially good. An un-oaked Chardonnay or a light red wine will also work. Fruit sorbet is all you'll want for dessert.

AÏOLI SAUCE

Make a double batch, one batch at a time. Use the freshest garlic you can find, and modulate amounts to your taste. This recipe will serve 12 hungry people.

8 to 10 garlic cloves, peeled
1 teaspoon salt
2 large egg yolks, at room temperature
4 teaspoons freshly squeezed lemon juice
1 tablespoon Dijon mustard
1½ cups extra-virgin olive oil, at room temperature

Puree the garlic and salt in a food processor or blender. Whisk the egg yolks in a small bowl until light and smooth, and add to the garlic. Add the lemon juice and mustard and process to a smooth paste.

With the machine running, pour the oil into the mixture in a slow, steady stream. If you add the oil too quickly, the mixture will not emulsify. Continue blending until the mixture is thick, and firm—a minute or so. It's best to have all the ingredients at room temperature. If the aïoli separates, stop adding oil and continue to mix until the ingredients come together. Taste for seasoning. Transfer to a storage container, cover with plastic wrap, and refrigerate until ready to use. Aïoli will keep for a few days but is best within 24 hours of being made.

AÏOLI PLATTER

The possibilities are limitless. These are some suggestions. Pick and choose what appeals to you or is fresh at the market. Choose three or four raw and three or four cooked vegetables; fresh fish (and salt cod if you use it); meat or chicken, and one hard-boiled egg per person. Use the smallest vegetables you can get and parboil those that need it. Everything should be served at room temperature.

Makes 12 servings

FISH (CHOOSE I OR 2)

2 to 3 pounds salt cod
1 small onion
3 sprigs fresh thyme
2 bay leaves
whole black peppercorns
2 pounds precooked squid, cut into ½-inch strips
½ pound periwinkles (tiny sea snails), cooked in salted water for 10 minutes and drained
3 pounds fillet of salmon, cod, halibut, or other fish, poached

Cover the salt cod with cold water and refrigerate. This may require more than 1 bowl. Change water 3 times a day for up to 3 days, depending on saltiness. When ready to cook, drain the fish and place it in a large pot. Cover with water and add a small onion, halved; 3 sprigs of fresh thyme; 2 bay leaves; and a few whole black peppercorns. Bring gently to a simmer and remove form heat. Using a slotted spoon, place the cod on a platter.

MEAT (CHOOSE I)

5 pounds roast chicken, cut into pieces
1 pound carpaccio (thin-sliced raw beef tenderloin)
4 pounds boned leg of lamb, roasted and sliced

BLANCHED VEGETABLES

(CHOOSE 2 OR 3)

½ pound snow peas or
    snap peas
˙½ pound thin green beans
2 pounds cauliflower, cut up
2 pounds broccoli, cut up
2 pounds thin asparagus
12 baby artichokes (chokes
    removed) or canned
    artichoke hearts
1 pound baby zucchini (or
    regular zucchini sliced
    into sticks)
1 pound baby pattypan
    squash (or regular
    pattypan or summer
    squash, cut into bite-
    sized pieces)

To blanch, place the vegetables in boiling water for just a couple of minutes and refresh in a bowl of ice water. Drain and store in the refrigerator until ready to use.

RAW VEGETABLES

(CHOOSE 2 OR 3)

1 pint cherry or grape
    tomatoes
1 pound baby carrots
3 red, yellow, and/or
    orange peppers, sliced
1 bunch of celery, cut into sticks

OTHER COMMON COMPONENTS

12 hard-boiled eggs
6 medium beets, baked and
    peeled or from a can
1 (15-ounce) can of chickpeas
    (garbanzo beans)
1 pound boiled new potatoes,
    unpeeled
4 sweet potatoes boiled,
    peeled, and cut into bite-
    sized pieces

FOREVER BREAKFAST

✳   ✳   ✳

I've long said that if I were about to be executed and
were given a choice of my last meal, it would be bacon and eggs.
JAMES BEARD

NEW JERSEY is perfect in at least one way. You can get breakfast all day almost anywhere. The Garden State is the diner capital of the world. For breakfast lovers, this is big.

Even though we all know, theoretically, that it's the most important meal of the day nutritionally, no one has time to cook or eat breakfast anymore. Convenience foods have made breakfast easy to grab and go.

Fortunately, there is absolutely no reason to eat breakfast only in the morning. Breakfast foods are right any time.

For me, the required ingredients are bacon, eggs, and starch. But I keep an open mind. I had never heard of hash browns until I visited the Northeast, and I first saw chili peppers in eggs in the West. I instantly took to them both.

The Pennsylvania Dutch are the practical people thought to have put holes in donuts to make them easier to dunk into coffee. They also brought scrapple to the breakfast table. Pork scraps, cornmeal, and seasonings are cooked into loaves, sliced and fried. Thrifty New Englanders take the leftovers from a boiled dinner, chop them up, and fry them together to make hash. A poached egg makes an ideal garnish.

The colonists learned about corn from the Indians and quickly worked it into breakfast. George Washington usually got up before sunrise and did paperwork before joining Martha at seven for his usual breakfast, described by his step-granddaughter Nelly Custis as hoecakes (made of cornmeal), swimming in butter and honey and accompanied by three cups of tea. The corn cakes were cooked on griddles known as hoes in front of the fire.

Early settlers learned about grits from the Indians who made a mush from hominy, kernels of corn soaked in lye, dried, and ground. Southern breakfasts to this day are naked without grits. Eggs and grits are to the South what eggs and hash browns are to the Northeast. Shrimp and grits is a traditional fisherman's breakfast in the low country of South Carolina, where it is sometimes just called "breakfast shrimp." The dish has gone uptown in recent years and is now served in trendy Southern-style restaurants for dinner.

Then there are pancakes, so popular they've become part of religious practice. Shrove Tuesday, for example, is often marked with a Pancake Supper. One story is that "pancake day" was instituted to use up the fat, butter, and eggs once forbidden during Lent.

Pancake houses are an American favorite. San Franciscans have lined up for Swedish pancakes for breakfast at Sears Fine Food since 1938—not only pancakes but also French toast made with the city's famous sourdough bread, waffles, baked apples, coffee cake, ham and sausage, omelets, and hash browns. They serve lunch but it's breakfast that keeps the lines long. Guidebooks call Walker Brothers Pancakes in Chicago the place for the city's best breakfast. (Note to Chicago's Lou Mitchell's fanatics: We're just talking about pancake houses here.) The "original" Original Pancake House in Portland, Oregon, has been serving its famous apple pancake since 1953.

Some people like sweets at breakfast. In addition to pancakes, there's coffee cake, chocolate-filled croissants, Danish. I prefer the savories, but always fall for a good sticky bun.

I learned about the Mexican breakfast in a dumpy, hole-in-the-wall café in Bryan, Texas, where I had my first breakfast burritos. Eggs with a choice of potatoes, sausage, beans, or peppers were rolled into flour tortillas.

Like everything Mexican, breakfast is colorful. Red or green

salsa, beans, tortillas, avocado, cheese, spicy chorizo, slices of cactus, mango, and papaya all show up on the plate. Arturo's Bakery
in Austin has fifty different kinds of breakfast burritos and at
Cisco's Bakery there I found migas (a Tex-Mex scramble of eggs,
tortilla, onions, tomatoes, cheese, and chilies), huevos rancheros
(poached or fried eggs on tortillas with red chili sauce and cheese),
and chilaquiles (a dish featuring stale tortillas).

Menudo is the only Mexican breakfast food I have not em-
braced fully. It is a stewish tripe soup famous as a hangover cure
and typically served on weekends. We spent New Year's Eve in
Mexico City one year with another couple and overdid it with the
tequila so we thought the "breakfast of champions," as menudo is
often called, was just the thing. There are very few foods I do not
eat. This is one.

New Mexico is serious about Mexican-style breakfast and
breakfast in general. Café Pasqual's in Santa Fe is a charming
restaurant named for the patron saint of cooks and kitchens. In
Café Pasqual's Cookbook, founder and chef Katharine Kagel writes:

> *I have always known that the great cafés of the world respect
> breakfast. At Café Pasqual's we serve this beloved meal all day.
> Even after the lunch menu is added at eleven o'clock, customers can
> still get corned beef hash and eggs, huevos motulenos [a Yucatecan
> dish made with eggs on tortillas with black beans and cheese],
> grilled trout with home-fried potatoes, or quesadillas filled with ba-
> con and eggs. If you feel like breakfast at two o'clock in the after-
> noon, so be it. . . . Breakfast-food lovers do not obey the clock.*

How can you not love this place?

Breakfast is important whenever you travel. My husband and I always plan car trips so we can stop for small-town breakfasts. We love
booths and counters. We assume the more plastic and linoleum, the
better the food. A table of local residents who look like they've been
sitting there every day for years is always a good sign.

If we're not near the Southern border, I usually get two eggs over easy, bacon, hash browns, and, if possible, biscuits. My husband gets the same with one pancake. My son adds some kind of hunk of beef. We are all very, very happy.

My husband spent years going for all-day fishing trips with his father. I think the high point of these outings was the little places they stopped for breakfast. Whenever we drive through a small town in Maryland, my husband points and says, "My dad and I used to eat breakfast there." I often wonder how much fishing they did.

After a few years in Washington, D.C., we found the country inn in the mind of God in the foothills of Virginia's Blue Ridge Mountains. The Ashby Inn is a one-hour drive from our house. The rooms are perfect. Each has a fireplace and no teddy bears, dolls, or lace. But it's almost worth going for the breakfast alone. The table is set with a pitcher of freshly squeezed juice and a basket of hot, just-baked muffins. Eggs come any way you want them with sausage, ham, or bacon and spicy sautéed apples. The coffee is hot and good. You should eat this breakfast, however, only if you have a three-hour hike planned.

We loved the Israeli breakfasts of chopped cucumber and tomato salad, olives, cheeses, and breads. The Brits, too, know how to throw a good breakfast. As a matter of fact, before England became a culinary hotspot, W. Somerset Maugham once said, "To eat well in England, you should have breakfast three times a day." That would be a lot of food. A hearty English breakfast consists of fruit, eggs, sautéed mushrooms, grilled tomatoes, baked beans, sausage or kippers. It's a good way to prepare for a ramble, as the English call a walk in the country.

I had the best breakfast I've ever eaten in Kenmare, Ireland, at a B and B run by a woman who also has a terrific restaurant in town. The eggs had just been taken from under the hens and the bacon brought in from the local smokehouse. Another morning we had steel-cut Irish oats with fresh cream and berries.

There's something about breakfast on the road, at a B and B, in a foreign country, that beats any brunch. The food's pretty much the same but the ambience is different. Breakfasts are for the people. Brunch is for the leisure classes. I do, however, like the now-standard brunch strata—an egg and stale bread dish you can assemble the night before. And my mother made something called hopple popple that I thought she'd invented until I saw similar recipes with the same name all over the Internet. It's another easy egg, vegetable, and meat casserole.

When my son was in high school, he spent a summer on the Caribbean island of Guadeloupe, helping restore a school garden. Every day the twenty students he lived with alternated shopping and making meals. For the Fourth of July, the student cooks decided the most American dinner they could make was breakfast. They had pancakes with strawberries, blueberries, and whipped cream to set the color theme, hash brown potatoes with peppers, and scrambled eggs. He says it was just right.

✳ HOPPLE POPPLE

I have no idea where the name came from. I've tried to find out but, so far, no luck. My mother often made this for breakfast when we had company.

Makes 8 servings

2½ cups hard salami, cubed

½ cup chopped onions

2 diced fresh tomatoes (if it's not tomato season, use 3 fresh Italian tomatoes)

½ cup diced green pepper

1 teaspoon salt

¼ teaspoon pepper

8 to 12 large eggs, slightly beaten

Preheat the oven to 350°F.

In a medium skillet, sauté the salami until slightly browned and pour off the fat. Mix with all the other ingredients and pour into a 13 × 9 × 2 buttered baking pan. Bake for 20 minutes or more, until the eggs are set.

✳ ALLISON'S CHEESE STRATA

This is an easy, no-fail version of the popular brunch dish. Add ham, sausage, smoked salmon, green onions, or anything else you like.

Makes 6 to 8 servings

8 slices white bread, cubed
2 cups grated sharp
  Cheddar cheese
8 large eggs
¼ cup (½ stick) butter,
  melted
2 cups milk
½ teaspoon dry mustard
Salt and pepper, to taste

Grease a soufflé dish.
Put in the bread and cheese in layers, ending with cheese.

Whisk the other ingredients and pour the mixture over the bread and cheese. Cover the dish and refrigerate overnight. Let it come to room temperature before baking.

Preheat the oven to 350°F.

Bake the strata for about an hour, or until the eggs are set and puffy, and the top is browned but not burnt.

GIVING THANKS

❋ ❋ ❋

An optimist is a person who starts a new diet on Thanksgiving Day.
IRV KUPCINET

THERE ARE no gifts, no department store music, no special rituals, no unachievable expectations. Plus, overeating itself is
an act of patriotism on this day. All you have to do is plan the
menu, go through recipes, make shopping lists, buy ingredients,
set the table, and cook for people you love at a beautiful time of
year. Thanksgiving is a perfect holiday.

I have more recipes for Thanksgiving than for any other occasion. There are recipes I make every year, recipes I've made from
time to time, and recipes I've never made but might want to make
someday. I spend innumerable hours in the weeks before Thanksgiving going through magazines, books, and the Internet looking
for more recipes to add to the mix.

My collection is founded on a piece of a brown grocery bag on
which is written, "Stuff turkey, season, and put in paper bag, breast
side up. Roast 2½ hours at 325°F. Raise heat to 425°F, tear open
bag, and roast another 30 minutes, basting frequently." We lived in
New Jersey and this was my first turkey at my first Thanksgiving. I
got the directions from my mother over the phone. In the late afternoon, my mother-in-law called from Baltimore to see how it
was going. I told her the turkey didn't seem done. Five minutes
later, my mom called from Minneapolis and said, "Ruth says your
turkey's raw." Thousands of miles cannot separate mothers from
their children at holidays.

My husband and I each brought family traditions to the marriage and some were incorporated into our Thanksgivings. The quest for the new and better, however, will never end.

Early in the week before the holiday one year, I was having coffee with a number of women friends at the neighborhood gym. We all started talking about what we were making for Thanksgiving and there was suddenly a frenzied recipe exchange. Everyone wanted Carin's sweet potato biscuits and her braised shallots. Gayle's cranberries with jalapeño and her apple pie with a cheese crust sounded fabulous. Lis did something with Brussels sprouts, garlic, oil, anchovies, and bacon that we all needed to write down. I have added these recipes—on business cards, napkins, and crumpled receipts—to my pile.

My husband and I and Allison and Larry like Thanksgiving so much, we've had a second one on Friday for twenty years. We pool our leftovers, cook a couple of chickens if there's not enough leftover turkey, and try some of those recipes you can't use at Thursday's dinner because of all the dishes required by family tradition.

For instance, on the first night of Thanksgiving, we always have two kinds of sweet potatoes. My mother-in-law's are candied with pecans and raisins and my brother-in-law Stevan's are whipped with about five pounds of butter. Stevan makes a nice squash and apple soup for a first course. He does a lot of the cooking. He, too, is a Thanksgivingophile and we alternate hosting years.

My son has two compulsory dishes for the main meal—my wild rice stuffing and Allison's white corn pudding. Once I cut way back on the butter in the stuffing and he called me on it right away. Another year, I made a different corn pudding and he was outraged. "Why, Mom, why?" Allison's pudding uses *three* cups of heavy cream, that's why.

Every year, I agonize over the green vegetable. I have pared it down to two choices—green beans or Brussels sprouts. I have recipes for green beans with hazelnuts or persimmons or shallots. I can go with braised Brussels sprouts with pearl onions and chest-

nuts, shredded Brussels sprouts with hickory nuts, Brussels sprouts
with red grapes. For several years in a row I made a good roasted
Brussels sprouts with walnuts.

I also have not settled on desserts, although my son has pumpkin and pecan pies in his contract. I found a recipe for a pumpkin-
pecan pie that kills two pies with one crust. To my astonishment, it
was acceptable to him. I've made harvest tarts, cranberry crum-
bles, and a pumpkin crème brûlée of my sister-in-law's that was a
real winner.

While I obsess over vegetables and pies, my husband fixates on
wine. He says it's the most difficult meal of the year to match with
wine. Nothing goes well with both candied sweet potatoes and
turkey. After thirty years of research, he has come to several con-
clusions.

No single wine works for the whole meal. He thinks a Gewürztraminer stands up the best because it's "big and spicy." But too
many people don't like it. While it's good with food, it's not a great
sipping wine and "people have trouble separating the two experiences," he says. So he has a Gewürztraminer for himself and a variety for the rest of us. He likes an Oregon Pinot Noir with turkey
and also has Riesling and Chardonnay available for white wine tra-
ditionalists. He offers Sauvignon Blanc with the gravlax he makes
as an appetizer. He uses only American wines on this über-
American holiday.

At my parents' Thanksgiving in Minneapolis, we always started
with oysters. While there are plenty of walleye pike in the land of
ten thousand lakes, there are no oysters. Fortunately, my grandfather had a lumber company that did business with the big paper
company Georgia Pacific in the 1950s, and every year at Thanksgiving they sent him a barrel of oysters. I find Thanksgiving without oysters a sad day.

After we were married, we lived in New Jersey for a few years
and Thanksgiving oysters were easy. Our next home, however,
was in College Station, Texas. It was much closer geographically to
the sea than Minneapolis, but further away psychologically. So

when we were planning our first Lone Star Thanksgiving—
outdoors, like the Pilgrims—I got panicky. No oysters. I finally
found a source, but I had to buy a bushel. That's about twenty
dozen oysters. Friends around town bought a few dozen, but my
husband still shucked nine dozen oysters for our guests. Everyone
was happy but him.

When we moved to Washington, oyster availability was not the
problem. Except for my husband, I married into a non-oyster-
eating family. So I start the holiday early. Sometime during
Thanksgiving week I go down to the wharf in southwest Washington, buy a half-dozen oysters, and eat them off a Styrofoam plate,
standing up outside in a parking lot.

Instead of oysters, we have my husband's gravlax and my
friend Susan's fabulous spiced pecans.

Since the paper-bag turkey, we have tried various turkeys and
cooking methods.

One year, we made a wild turkey that is probably closer to what
the Pilgrims ate. All we really know about the food at that first harvest celebration comes from the writing of colonist Edward
Winslow, who recorded that the governor sent "four men fowling"
and that the Wampanoag Indians "went out and killed five deer."

So we know they had venison. They might have had some kind
of waterfowl—goose, duck, swan, or eagle. (Best not to think
about those last two.) The fowl also *could* have been wild turkey.

That bird in the supermarket case is a very distant relative of
the wild turkey of 1621. Turkeys have had most of the wildness
bred out of them. In the quest for more white meat, they have
been "genetically improved" with abnormally large breasts. They
are too top heavy and fat to get off the ground.

Wild turkeys, however, run and fly so they're quite trim. They
also have longer legs than domesticated turkeys. The wild birds are
smaller, firmer, and have a rich, intense flavor since they are mostly
dark meat. They are expensive and far less meaty than commercial
birds, but they are delicious.

They can be stuffed and cooked like any other turkey, but you have to take more care not to overcook them or dry them out since they have no extra fat. Barding with bacon is often recommended.

Domestic or wild, our turkey gets cooked outdoors. We brine the bird—in a really big bucket—overnight. We marinate whatever herbs we have in the garden—usually rosemary, oregano, and thyme for at least three hours in olive oil, kosher salt, and a couple of garlic cloves and stuff the mixture under the turkey skin. Then my husband cooks the bird in a Weber kettle over indirect heat.

Ordering and buying the turkey is part of the holiday ritual. Early in November, I go to Eastern Market Poultry, put in my order with Melvin, and get my number. Melvin sells two thousand turkeys at Thanksgiving. At 7:00 A.M. the day before the holiday, Stephanie and I take our numbers and our market carts and get in the long, long line in front of the refrigerated cases piled high with fresh, numbered turkeys.

Then we have coffee and muffins, drop our turkeys at home, pick up large trash bags and garden shears, and set out for our annual trip to "prune" the bittersweet that grows wild in a large, forested park that snakes for miles from the Potomac River into the Washington suburbs. I am mad about bittersweet. The woody vine with bright orange berries grows by winding itself around trees. It can become a parasite and choke the trees so we truly believe we are performing a public service. The bittersweet goes into flower arrangements, door decorations, and table settings. I sometimes put a gigantic vase filled with nothing but bittersweet on the piano. If I weren't so old, I'd wear it in my hair.

I like to set the Thanksgiving table and autumnize the house almost as much as I like to cook the Thanksgiving dinner. The outdoor planters are filled with russet and maroon mums and the Indian corn is hung on the door. Inside, gourds and pumpkins. Everywhere. On the fall-colored tablecloth my mom made years ago, I put the wicker cornucopia I got at a yard sale. It overflows with oranges, grapefruit, apples, pears, bananas, pomegranates, and grapes. Then I take handfuls of nuts and sprinkle them all over the fruit and the table. My mom used to have us slice pitted dates, insert a walnut half, and roll each in sugar. I do that if there's time. I also throw in some figs. Amidst the table crops are nutcrackers and the metal turkey candleholders I got in Mexico.

The table looks bountiful and the house is filled with cooking smells. This is a perfect moment. In a few hours, the table will be covered in nut shells and globs of sweet potato, bittersweet berries will be crushed into the rug, the dishes will be piled high in the kitchen, and children's abandoned toys will peek out from under the couch.

The toys no longer belong to our children or nieces and nephews, but to their kids. Our family has grown since I cooked the turkey in a paper bag. My husband and I are fortunate to have all our parents and we and our siblings have nine children. Some of our children have children, so we have relatives at the table from age six months to ninety-five years. There's a lot to give thanks for.

※ SUSAN'S SPICY PECANS

Until she moved back home to New Mexico, my friend Susan Lindeborg was one of the top chefs in Washington, D.C. She served these pecans when she was the chef at the Morrison-Clark Historic Inn and Restaurant. She says all the following measurements are approximate and you should adjust to taste. I use less butter. People can't get enough of these pecans.

Makes 8–10 appetizer servings

4 cups pecan halves
⅔ cup warm melted butter
¼ cup Worcestershire sauce
6 dashes Tabasco sauce
Kosher salt

Preheat the oven to 350°F.

Spread the pecans on a cookie sheet and lightly toast them in the oven. Transfer them to a large bowl and add the butter. Mix gently until the butter is absorbed. This takes a little while—both the butter and the pecans need to be warm. As you work in the butter, add the Worcestershire sauce and Tabasco sauce.

Continued

When the liquids are mostly absorbed, spread the nuts out on the cookie sheet and return to the oven. Toast the nuts until they are crisp and dark brown, stirring occasionally. This takes 10 to 20 minutes. (Take care not to burn them.) Cool until warm and toss with kosher salt to taste.

Store the finished pecans in an airtight container at room temperature if they are to be used in a day or so or freeze them. If you freeze the pecans, toast them lightly before serving.

✳ RUTH'S SWEET POTATOES

Makes 8 servings

8 medium sweet potatoes
1 cup brown sugar
2 tablespoons cornstarch
½ teaspoon salt
½ teaspoon shredded
    orange peel
2 cups orange juice
½ cup black raisins
6 tablespoons butter
⅓ cup dry sherry
¼ cup chopped walnuts

Preheat the oven to 325°F.
Butter a 13½ × 8¾ × 1¾-inch pan.

Cook the potatoes in salted boiling water until tender. When cool enough to handle, peel and cut the potatoes lengthwise into ½-inch-thick slices. Lay them in the pan and salt.

Cook the brown sugar, cornstarch, salt, orange peel, orange juice, and raisins until bubbly and thin, then 1 minute more.

Add the butter, sherry, and walnuts to the sugar mixture and cook until the butter melts. Pour over the potatoes. Bake, uncovered, about ½ hour or until well glazed. Baste occasionally.

✳ ALLISON'S WHITE CORN PUDDING

Makes 8 to 10 servings

3 cups frozen white corn
  kernels
6 large eggs
3 cups heavy cream
½ cup sugar
½ teaspoon salt
½ teaspoon baking powder
1 teaspoon flour
2 teaspoons melted butter

Defrost the corn and process to rough chop. Place in a colander to drain for several hours or overnight.

Preheat the oven to 350°F.
Grease a 13 × 9-inch ovenproof dish

Beat the eggs lightly. Add all the remaining ingredients, including the corn, and mix well. Pour into the ovenproof dish. Bake for 1 hour or until set.

✳ BRUSSELS SPROUTS WITH WALNUTS

This is my current vegetable enthusiasm.

Makes 6 to 8 servings

½ cup walnuts
24 Brussels sprouts
Olive oil
Salt and pepper, to taste
Lemon wedge
Shaved aged Pecorino for
  garnish

Preheat the oven to 450°F.

Toast the walnuts for 10 minutes. (I use the toaster oven at 350°F.)

Cut the Brussels sprouts in half, put in a medium bowl, drizzle with olive oil, and toss. Season with salt and pepper.

Spread the sprouts on a cookie sheet with sides and roast until fork tender, about 20 minutes. Let cool, then toss with the walnuts. Drizzle liberally with olive oil, a squeeze of lemon, and salt and pepper to taste. Top with pecorino.

DINNER DISASTERS

❋   ❋   ❋

Mistakes are part of the dues that one pays for a full life.
SOPHIA LOREN

OUR HOST at a Saturday night dinner party greeted us with this news of his wife: "Megan's at the hospital emergency room."

She had suffered an esophageal spasm and was unable to swallow. Her husband, Duncan, said she had driven herself to the hospital and instructed him to insist we stay. She had spent all day preparing a multicourse Indian dinner for us and another couple and thought she would be back from the hospital by the time we got to the kharu gos (lamb with spices). She'd had these attacks before and usually responded quickly to medication.

The food was all made and warming on the stove. I turned the burners down from high to simmer. We had a drink and called Megan's cell phone every twenty minutes. No answer. We told Duncan we should leave and he should go to the hospital. Nope. So he set all the food on the dining room sideboard. There were candles everywhere—little ones on the tables, candelabras and candlesticks all over the room. I lit them and dimmed the lights. Duncan said, "I would never have thought of that."

The food was delicious and the conversation pleasant. We continued to phone Megan. She never answered and she never showed and we finally got up to leave. At the door, Duncan thought again of his wife. "There was probably dessert," he said.

Megan was in the hospital for two days. She was glad we lit the candles, which she had put out to celebrate Diwali, the Indian festival of lights. Of course, she had prepared dessert, mango fool. I'm sure it was lovely.

As carefully as you plan for a dinner party, the unexpected is always lying in wait. Megan told me about a newly married friend who for some reason or other had Dr. Benjamin Spock and his wife for dinner. Just before they were to arrive, the ceiling fell onto the dining room table. The newlyweds cleaned it off and served dinner with a gaping hole above the famous baby doctor and his wife.

Having the sky fall in or your throat close up is hard to predict. But some things are not and we can, presumably, learn from experience.

Fire, for example, is always a possibility. After several close calls. I cook on constant blaze alert. I have set fire to my hair when bending too close to a gas burner, have lit wrapping paper from birthday gifts while blowing out the candles on my cake, and have set on fire every pot holder I've ever owned.

Far worse things have happened to others. Annette invited some fellow graduate students for dinner. They were Greek so she made moussaka. In her enthusiasm, she overfilled the pan, it overflowed, and steam was coming out of the oven. She asked her husband if it was baking soda or flour you throw on a fire. He said flour. Wrong answer. Flour accelerates fire. Flames leaped from the oven. It took months to get it clean.

Disaster usually strikes when you are making dinner for people you don't know, your in-laws, or the boss. This is especially true for those of us who always try something new for a dinner party.

I once read about cooking a whole chicken in salt, thereby sealing in its moisture. I had done this successfully with a whole fish so thought I'd give it a try on a night when I was having six complete strangers for dinner. The recipe called for "coarse rock salt." I had sea salt, kosher salt, and pink salt mined in the foothills of the Himalayas but nothing labeled "coarse rock salt." Then I remembered the salt in the garage. Sure enough, "rock salt." Even though "rock salt" can refer to table salt under some circumstances, the salt in your garage is not that kind of rock salt. What you find on the shelf next to the antifreeze is the dried-up remains of ancient oceans that will melt the ice in the driveway and work in the ice cream maker. It is not edible.

I'd had these brain shutdowns before. This, however, was the worst. Even though they looked a little gray, I brought the chickens out to the dining room to be admired before cutting. Unlike the salt-entombed fish, the crust on the chickens didn't break easily and a lot of it got on the meat. I did, however, carve and serve the chicken, piling fresh parsley on the platters in an effort to make it look more appetizing. It was not fit for human consumption. Even the dog turned up her nose.

Meanwhile, my guests politely picked at their food while I apologized for breaking the salt crust and making the chicken too salty. This is where you want to stand up and scream: "I'm really a good cook. This was a terrible mistake. Let's get a pizza. Ha-ha-ha." The moment never seemed right. The steamed pudding dessert with the whole orange inside was a complete flop. Even the green salad was off. My guests smiled and told me how good dinner was. We never bonded with these people.

Then there is the dinner that turns to farce for no discernible reason. A dish you've made many times with great success bombs. I have a recipe for bouillabaisse I've made successfully a dozen times. I made it for ten people one night and it looked and tasted like dishwater. Actually, dishwater might have been an improvement. Clearly, I did something wrong, left something out. But I still don't know what. Allison has a standard lasagna recipe she once made for us and had to serve in bowls because it came out like soup. She, too, was clueless. It does keep complacency at arm's length.

Some problems stem more from lack of experience than lack of common sense. For example, if you've never cooked a whole chicken, you might think that little bag full of giblets is supposed to stay in the cavity of the bird, you might not even notice it's there. If you're asked to warm up the rolls, how would you know you're supposed to take them out of the plastic bag first? Don't be too hard on yourself. We've all been distracted and left the leavening agent out of the cake or put in twice too much sugar. All you can do is try to focus and hope for forgiveness. Sometimes you will get it.

Overexuberance also can be a problem. My husband opened a bottle of Champagne for our first dinner party in our first home and in an effort to be festive and dramatic, let the cork fly. It hit the ceiling, rebounded onto his china dinner plate, and cracked it in half. One plate—a wedding gift—cost more than I made in a week. I heard about a hostess getting so caught up in fluffing the mashed potatoes that she sent the whole pile of them flying through the air and onto the middle of the table. Talk about a dramatic centerpiece.

Of course, child-related disasters are common. Pam's sister and her husband had small children and hadn't had anyone for dinner in years. Finally, they invited people over and cooked a stuffed turkey. As they scooped the stuffing out at the table, they found that somewhere between preparing it and putting it in the bird, a child had added some colorful ingredients. Several crayons were nestled in the stuffing.

I know someone else whose kids turned the refrigerator thermostat so low all the soda pop froze. The discovery was made when a loud sound came from the kitchen—the pop exploding all over the dishes she had cooked ahead of time and refrigerated for a party later. Neither Diet Coke nor glass improves pasta salad. These things always happen when you have childless people for dinner. There's a law.

Haste, of course, makes waste. You have to be patient and let the cake layers cool before inserting the doll on top for the beautiful birthday cake or the doll's legs will melt and give the kitchen that nice liquid plastic smell. When you're ready to do the dishes after all the guests go home and can't find the sink stopper or the sponge, check the cavity of the turkey.

Thanksgiving is particularly accident prone, probably because with so many dishes there are exponentially more things that can go wrong. You grab a glass pan to cook the gravy and it explodes all over the cranberry sauce. You decide to deep fry the turkey without reading the directions. You find the cat licking the sweet potatoes or the dog dragging the bird through the house by a wing.

My friend Jen left no disaster untested in her first Thanksgiving. As a young bride in Dubai, where her husband was working on an oil rig, she invited the boss and his wife for the traditional American meal. At twenty-one, Jen hadn't cooked many dinners, let alone a multidish Thanksgiving. The turkey and sweet potatoes were both raw. Jen had told her helper to "cook the rice." He found a ten-pound bag, used every pot in the house, and cooked it all.

"I had good pies and thought I'd redeem myself with dessert," Jen says. She invited everyone into the living room and brought out the big silver Victorian coffeepot her mother had given her. She served the pie, picked up the coffeepot by the handle, and, with a yelp, dropped it so that scalding coffee went all over the boss' wife's white dress. Silver is the best-known conductor of heat.

These lemons can sometimes be made into lemonade. Mike's mom was preparing for a big political fund-raiser at her house when the electricity went out. She farmed out two turkeys and all the side dishes to cook in neighbors' ovens up and down the block. She collected the food when it was done, lit lots of candles, opened the bar, and her guests, and their wallets, stayed longer than they might have otherwise.

Part of what makes cooking and entertaining fun is the element of surprise. Even if you've done something the same way many times, you never really know how it will all turn out. When all systems collapse, sometimes you can save the evening and sometimes you can't. At least you have the comfort of knowing you're not alone.

And then, of course, there's the last resort. If you've cooked with the salt from the garage, you can always escape by going to the emergency room.

✻ JEN'S ROAST PORK WITH PRUNES AND PORT

Jen Wilkinson has come a long way since her Dubai Thanksgiving disaster. She has been a food writer and editor for years and swears that the following recipe *never* fails. She serves this dish with a bulgur wheat mixture including sliced celery, chopped red sweet pepper, sliced spring onions, parsley, garbanzo beans, currants, and finely shredded orange peel.

Makes 6 to 8 servings

2 pork tenderloins (1 pound each)
1 cup tawny port
½ cup prune juice
2 tablespoons soy sauce
2 tablespoons orange juice
2 cloves garlic, minced
¼ teaspoon ground black pepper
¾ cup pitted prunes

Place the pork tenderloins in a self-sealing plastic bag set in a shallow dish. In a small mixing bowl, combine ½ cup port, prune juice, soy sauce, orange juice, garlic, and black pepper. Pour over the meat. Close the bag. Marinate in the refrigerator for 2 to 4 hours, turning occasionally.

Preheat the oven to 425°F.

Drain the meat, reserving the marinade. Place the tenderloins on a rack in a shallow roasting pan. Pour the reserved marinade into the roasting pan. Roast the tenderloins, uncovered, for about 15 minutes.

Meanwhile, cover the prunes with boiling water. Let stand for 5 minutes and then drain. Add the prunes to the pan juices. Roast for 15 to 20 minutes more, or until a meat thermometer registers 160°F. Using a slotted spoon, remove the prunes from the roasting pan. Transfer the meat and prunes to a serving platter. Cover with foil and let stand for 10 minutes before slicing.

For the sauce, stir the remaining ½ cup port into the juices in the roasting pan, scraping up the crusty browned bits. Transfer the mixture to a small saucepan and bring it to a boil. Pour over the sliced meat and prunes.

'TIS THE SEASON

✻ ✻ ✻

Everybody knows a turkey and some mistletoe
Help to make the season bright.
"THE CHRISTMAS SONG"

IF YOU think the true spirit of Christmas has been lost, check in the kitchen. It's one of the few places on earth to escape the holiday's extensive commercialization and cleave to the traditional ways.

Of course, it still makes us crazy that as soon as the pumpkin is off the stoop, the Santa is on the roof, that we are whipped into a shopping frenzy while being told there are only seventy-two shopping days until C-day, that as heroes of mass consumption we must run amok in overcrowded stores to the sound of canned carols.

But while the gingerbread house may come in a kit, it's still put together in the family kitchen with small helping hands. This is where we bake cookies for family and friends using dog-eared, butter-stained recipes. It's in the kitchen that we prepare a dinner that is based on custom and family.

That holiday dinner varies from home to home. In the United States, however, this is the season the melting pot really heats up.

Baked goods in particular reflect the cultural heritage of the baker. There are steamed puddings, stollen, fruitcakes, panettone, sweet rice desserts, donuts, mince pies, kransekake, rum balls, bûche de Noël, molasses cookies, gingerbread, shortbread, sugar cookies, pastries in banana leaves.

While there is no standard main dish for the holiday it is always something considered out of the ordinary. This is the night for the standing rib roast, the tenderloin of beef, the goose, the duck, the tamales, or the empanadas.

I was brought up in a different religious tradition, but I like that Christmas is all around me. I love the weather, the music, and the feeling of celebration. The air feels like winter and smells like pine boughs. Luminarias light the dark paths to open houses loaded with platters of baked goods and vats of eggnog. Chestnuts roast on an open fire. Jack Frost nips at your nose.

On Christmas Eve, we are always invited to someone's home for dinner. Christmas Day is different. Everything is closed, the streets are silent, and everyone stays home with their families. I like to be home with my own family on this quiet, peaceful day and think we should have a wonderful dinner, too.

I started with a goose after years of singing, "Christmas is coming, the geese are getting fat." While goose is a traditional holiday choice in many countries, it never caught on in the United States. So it was hard to find a goose and hard to find a goose recipe. Times have changed. Geese are now available, sometimes even fresh, at least around the holidays. Christmas is coming, the geese are getting fat.

My first goose didn't fly. It was a disaster. Geese are very fat, which presents several problems. As the fat accumulates, it can smoke or catch on fire, so you need to pour it off every now and then. Because a goose is almost half fat, if you don't watch carefully, there's not much of the bird left by the time the fat is all out of it. We had a pretty scrawny bird that was a little dry but still fatty tasting. Yum.

I finally found a good goose recipe from, of all places, an early American cookbook. The first settlers ate whatever they could shoot and this, apparently, is what they did with it. It was a fabulous goose, stuffed with onions, apples, and sage.

Then one year my mother suggested a stuffed veal breast. I had never heard of such a thing. She gave me a recipe, I tried it, I loved it. It became the dinner I made on Christmas Day.

Veal breasts are not easy to find. Stuffed veal breast is an old-fashioned dish in a newfangled culinary world. My butcher says he is rarely asked for the cut. The day I went to see him about ordering one, he said he had suddenly sold several in the last few weeks though, so maybe there's a revival. There should be.

The veal breast is an economical cut of meat, feeds up to twelve adults, and looks absolutely spectacular when finished. It's tender and moist. It can be served hot, at room temperature, or chilled. Did I mention that it's incredibly easy to assemble and cook?

Whole breasts vary in size, depending on the size of the calf. The proportion of meat to fat and bones is small, so you should figure on about a pound (including bones) per person. You will have to ask the butcher to cut a deep pocket in the breast. That's where the stuffing goes.

Stuffed veal breast is part of both Eastern European and Italian culinary traditions. My grandmother-in-law from Ukraine was famous for her stuffed veal breast. Sadly, the recipes she handed down always left out several ingredients. Stuffings made with pancetta or sausage and olives testify to the Italian connection. I've also seen recipes calling for stuffings of spinach and mushrooms, buckwheat and mushrooms, bread and nuts. You can really use any stuffing you like.

I usually make a simple savory potato stuffing in the Eastern European tradition. It's so good—especially drenched in veal fat.

The golden brown, incredibly aromatic, whole veal breast makes quite an entrance. It is carved between the wide ribs so portions look impressive. The only other thing you need for a complete meal is a nice green salad.

In the spirit of the season, I make my mother's gingerbread or Gayle's steamed cranberry pudding for dessert. Sometimes both. And we have ourselves a merry little Christmas.

✳ STUFFED VEAL BREAST

Makes 10 to 12 servings

1 whole veal breast (12 to
14 pounds) cut with a
deep pocket

Preheat the oven to 350°F.

FOR THE STUFFING

6 medium Idaho potatoes
1 medium onion, finely
chopped
2 cloves garlic, minced
2 large eggs, slightly beaten
½ cup flour
⅓ cup chopped celery
2 teaspoons salt
1 teaspoon ground thyme
½ teaspoon freshly ground
pepper
¼ cup chopped parsley
½ cup (1 stick) butter

Peel and grate the potatoes. Place them in a
bowl of cold water. Let sit for 5 minutes.
Drain well, squeeze out the excess water,
and return to a clean, dry bowl. Mix in the
onions and the garlic. Add the eggs, flour,
celery, salt, thyme, pepper, and parsley. Mix
until well combined. I do this with my hands.

Heat the butter in a roasting pan large
enough to hold the veal breast; then add to
the potato mixture, combining well. This
greases the pan as well as melts the butter.
Let the stuffing sit until it comes to room
temperature.

FOR THE RUB

2 cloves garlic, minced
1 tablespoon chopped fresh
thyme
1 teaspoon salt
½ teaspoon freshly ground
pepper
1 tablespoon olive oil

Meanwhile, combine the ingredients for the
rub in a small bowl and set aside.

Fill the veal pocket with the stuffing and fas-
ten with metal skewers tied with kitchen
string. Don't overstuff, because the stuffing
will expand. Rub the meat all over with the
garlic-thyme mixture. Spread the onion,
carrots, and garlic on the bottom of the
roasting pan. Sprinkle with salt and pepper.
Lay the breast, bone side down, on top of
the vegetables and pour the wine and broth
around it.

FOR THE PAN

1 onion, chopped
2 carrots, chopped
2 cloves garlic, chopped
Salt and pepper, to taste
½ cup white wine
½ cup chicken broth

Cover with foil and roast for 2½ to 3 hours, until the meat can be easily pierced with a fork. Remove the foil for the last half hour and baste the veal with the liquid in the pan to brown the meat. Add more chicken broth to the pan if necessary.

Let rest for 10 to 15 minutes after removing from the oven. Slice between the ribs and serve.

✳ FERN'S GINGERBREAD

Makes 8 servings

2 cups apples, peeled, cored, and diced
¼ cup dark brown sugar, firmly packed
1 tablespoon butter
1¼ cups all-purpose flour
1 teaspoon ground ginger
1 teaspoon ground cinnamon
Pinch of ground cardamom
¾ teaspoon baking soda
¼ teaspoon nutmeg
⅛ teaspoon salt
¼ teaspoon finely ground black pepper
⅛ teaspoon cloves
½ cup chopped dates
¼ cup canola oil
⅓ cup sugar
⅓ cup molasses
1 large egg
½ cup strong, brewed coffee
½ cup plain yogurt

Preheat the oven to 350°F.

Butter an 10 × 8-inch loaf pan.

Mix the apples, brown sugar, and butter and place in the pan.

In a bowl, mix the flour, ginger, cinnamon, cardamom, baking soda, nutmeg, salt, pepper, cloves, and dates. In another bowl, combine the oil, sugar, molasses, egg, coffee, and yogurt and add to the dry mixture. Pour this mixture over the apples in the pan. Bake for 35 to 40 minutes, or until the cake feels done when pressed. Cool for 5 minutes before serving. Serve with whipped cream flavored with Calvados, or with warm applesauce.

✳ GAYLE'S CRANBERRY PUDDING

Gayle Krughoff grew up in a small town in South Dakota. She says this pudding always made her think of exquisite homes and wealthy people with beautiful dining rooms. It came from Muriel, a family friend who had such a home. Muriel, now in her nineties, still makes the pudding from a recipe she got from her husband's aunt Emma.

Makes 8 to 10 servings

2 cups fresh cranberries, chopped
1⅓ cups all-purpose flour
¼ cup molasses
¼ cup light corn syrup
2 teaspoons baking soda
⅓ cup hot water

Mix all the ingredients together and pour into a lightly buttered 10-cup mold. The pudding will not fill the mold. Place the mold on a rack in a heavy saucepan over 1 inch of boiling water. Cover. Use high heat until steam begins to escape; then lower the heat. Cook for 1½ to 2 hours, or until a toothpick inserted in the pudding comes out clean. Let the pudding rest for 10 minutes before unmolding.

Put a little hard sauce on each serving and pass the rest.

HARD SAUCE
½ cup (1 stick) butter
½ cup cream
1 cup sugar

Mix the ingredients together and cook over medium-low heat, stirring, until the sugar dissolves and the butter melts.

NOTE FROM GAYLE: If you run out of the pudding, serve the hard sauce over shoe leather.

THE CHICKEN CHALLENGE

❋ ❋ ❋

A perfectly roasted chicken is as fine a dish as one can have.
JAMES BEARD

A T FIRST glance, a recipe for roast chicken looks like something a child could make. Put a chicken in a pan, season it with salt and pepper, and stick it in the oven. What could be easier? Almost anything.

To make a perfect roast chicken takes an understanding of chemistry and thermodynamics, insight into the politics and history of the poultry industry, and an awareness of changes in American agriculture. Reputations rise and fall on the quality of a roast chicken. According to Julia Child, "You can always judge the quality of a cook or a restaurant by roast chicken."

I've roasted flocks of chickens. But I've never achieved anything near perfection. My roast chickens have always been closer to "fine" than "great."

A *great* roast chicken has moist, juicy white meat; thoroughly cooked dark meat, browned, crispy skin, and lots of flavor. The reality is often the dreaded rubber chicken—overcooked or undercooked, stringy, tough, dry, and flavorless.

What's the secret? I looked at recipes in cookbooks, on the Internet, and in newspapers and magazines. I asked friends, relatives, neighbors, and people I barely know how they roast their chickens. There's really no mystery. There's just a principle: Less is more. The beauty of the roast chicken is its simplicity.

In the beginning, chickens pecked and scratched in the yards and on the farms of early American homes. Their job was to lay eggs. Every now and then, one of them would be a special Sunday or holiday dinner. They were considered a rare luxury by the non-farm community. Then the commercial broiler industry began raising chickens specifically for their meat. Business boomed and by the 1990s, Americans were eating more chicken than red meat.

As the numbers went up, the flavor went down. There were charges of inhumane practices and now we're back where we started. We want chickens that peck and scratch in the yard. Does a chicken that's not stressed out taste better? It's a matter of opinion. I usually buy organic chickens and have always enjoyed them. My only bad experience was with a bird I bought at a farmer's market that was described as "more organic than organic, more free range than free range." I have no idea what that means, but I bought it. I took the super organic chicken home and unwrapped it to find a scrawny, pale chicken. I cooked it and it tasted scrawny and pale. At least it was happy.

My mother-in-law has always maintained that the best chicken is a kosher chicken. I admit that for most of my marriage I dismissed this as a parochial reaction based on limited experience. Then I read about a blind chicken tasting done by *Cook's Illustrated* magazine in which at least four national free-range, organic chicken brands came in behind a supermarket brand. First place: kosher chicken. Which brings us to the important issue of salt.

A kosher chicken is buried in salt for an hour, then rinsed to rid the bird of all blood, impurities, and salt. And that, many cooks say, is why it's so good.

Judy Rodgers, chef-owner of San Francisco's Zuni Café, may make the most famous roast chicken in the country. Many consider hers the gold standard. So I called her. She is very, very serious about salt. Success, she says, has less to do with the bird than with the method. She does, however, recommend using a small bird—2¾ to 3½ pounds. I agree that smaller is better, but I will go up to 4½ pounds.

Judy coats her chickens with salt and some pepper, covers them loosely, and refrigerates them for at least 24 hours. She uses ¾ teaspoon of sea salt per pound of chicken. There is a scientific explanation for the process that involves osmosis, diffusion, and denaturing. It's way over my head. Basically, salting hydrates the cells so they hold on to water while they're cooking. In *The Zuni Café Cookbook,* Judy talks about salting at great length. Brining— soaking meats in salt and water—has the same effect. The process, she says, works whether the salt is wet or dry. The end result is tender, moist, evenly seasoned meat. And, strangely, salting the bird this way doesn't make it taste salty.

If you brine your chicken, about an hour a pound, rinse and dry it thoroughly when it comes out of the brine. If you don't dry a chicken well enough, the skin will steam instead of brown. Don't brine a kosher chicken. It's been there, done that.

The only possible downside to brining is that adding moisture to the skin may keep it from getting as crisp as you like. Letting it dry uncovered in the refrigerator will keep it drier.

If you've brined the bird, the chicken experts say, you don't need to do much of anything else except rub a little oil or butter on the skin. If the bird is not brined, salt and pepper inside and out and rub the skin with butter or oil. I tried this simplest of all approaches several times and always found the result a little bland. So I added some fresh herbs. Better.

At my friend Carin's suggestion, I rubbed a chicken inside and out with lemon juice and lightly crushed garlic. I then put the shells of the squeezed lemons and what was left of the garlic into the cavity of the chicken. I also tossed in handfuls of herbs. I rubbed the skin with a little olive oil to ensure a browned, crispy skin. I thought this chicken was delicious. The lemon and garlic seem to bring out the best in a chicken and the flavor was just right. I have also slipped herbs and oil under the chicken skin with good results.

Next comes a big decision: to truss or not to truss. I'm antitrussing. Too much trouble. You need to find the little metal skewers, the kitchen string, and figure out how to hold it all together at the same time you sew. Instead, I throw a bunch of stuff inside the chicken and leave it untrussed.

I think one of the most important things in chicken cookery is thoroughly cooked meat. This is not a universal attitude. James Beard, for example, liked chicken "pink." The problem is that dark meat and white meat cook at different rates. "Therefore," Beard wrote, "either resign yourself to a bit of pink or roast the dark and white meat separately." This is somewhat impractical if you want a whole roast chicken. Kitchen scientist Harold McGee straps ice packs on his chicken breasts. Chilling the white meat, he says, makes it cook more slowly.

Rotisseries work well because the chicken is continually turned, which helps it to roast evenly. To get the same result in a roasting pan, you have to turn and baste the chicken.

I feel the same way about basting and turning that I do about trussing. I'm lucky if I remember there's a chicken in the oven, let alone if I've turned or basted it. Basting flavors the meat and keeps it moist, and turning helps guarantee even roasting.

So what to do? My friend Beth told me to try a vertical roaster. This simple, inexpensive device looks like a small metal Eiffel Tower. The principle is similar to that of the beer can chicken. You slip the beer can or roaster (you could even use the insert from an angel food cake pan) through the chicken's cavity and out the opening at the top. (Spray some oil on the vertical roaster first.) The visual is disconcerting. It looks like a headless chicken Buddha. Season as you like, set it in a pan with a little water, put it in the oven, and walk away. The fat drains away and the chicken sits above the fat. There's no trussing or basting. The dark meat comes out just right and the white meat is wonderfully tender and juicy. Doesn't get much easier than this.

One key to success with the vertical roaster—and, I think, for chicken roasting in general—is steady high heat. Every chicken chef has a heat theory. Some start high and then lower the heat after a time. Others cook at a steady low heat. In my search for simplicity, I sit my chicken on its roaster, season it, and put it in a 475°F oven. (Be sure the oven is really preheated—15 minutes or so.) You get crisp skin and moist meat. If you use a vertical roaster, don't leave it in the oven too long. The chicken really cooks fast on this thing, about 15 minutes a pound.

My alternative to the vertical roaster is the V-rack. It keeps the chicken higher up than a flat rack. Any rack will allow hot air to circulate all around the chicken so it browns evenly. Judy Rodgers puts her celebrated chicken in a snug pan with no rack.

What you do after taking the bird out of the oven may be one of the most important steps in achieving roast chicken perfection: What you do is nothing. Let the chicken sit for 15 minutes to a half hour before carving. Cover loosely with foil to keep warm. More complicated scientific processes occur during this time. Essentially, the juices go back into the meat and the muscles loosen.

To recap:

1. Buy a good, small chicken and brine it or get a kosher chicken.
2. Season as you like and rub a little oil or butter on the skin for browning. Do not truss.
3. Place the chicken on a vertical roaster or a V-rack in a roasting pan.
4. Preheat the oven to 475°F for at least 15 minutes.
5. Place the chicken in the oven and cook until nicely browned and an instant-read thermometer inserted in the breast reads 160°F and in the thigh reads 165° to 170°F.
6. Do not open the oven. Do not baste. Do not turn.
7. When the chicken is done, remove it from the oven, and let it sit for 15 to 30 minutes.
8. Carve, serve, and graciously receive compliments.

TAKING POTLUCK

✳ ✳ ✳

Necessity is the mother of taking chances.
MARK TWAIN

MISS MANNERS does not approve of the potluck. "How did the charmingly homely phrase 'potluck' come to stand for such an unfortunate situation?" she asks.

She says, and I paraphrase, that potluck used to mean come on over for family dinner, nothing fancy, take your chances. Now, she says, it's come to mean: We consider it too much trouble and expense to make any effort for you, so if you want to eat with us at our house bring your own food.

Miss Manners excepts "cooperative entertaining," which includes picnics, meetings, and regularly convened dinner groups. These events, she says, have "organizers" rather than "hosts."

Too often, though, the exception is the rule. Potlucks are facts of modern life. There's the fourth-grade parents' potluck, the high school football potluck tailgate, the church potluck, the birthday-at-work potluck. We bring food to friends and relatives when they move into a new house, have a baby, or suffer a loss. Pam and Matt met in graduate school and regularly had potlucks with their friends. So at their wedding, they provided the Champagne and cake and everyone brought a dish.

It was under the rubric of "cooperative entertaining" that I asked thirty-two people over for dinner and asked them to bring their own food. Other than Thanksgiving where guests want to bring a special dish or pie or a major religious holiday involving a multicourse sit-down meal for forty, this was the first time I have ever asked anyone to bring food to my house. I like to invite people over and be a hostess, cook their dinner, and take care of their needs. I like to eat their food at their homes and have them take care of mine.

I love to prepare food for others. I am at ease in the kitchen. But when I'm asked to bring something for a potluck, I panic. Suddenly, I forget how to cook. I can't think of anything to make. I bring cheese and crackers. I buy prepared deli salads. I put store-bought hummus in a bowl surrounded by store-cut vegetables.

I can't explain my discomfort. Is it all a control issue? Maybe it's the element of competition at the potluck. You surreptitiously look over every few minutes to see whose dish is going the fastest. You calculate who worked the hardest on their offering. You look at the platters people brought things on.

So why did I inflict this unease on thirty-two people I like? I was looking for new recipes. I was curious to see what people would bring. It seemed like a good idea at the time. Everyone was incredibly gracious and even enthusiastic. No one was offended. I made five dishes, bought lots of wine and beer, and used real plates and napkins to assuage my guilt. I rearranged the whole house so everyone would have a seat at a table. I spent a good part of the evening apologizing for asking people to cook their own dinner.

I did, however, learn a number of things from the experience.

First, no one brings a green vegetable. We all think in terms of balance when planning meals and know the important place of fruits and vegetables in a healthful diet. But steamed broccoli doesn't seem like a fun date at a potluck. Consequently, there were no green beans or Brussels sprouts. I asked one person to make a salad and she did a lovely job with pears, cheese, and a nice vinaigrette. I had bags of lettuce in the refrigerator for backup. No one demanded more salad. The only fruits appeared in desserts with plenty of sugar, such as Nancy's apple chocolate cake. This is probably not what the USDA has in mind when recommending numerous servings of fruits and vegetables each day.

Another lesson learned: Almost everyone brings a casserole with noodles. This was a problem for the one guest who hadn't heard that low-carb diets are passé. One woman brought the comforting noodle, tomato, and hamburger dish she brings to all new mothers. Another made the lasagna she used to make regularly for her now-grown children. Carin brings Orzo with Everything to all potlucks. "It's simple and it's like eating candy," she says.

Potluck dishes often tap into food nostalgia. Susan grew up in a two-family house in Brooklyn. She lived on the first level and Mrs. Castino and her son, Matty, who was wounded during World War II, lived upstairs. "Mrs. Castino was Italian Catholic and my grandmother was Eastern European Jewish," Susan says. They had a lot in common, though, especially in the kitchen. But Susan remembers that their kitchens smelled different. "Mrs. Castino browned her garlic and onions with pork drippings she kept in a can on the stove. My grandmother used chicken fat that she kept in a jar in the fridge. Mrs. Castino made pasta with her special tomato sauce that simmered for hours on a rear stove burner. My grandmother made the Jewish equivalent of Italian pasta—savory noodle kugel. It was like ravioli." Susan brought a kugel like her grandmother would have made.

Regions of origin also come out at a potluck. The two Minnesotans I invited both had recipes for wild rice casseroles. In response to my invitation, I got this e-mail from Danelle: "Just name the category. Of course anything—main dish or appetizer (or dessert)—will probably include seafood from our house." She and her husband are from Louisiana. What she brought was something called Shrimp LeBlanc that she got from a friend who got it from a friend who got it from her aunt. It uses Velveeta cheese and crispy fried onions from a can. It was very southern, very sinful, and a big hit.

Danelle has young children and clearly knows the potluck rules. She brought her dish in a beautiful basket covered in an elegant tea towel. People with children at home are in an intense potluck period and find a request to cook their own meals, wrap them up, and bring them to someone else's house par for the course. Another woman with children the same age brought a carrot cake—the third she'd made that week. She even has a large plastic-covered cake carrier.

Barbara has grown children but obviously knew how to approach the occasion. She brought delicious coq au vin in a Crock-Pot (now called a slow cooker). This is a perfect way to transport your food to someone else's house. You just plug it in when you get there to reheat, considerately leaving oven space to others. Barbara was so appalled I didn't have a slow cooker, she left the one she brought as a gift.

I also learned that, by a margin of 2 to 1, people drink more white than red wine regardless of what they're eating or the time of year. The quality of the wine seems to be irrelevant in this setting, so hang on to those special bottles for another time.

It occurred to me halfway through the evening that I could have made the Working Meat Loaf. Years earlier, the neighborhood arts workshop put on a production of the musical adaptation of *Working*, Studs Terkel's oral history of working life. I was in charge of food for the pretheater dinners. The menu included meat loaf and mashed potatoes. I devised a meat loaf that could be made in bulk. It can be scaled down to serve ten and is good hot or cold. Maybe I'll remember next time.

Apparently, my potluck was a good party. People stayed late, were in high spirits, and loud voice. The thank-you e-mails and calls seemed sincere. It appears that a potluck where you invite everyone in your address book becomes less about the cooking than the company. The guests were not connected by soccer, the lousy principal, the neighborhood library, the political campaign, or the Save the Trees project. While some knew each other, the only real common ground was that I had all their e-mail addresses.

The food thereby became an instrument for introduction. "What did you bring?" "Oh, *that* looks good." "Where did you get cranberries this time of year?"

I still prefer cooking everything myself for guests in my home. I'm a calmer hostess that way. I do not, however, agree with Miss Manners's characterization of the potluck as a "misfortune for the noble institution of hospitality." I have been to the home of everyone who came to my starter potluck. They are all good cooks and gracious hosts. They have never asked me to cook my own food for their parties, but I'm sure if they held potlucks they would be lovely. I just have no idea what I would bring. Probably cheese and crackers.

✳ CARIN'S ORZO WITH EVERYTHING

Use oil and vinegar to your taste; just keep a 3-to-1 ratio.

Makes 10 to 12 servings

16 ounces orzo
1 cup oil-packed, sun-dried tomatoes, drained and chopped
¾ cup olive oil
¼ cup balsamic vinegar
½ cup chopped, pitted Kalamata olives
2 small (or 1 medium) heads radicchio, chopped
½ cup toasted pine nuts
½ cup fresh basil, slivered
1 cup grated Parmesan
2 large cloves garlic, minced
Salt and pepper, to taste

Cook the orzo according to the directions on the package. Be careful not to overcook. Drain. Transfer to a large bowl. Add the tomatoes, olive oil, and vinegar and mix. Cool. Mix in everything else and add the salt and pepper.

✳ WORKING MEAT LOAF

Makes 10 to 12 servings

3 tablespoons unsalted
butter
¾ cup finely chopped onion
¾ cup finely chopped
scallions, white bulb and
3 inches of green
½ cup finely chopped
carrots
¼ cup finely chopped celery
½ cup minced red bell
pepper
2 teaspoons minced garlic
Salt, to taste
1½ teaspoons freshly
ground black pepper
¼ teaspoon cayenne pepper
1 teaspoon ground cumin
½ teaspoon nutmeg
3 large eggs, well beaten
½ cup ketchup
½ cup half and half
2 pounds lean ground beef
12 ounces sausage meat
(not fennel-flavored)
¾ cup bread crumbs

Preheat the oven to 375°F.

Melt the butter in a heavy skillet and add
the onion, scallions, carrots, celery, bell pepper, and garlic. Cook, stirring often, until
the moisture from the vegetables has evaporated, about 10 minutes. Set aside to cool.
Refrigerate, covered, until chilled, at least 1
hour.

Combine in a mixing bowl the salt, pepper,
cayenne, cumin, nutmeg, and eggs and beat
well. Add the ketchup and half and half.
Blend thoroughly.

Add the ground beef, sausage, and bread
crumbs to the egg mixture. Add the chilled
vegetables and mix thoroughly with your
hands, kneading for 5 minutes.

With damp hands, form two loaves. Place the loaves in a baking dish and
place that dish inside a larger pan. Pour boiling water into the larger pan
until it reaches halfway up the sides of the baking dish.

Place the pan in the oven and bake 35 to 40 minutes.

Remove the baking dish from the water bath and let the meat loaf rest for
20 minutes before slicing and serving.

⚹ NANCY'S APPLE CHOCOLATE CAKE

Nancy's mother got this recipe from the annual apple festival at Kirby's Mill in Medford, New Jersey. Nancy brings it to all potlucks.

Makes 10 to 12 servings

1½ cups sugar
4 cups peeled, chopped
   apples
3 cups all-purpose flour
2 teaspoons baking soda
1½ teaspoons cinnamon
¼ teaspoon salt
1 cup vegetable oil
2 large eggs
10 ounces semisweet
   chocolate chips

Preheat the oven to 350°F. Grease a 13 × 9-inch baking pan.

Mix the sugar and apples in a large bowl. Let stand for 15 minutes. In a bowl, mix together the flour, baking soda, cinnamon, and salt.

Add the oil and eggs to the apple mixture. Add the dry ingredients to the apple mixture. Add the chocolate chips. Pour the mixture into the greased baking pan.

Bake for 40 minutes. The cake is done when a toothpick inserted into the center of the cake comes out clean.

LIGHTS AND LATKES

✳   ✳   ✳

What I say is that, if a fellow really likes potatoes,
he must be a pretty decent sort of fellow.

A. A. MILNE

O NE DECEMBER night, my son came home from walking the dog in Lincoln Park near our house and said, "Mom, I need to take some latkes to the park tomorrow." He was twelve, and he belonged to a regular group of dog owners who gathered each evening to walk their dogs and visit beneath a colossal statue of Lincoln freeing the slaves.

My son usually came home with information on the romantic breakups or work problems of people he knew only by the names of their dogs. "Maxie's mother got fired" or "Taffy's father broke up with his girlfriend." On this winter night, they had been talking about the holiday season and my son announced: "My mom makes the best latkes." There was dissension, particularly from the owner of Joy, a ten-year-old, one-hundred-pound rottweiler, who claimed she made the best latkes—the fried potato pancakes traditionally served on Hanukkah. She also said Joy was a lap dog.

The taste-off was the next night. I was instructed to make the latkes but not come to the park. My son came home a half hour later with the news that I had lost. Freezing temperatures kept all but the hardiest latke enthusiasts home so I'm not sure how big a defeat I suffered. I chalked it up to a win for the familiar. Joy's mom finely grated each potato by hand in the traditional fashion. I do mine in the food processor with the grating blade on the thickest cut. Mine turn out like hashed brown patties while hers are more pancakelike. I met her years later and had her latkes. She cooks them in goose fat. They were *quite* good.

My son based his high opinion of my latkes on the annual Hanukkah party we have with family, friends, and neighbors (only about half of whom are Jewish). I spend most of the day and most of the party in the kitchen preparing and making the latkes.

For the record, Hanukkah is a minor holiday. Its status has been raised by its proximity to Christmas. The tradition of gift-giving at Hanukkah is just an excuse for Jewish children to get as many presents as their classmates.

I remember when the neighbors started baking Christmas cookies, my mother made sugar cookies in the shape of menorahs with red maraschino cherries as the flames. She sprinkled them with blue sugar someone had sent her from Neiman Marcus—in those days, a store found only in Dallas.

The holiday is particularly appealing to me because feasting is part of the celebration. Singing and rejoicing are also encouraged. It's a good excuse for a big party. And because Hanukkah is a festival of lights, it's a big party with a lot of candles.

Since we moved to Washington in 1985, we've gathered with the same group of friends and their children to celebrate the victory of Judah Maccabee and his followers over King Antiochus Epiphanes, who was trying to wipe out Judaism, the first time Jews had taken up arms to defend their religion. When they chased the enemy out of Jerusalem, the Maccabees found their temple had been desecrated. They had only one small vial of untainted olive oil—enough to burn for one day. They lit it and it lasted the eight days they needed to get more consecrated oil and rededicate the temple. This miracle is celebrated by lighting a candle for each of the eight days of Hanukkah.

My husband always tells the children the story of Hanukkah, something he was asked to stop when they got into their teens, but he persists. We always serve the same dinner: brisket and

latkes. I usually make a green salad, but it's fairly irrelevant.
Dessert is a big platter of the Christmas cookies and cakes I've
been given during the holiday season garnished with a sprig of
holly. No matter how much brisket I make or how many latkes I
fry, there are never any leftovers. Never.

I decorate the house with blue and silver Christmas balls for a
little crosscultural touch, set the table in blue and white (the colors
of the Israeli flag), light millions of candles, dim the lights, and go
into the kitchen, where I fry latkes all night.

In the kitchen, the miracle of the oil is celebrated in a frying
pan. I have a huge cast-iron skillet and borrow a second one. I am
smitten with these pans. They cook evenly and retain heat. You
also get a great workout since they weigh about a ton each. I can't
believe I threw out my husband's grandmother's cast-iron pan
when we got married. I thought it was so old-fashioned and nasty-
looking (due to years of careful seasoning).

You can apparently make latkes ahead and reheat them in the
oven, but I think this is wrong. They'll never be as hot, as greasy,
or as crisp as they are freshly fried and served. I do make the
brisket in advance so I can skim off the inch or so of fat that con-
geals after a day in the refrigerator. Brisket only gets better the
longer it sits.

Latkes provide the exception to the rule that hosts should plan
a meal so they sit down with their guests to eat. The latke fryer be-
longs in the kitchen. I stand at the stove in my apron that covers
an old workshirt (it's a dirty business) with a spatula in one hand
and a glass of bourbon on the rocks in the other while everyone
else sits down in the dining room. I have plenty of company.
Guests of all ages come in to "test." Personally, I think latkes taste
best while they're sitting on the paper towel–lined cookie sheet,
just out of the frying pan. When I make latkes. I run through at
least ten pounds of potatoes. It's never enough. I could use thirty
pounds and they'd all be eaten.

I heard about someone who made what she thought would be

healthier latkes by "frying" them in a pan coated with Pam. Not even close. For the right texture and flavor, latkes must be fried in oil. Period. If the temperature is hot enough, the pancakes don't absorb much fat. I use peanut oil, which has the high smoking point desirable for frying. Use oil about ½ inch deep to reach and keep the high temperature you need. If the oil starts smoking, turn down the heat. No matter how well regulated the temperature, your house will smell like oil for about a month.

Some people like sour cream with their latkes. However, I think applesauce is even better. Jarred applesauce isn't bad if you heat it up and add a little cinnamon. But it's easy to make your own applesauce in the microwave. It's not only better, but prettier. I leave the skin on, and the sauce has a pink tinge. You can also make a chunkier sauce if you do it yourself.

Everyone has an opinion on how to make latkes. There are recipes for latkes made with apples, zucchini, and sweet potatoes. Nothing is wrong with these additions. They just don't belong in latkes. Then there's the question of variety of potato. I think oblong baking potatoes (also called russet or Idaho) work best. They have less moisture than boiling potatoes, ergo, crisper latkes. I have eaten latkes made from a mix. They are a crime against man and a crime against nature.

We're on our third dog since my son's Lincoln Park days. Some of the children who listened to the story of Hanukkah now have children of their own. One year Hanukkah was very early, right after Thanksgiving. Some of the now-grown children who had always come to our party weren't in town until the Christmas holidays. They wanted their brisket and latkes as usual, so we had a thirty-fifth night of Hanukkah party. The world may change, dogs may come and go, but you never outgrow your need for latkes.

❉ LATKES

Makes 20 to 24 pancakes (3 inches each)

The following recipe is a guide only. Be careful not to put in too much flour or the pancakes will be heavy. Add flour slowly until you just bind the batter. Also watch the eggs. You shouldn't use more than one per pound of potatoes. I like to add grated onion. Many people don't. The only other ingredients are salt and pepper to taste. Serve with simple homemade applesauce.

2 pounds baking potatoes
1 onion, grated
2 large eggs, lightly beaten
1 cup (or less) all-purpose
  flour
1 teaspoon salt
Freshly ground black
  pepper to taste
Peanut oil, for frying
Simple Applesauce (recipe
  follows on page 164)

Peel the potatoes and place in a bowl of cold water to cover.

Place a shredding disk the width of your choice into a food processor. As you grate the potatoes, submerge them in another bowl of cold water. After grating all the potatoes, set the bowl aside for a few minutes. The water will be pink and starchy. Drain and rinse the potatoes under cold water. You've taken out a lot of the starch and prepared them so they won't discolor.

Put the drained potatoes in a large bowl. Add the grated onion, eggs, flour, salt, and pepper. The best way to mix this is with your hands.

Place about ½ inch of oil in a large, heavy skillet. I've found cast iron works the best. Heat until when you flick in a few drops of water, the oil hisses.

With a large tablespoon or ¼-cup measuring cup, drop the batter into the hot oil, making pancakes about 3 inches in diameter. Fry until brown on the underside. Turn to brown the other side. Lift out with a slotted spatula and place on a paper towel–lined cookie sheet to drain.

Serve hot with applesauce.

✳ SIMPLE APPLESAUCE

6 medium apples (you can
  mix varieties)
¼ cup water
½ teaspoon ground
  cinnamon, or to taste
1 tablespoon sugar, or to
  taste (optional)

You can peel the apples, but leaving the skin on gives the sauce a nice color and more fiber.

Core and thinly slice the apples, and put them in a large microwave-safe bowl. Add the water. Cover with plastic wrap and microwave on HIGH for 10 minutes. Stir the apples. Microwave, uncovered, until the apples are very tender, about 5 minutes more. Using a large fork, coarsely mash the apples to the desired consistency. Mix in the cinnamon. Add the sugar, if desired.

ENTERTAINING IN COLOR

※ ※ ※

I found I could say things with color and shapes
that I couldn't say any other way. . . .
GEORGIA O'KEEFFE

KATE IS the queen of the theme. By early October, Indian corn is hanging on her door, candles shaped like candy corn are on the table, gourds and baby pumpkins spill off the mantelpiece. At a birthday party for an equestrian friend, place mats were horse puzzles from the dime store. For parties after her son's high school football games she served hot dogs, chips, and other stadium foods.

When her friend's daughter had a baby, Kate immediately began planning a grandmother shower. Because the baby was a girl, the theme was obvious: pink. Kate served pink lemonade and sparkling Burgundy, which is, essentially, pink champagne. A large pink tub in the center of the table held gift bags for the guests— pink soaps wrapped in pink toile. She served pink salmon, pink champagne truffles and petit fours, and pink gelato. Guests were directed not to bring practical gifts—no bibs or blankets. Indulgent presents like pretty dresses were recommended. Kate wore hot pink and pale pink.

She just can't help herself. She thinks thematically.

No, Kate is not someone with too much time on her hands. She runs a successful marketing agency. Her thank-you notes are always sent immediately, she never forgets a birthday, and has an incredibly orderly house.

To think like Kate, color is a good place to start. Extend the theme as far as possible, stopping at colors that are not found in nature.

Most color themes are obvious.

St. Patrick's Day is green. You can make a centerpiece with pots of clover or the ornamental grass now inexplicably grown in pots. Sprinkle shamrock confetti on the table and hang green Christmas lights from the chandelier. Start the meal with spring pea soup, but don't push the green food *too* far. Kelly green is not a good color for beer or for foods that weren't born that way. Leave the Irish stew and soda bread in their natural hues. Play Irish music. Have a glass of Irish whiskey or a room-temperature Guinness in their natural shades of brown. Guinness, by the way, is excellent with oysters.

The Fourth of July, of course, is red, white, and blue. Everything from invitations to backyard torch candles come in patriotic mufti so decorating is a breeze. There are plenty of summer fruits and vegetables that are also red, white, and blue. Serve them alongside your burgers and bake that cake that looks like a flag that's in every food magazine in July. If you want to follow a road less taken, do Flag Day on June 14 or Bastille Day on July 14—the same color scheme as the Fourth of July but you get credit for originality and can make bouillabaise or chicken with forty cloves of garlic with a fruit tart for dessert. Make all food in their natural colors.

Valentine's Day is even easier. Red candles, red place mats, hearts, and flowers. Nearly every food from artichoke to zucchini has been considered an aphrodisiac, so menu choices are unlimited. Oysters were first identified as sexually stimulating by the ancient Romans who wrote about the wanton behavior of women who ate oysters. That's your first course. The Aztec emperor Montezuma drank fifty goblets of hot chocolate before visiting his harem of six hundred. Be sure to serve some chocolate with coffee. You get the idea.

A home-based bacchanal for Mardi Gras requires only a trip to the party store, where you can get beads, masks, and decorations in the carnival's signature colors: green, purple, and gold. Play loud zydeco music, make gumbo, and get a king's cake for dessert. These braided, coffee cake–like pastries were brought to New Orleans by the early French settlers, continuing a custom dating from the Epiphany cakes of the Middle Ages in Europe. They are covered with colored sugar—purple for justice, green for faith, and gold for power—and inside each is baked a plastic baby doll or bean. Whoever gets the prize has to host the next year's king's cake party. If you can't find one where you live, there are a number of New Orleans bakeries that ship the cakes in special boxes. Some even come with beads.

As a case study one year, I decided to do an adult Halloween party. Colors are obvious, but there's no traditional food. So while Halloween has become one of the biggest party nights of the year, right behind New Year's Eve and the Super Bowl, there's no Champagne, no chili, and no wings to fall back on. If you're older than twelve, you can't make a whole meal of candy.

Decking out your house for the holiday is almost too easy. Paraphernalia starts showing up in stores toward the end of summer, and the choice is vast: spiderweb cocktail napkins, foam tabletop tombstones, pumpkin candleholders, wire trees with faces, black plastic spiders. You don't have to go any farther than the corner drugstore. The decoration shopping for Halloween is second only to Christmas.

I decided to extend the color scheme to the food and serve an all black and orange dinner.

I used an orange tablecloth, black napkins, and black plates, all of which I found at yard sales. I got a black plastic cauldron from the drugstore and filled it with orange mums. I used orange tapers and lots of candles in pumpkin shapes. The table, of course, was sprinkled with candy corn. At each guest's place was a little orange-and-black plastic jack-o'-lantern full of black licorice sticks.

Appetizers were baby carrots and orange pepper slices with a black olive tapenade; red fish roe and smoked salmon on squares of black bread; orange Cheddar cheese encased in black rind with dark rye crackers or pumpernickel bread; black olives; blue corn tortilla chips (they look black) and red pepper hummus. If you want to go downscale: Cheetos.

A first course of black squid ink pasta with orange peppers would be nice, but it's hard to find the pasta. Substitute a salad of shredded carrots and currants. For the main course I made a black bean and pumpkin soup with spicy chorizo sausage and served it from a hollowed-out pumpkin. Dessert was simple—orange sorbet with Halloween Oreos, made with orange cream centers. Full disclosure: I served a green salad.

Even Kate was impressed. And I think it lifted her spirits. She had just been to New York, where her twenty-four-year-old son is a financial analyst with a big firm. "He's so mature and serious," she said. "I think this may be the year to stop putting together a Halloween bag to send him." But she can surely use green for the financial analyst for the next bank holiday.

✳ BLACK BEAN PUMPKIN SOUP

Makes 8 to 10 servings

3 (15½-ounce) cans black beans, rinsed and drained

Coarsely puree the beans and tomatoes in a food processor.

1¼ cups canned tomatoes with green chilies, drained and chopped

3 to 4 tablespoons combination olive oil and butter

1 medium yellow onion, chopped

6 shallots, minced

Heat the oil/butter in a heavy soup pot. Add the onion, shallots, garlic, salt, and pepper and cook over medium heat until softened. Add the chorizo and cumin and stir to mix. Stir in the broth and bring to a simmer. Add the bean puree, pumpkin puree, and sherry and simmer, uncovered, for 30 to 40 minutes. Stir occasionally. Add the vinegar and check the seasonings.

4 cloves garlic, minced
1½ teaspoons salt
½ teaspoon freshly ground
   black pepper
¾ pound chorizo, sliced and
   cooked through
1 tablespoon ground cumin
4 cups chicken broth
One 15-ounce can pumpkin
   puree (not pumpkin pie
   filling)
½ cup dry sherry
2 teaspoons red wine
   vinegar

Serve with sour cream (leave it white).

✳ PUMPKIN TUREEN

You'll need a big, squat pumpkin. Try to find one with a nice handle.

Wash the pumpkin in warm, soapy water and dry well.

Preheat the oven to 325°F.

Using a sharp knife, cut off the top to make a lid. You can do it in a straight line or in a zigzag pattern. Scoop out the strings and seeds. (Keep the seeds for roasting.) Oil the pumpkin lightly inside and out with vegetable oil.

Place the pumpkin and lid on a heavy baking sheet lined with parchment paper or sprayed with oil. If you don't have a heavy enough pan, use two baking sheets on top of each other.

Bake the pumpkin and its lid for under an hour, depending on the size of the pumpkin.

Continued

IMPORTANT NOTE: Don't overcook the pumpkin or it will be too soft to hold the soup. The shell should be warmed through and slightly soft, but still hold its shape. So watch it carefully; start checking after 30 minutes. Remember, it will keep cooking when you take it out of the oven, so err on the side of undercooking.

Let the shell cool. Ladle the hot soup into the pumpkin and use the lid as a cover if you wish.

If you do overcook the pumpkin and company's on the way, find a large bowl that fits the pumpkin and slip it inside.

FOOD ON FIRE

O! for a muse of fire, that would ascend the brightest heaven of invention.
WILLIAM SHAKESPEARE

O NE OF the big attractions of cooking is that you are not only
allowed but encouraged to play with fire.

It's usually subtle—the burner on the stove, the backyard barbecue, a campfire. Sometimes, though, we really let ourselves go
and actually light food on fire, on purpose, in front of people we
know.

Food flambé is not so fashionable as it was from the 1930s
to the 1960s. Every now and then, though, someone will light a
Christmas pudding or some Greek cheese and diners of all ages
will squeal with glee. It's unexpected. It's dramatic. It's primal.
And it's easy.

While setting food on fire is something you can do at home, it
was once the province of what in the United States were called
"continental" restaurants. In Minneapolis, a special-occasion dinner often took place at the Flame Room at the Radisson Hotel,
once the only Radisson Hotel in the world.

The Flame Room was an opulent dining room modeled after
small New York nightclubs. The hotel itself featured a kind of
French Renaissance décor, possibly a tribute to the hotel's namesake, Pierre Radisson, a French explorer who somehow got to
Minnesota in the seventeenth century.

One of the big draws of the Flame Room was the Golden
Strings, eight violins, a bass violist, and two baby grand pianos. An-

other was that many foods came out of the kitchen engulfed in flames.

The Flame Room had flaming entrées such as ham with pine-apple Coca-Cola sauce. One of the most amazing spectacles was when the waiter brought out cherries jubilee, a dessert completely ablaze.

Cherries jubilee was created by Auguste Escoffier—probably the world's most famous chef—in honor of Queen Victoria's Diamond Jubilee. Cherries were then considered an extravagance be-cause their season was so short and there were no refrigerated trucks or cargo planes. This was not just a showstopper, but one with a royal pedigree.

To make cherries jubilee you put some pitted dark cherries in a chafing dish, pour in a little cherry brandy and sugar, and light a match. When the flame dies you pour the whole thing over vanilla ice cream.

When he was in high school, my husband worked as assistant to the maître d'hôtel at the Chesapeake Restaurant in Baltimore, the premier restaurant in that city in the mid-sixties. He wore a gold jacket and a black bow tie. I'm sure he looked adorable. He remem-bers the first time he saw cherries jubilee come out of the Chesa-peake's kitchen. The lights were dimmed throughout the restaurant for dramatic effect.

Savory dishes, too, can be flamed. In addition to ham with flaming Coke sauce, there are recipes for flaming chicken, fish, meat, and even salad. But it is fiery desserts that really spark the imagination.

Sometime in the 1960s, my parents went to a fancy dinner party. On the dining room table was a big Steuben glass bowl filled with oranges and lemons. My mother thought it was just a center-piece. When it came time for dessert, a little bowl of sugar cubes was passed around. Guests were asked to rub a lemon or an or-ange with the sugar cube and then toss the sugar into a bowl. Next, chafing dishes filled with melted butter were put at each end of the table and the sugar cubes were thrown into the hot butter. Then some orange juice went in and finally liqueur was added and the whole thing was ignited.

When the flames died down in the chafing dishes, the crêpes were brought out and gently placed in the sauce to coat them.

The crêpes themselves are easily made in advance. They can even be frozen. Just bring them to room temperature before cooking. They'll be reheated in the sauce.

Not surprisingly, French crêpe pans make the best crêpes. La Cuisine, the Cook's Resource, is a small, independent cookware store in Alexandria, Virginia. I've found that if they carry a product, it's usually the best. La Cuisine recommends a traditional French carbon steel crêpe pan. They are reasonably priced and come in several sizes. A crêpe pan has angled sides so you get perfectly round crêpes.

I have, however, used my seven-inch stainless steel skillet with fine results. Just don't use anything with Teflon. At the table, you need a 12-inch pan put over the flame. My chafing dish is copper, as are traditional French crêpe finishing pans.

My mother was so taken with these sweet little pancakes in their boozy citrus sauce that crêpes Suzette became her standard dinner party dessert. My little brother sometimes hid under the table. I would watch the spectacle from a cracked bedroom door. It seemed so glamorous.

Like cherries jubilee, crêpes Suzette has royal connections. The story is that Henri Charpentier, a fourteen-year-old assistant waiter in Paris in 1895, was making dessert for the Prince of Wales, the future King Edward VII, of England. According to Charpentier's memoirs, the cordials in the chafing dish accidentally caught fire. He thought the dish was ruined. But he tasted it and declared it was the most delicious thing he ever tasted.

"That accident of the flame," he wrote, "was precisely what was needed to bring all those various instruments into one harmony of taste." The prince really liked it and asked Charpentier to name the dish after his dinner companion, Suzette, a French actress. "Thus was born and baptized," writes Charpentier, "this confection, one taste of which I really believe would reform a cannibal into a civilized gentleman." The next day the prince sent Charpentier a jeweled ring, a Panama hat, and a cane.

Charpentier became John D. Rockefeller's chef in the United States and brought crêpes Suzette with him. They were popular in restaurants—and at my house—in the 1950s and 1960s.

Flaming desserts were extinguished by the 1970s when restaurant styles began the change from gold and velvet to sleek and modern. Waiters no longer wore white jackets and remained unobtrusive. They now told you their names and had a lot of opinions.

Then in the early 1980s, we were in New Orleans, a city impervious to food fads. This is a place where you can get fried donuts twenty-four hours a day.

One Sunday, we had brunch at Brennan's restaurant, where we found that food was still ablaze. After a light meal of eggs with hollandaise and brandy-cream sauce, oysters with bacon, grits with butter and cheese, and a few glasses of bourbon milk punch, we were ready for dessert. At Brennan's, dessert means bananas Foster. It was invented there in the 1950s and named for Richard Foster, a regular customer, which made him part of the Brennan's royal family.

Bananas Foster starts with butter, sugar, and cinnamon in a flambé pan. Then banana liqueur and sliced bananas are put in the pan. When the bananas begin to brown, you add rum. When it's hot you set the whole thing on fire. Serve over ice cream. Like all flaming desserts, bananas Foster is rich and delicious, what Charpentier might call "a harmony of taste."

I tried, and failed, several times to create these dishes at home. In the process, I learned a few things:

• Beer doesn't work. Only booze with high alcohol content (about 80 proof) will burn. Brandy, cognac, rum, bourbon, for example.

- The liquor must be hot but not boiling. If it boils, the alcohol burns off and it won't light.
- If it doesn't light, it also might not be hot enough.

There are also inherent safety hazards in playing with fire. We once had dinner at the home of a neighbor and excellent cook. He made bananas flambé for dessert at the table in the sterling silver flambé dish his father brought home from Paris after World War II. He put in a stick of butter, sliced bananas, brown sugar, cinnamon, and then warmed crème de banana and black rum. He overdid it a little on the liquor and flames jumped out of the pan and onto his shirt. We poured a pitcher of water on him; both he and the bananas were fine.

My friend Trish was working as a waitress and slipped as she was serving a flaming baked Alaska to a customer. No one was hurt. Her next job was in government work.

A few safety tips:

- Stay as far away from the flame as possible. Use long matches and a long-handled pan.
- Keep the lid of the pan close by to extinguish the fire if necessary.
- Wear an oven mitt. It can't hurt.

When my parents were in their eighties, they came to visit us in Washington. They wanted to have a dinner party at our house for our friends who had always been so hospitable to them. My mother sewed a special tablecloth. They cooked everything. My son and his friend Charlotte got all dressed up and were the servers. The dinner ended beautifully with crêpes Suzette.

✳ CRÊPES SUZETTE

Makes 16 crêpes

¼ cup unbleached
  all-purpose flour
5 large eggs
Scant ½ teaspoon salt
¼ cup low-fat milk
1 to 2 tablespoons Grand
  Marnier
1 teaspoon butter (or more
  as needed)

By hand or in a food processor, mix all the ingredients, except the butter, until smooth. Refrigerate at least 1 hour and up to overnight. Bring to room temperature before cooking crêpes.

Heat about a teaspoon of butter over medium heat in either a crêpe pan or small (7 to 8 inches) non-aluminum frying pan. Pour a thin layer of batter into the pan and evenly coat the bottom. When the batter begins to come away from the side of pan and the crêpe is slightly browned, turn to the other side. The crêpes should be very thin. The pancakes can be made ahead. Just pile them between pieces of waxed paper. They will be reheated later in the sauce.

FOR THE SAUCE
½ cup (1 stick) unsalted
  butter, at room
  temperature
1 tablespoon sugar
3 lemons
3 oranges
6 sugar cubes
3 to 4 tablespoons rum
¼ cup Grand Marnier

In advance, cream the butter and a tablespoon of sugar in a bowl using the back of a wooden spoon. Cover and put aside.

Place the lemons and oranges in a bowl and pass around to guests. Pass around a bowl of sugar cubes. Each guest should rub his or her sugar cube over citrus fruit. All sides of the sugar cube should be rubbed.

The chafing dish, creamed butter, rum, liqueur, and crêpes should now all be at the table.

While the guests are infusing their sugar cubes, light the burner on the chafing dish. Set a 12-inch copper pan over the burner. Put the creamed butter in the pan to warm. Watch that it doesn't burn.

When the guests are done rubbing their sugar cubes, ask them to toss the sugar cubes into the pan over the burner. Then squeeze the oranges until you have a ½ cup of juice and add that to the pan. Stir the mixture until the sauce is reduced to about ½ cup.

With a long-handled fork, pick up a crêpe and lay it in the sauce. Spoon the sauce over the crêpe and turn. Spoon the sauce over the other side. Fold the crêpe in half and then half again, making a triangle, and move to the side of the pan. Repeat with the remaining crêpes.

When all the crêpes have been sauced and folded, carefully pour the rum and liqueur into the pan. It is possible the sauce may burst into flame. If it doesn't, light with a match. Slide the pan back and forth over the heat until the flames die. Spoon the sauce over the crêpes and serve immediately.

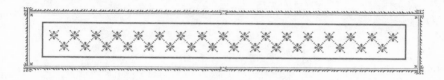

FOREIGN FOOD

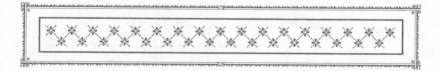

THE RUNNING OF THE SHAD

✳   ✳   ✳

Shad is one of the very few things left to enjoy
that still comes but once a year.
EDNA LEWIS

EVERY YEAR by mid-March, I get a call from Allison, who says simply, "It's in." We check our calendars, figure out whose turn it is to host, and begin preparing for our annual shad roe dinner.

Some people wait for the first crocus. Allison and I wait for the shad to start their run from the ocean to freshwater rivers as a sure sign of spring. We are not alone. All along the East Coast, people are waiting.

Fishermen's lore holds that when the forsythia blooms, the shad are in the river. So shad fanatics begin hanging around fish counters in mid-March.

Like salmon, shad (the largest member of the herring family) are anadromous, a fancy word that means they migrate from the ocean to rivers in the spring to spawn in the fresh water where they were born. After a long, hard winter, they gorge themselves to get ready for the trip and are fat and juicy by the time they get home.

Early Americans relied on shad as a staple of their diet. Over-fishing and environmental problems, however, have cut down the shad population. They've suffered from a fickle public as well. Shad roe has gone from being a common Atlantic coast meal to being an upscale delicacy to relative obscurity.

Why shad and its roe fell out of favor is a mystery. But the devoted are unwavering.

Those most passionate about shad grew up eating them. When

I moved to Washington in the mid-1980s, I found that my college friend Allison had married Larry, a native Washingtonian and serious shad roe lover. My Baltimore-born husband used to go shad fishing with his father—another rite of spring—but, being strictly catch and release, had never eaten either the fish or the roe.

Allison said the first time she saw shad roe her reaction was: "It was the most disgusting thing I'd ever seen." To the uninitiated, it's not a pretty sight. Shad roe comes in sets of two connected sacs of eggs—hundreds of thousands of eggs in each sac. The roe varies in color from blond to deep maroon, depending on the fish and its diet. You can see the veins. But if you can get past your initial shock, you may learn to love it. Larry showed us the inner beauty of shad roe, and we have never looked back.

I buy fish a block from my house at the Eastern Market, the last of Washington's nineteenth-century public markets. The fish sellers there say when the shad roe comes in, they have customers who buy it every week for its short season.

My friend Carla is one of them. She waits for the shad the way I wait for its roe. And when it's in, she drives crosstown as often as she can to get it. The fish is sweet and flavorful. The Latin name for American shad is *sapidissima,* which means "most delicious."

Some people stay away from shad, though, because they are the boniest of all eating fish, so bony the Indians called them porcupine fish. The legend is that a crabby porcupine complained about its lot in life to the Great Spirit, who responded by turning the porcupine inside out and throwing it into the water. Boning shad is considered an art, and boned shad fillets are available at some markets.

American Indians taught the Pilgrims to cook shad by "planking" it. As the unfilleted shad cooks slowly on cedar planks over an open fire, the seven hundred tiny bones soften or dissolve. Shad plankings today are social events that symbolize not only the beginning of spring but also the beginning of the political campaign season.

Every year on the third Wednesday in April, the Wakefield, Virginia, Ruritan Club sponsors a shad planking. The folks of Wakefield, which is about sixty miles south of Richmond, have been getting together to eat planked shad since 1939 when a few men went out, caught some fish, and cooked them outside. They had such a good time, they did it again the next year and invited some friends. The event now attracts up to four thousand people. The food committee cleans a couple of tons of shad on Tuesday afternoon and then treats itself to the roe deep fried for supper that night. Another well-known annual shad bake is held in Essex County, Connecticut. The Rotarians there serve five hundred pounds of fillets, two hundred pounds of potato salad, one hundred apple pies, and forty-five pounds of tomatoes. Connecticut recently made shad the state fish.

Enjoying shad is as old as the nation. Without shad, actually, there might have been no United States. Starving troops at Valley Forge in the winter of 1777–78 were rejuvenated by a large shad run that spring on the Schuylkill River. Or so the story goes.

Shad also played a role in the Civil War. The Virginia Battle of Five Forks on April 1, 1865, was such a big defeat for the Confederacy because of the shad run that day. General George Pickett of Gettysburg fame had orders: "Hold Five Forks at all hazards." But Pickett and Fitzhugh Lee—General Robert E. Lee's nephew and the cavalry commander—were invited to a shad bake and left their subordinates to battle General Phil Sheridan's troops without them. The generals stayed at the shad bake for three hours, by which time the Confederate soldiers were overrun.

Part of the appeal of both the shad and its roe is its ephemeral nature. It's here, and then it's gone.

The late Edna Lewis, the southern African American food writer and chef, grew up in a small Virginia Piedmont farming community. Her family awaited the first shad roe so eagerly that they couldn't wait to eat it for dinner. They'd fry the shad and its roe for breakfast. "We always served shad with scrambled eggs, bacon, steamed hominy, newfound honey, soft, rich batter bread, delicious cold milk, hot coffee, and a sip of dandelion wine. It was truly a meal to celebrate the coming of the spring," she writes in *The Taste of Country Cooking*. Shad roe cooked in bacon drippings and served with grits and eggs was a common spring breakfast along the Atlantic Coast.

I sometimes serve the roe topped with tiny fried quail eggs. I buy boned shad fillets and grill them under the broiler. But the Allison-and-Larry dinner never changes.

Every spring, the four of us sit down to the same meal: sautéed shad roe slathered with anchovy butter, lemon dill rice, and quickly steamed tiny asparagus drizzled with browned butter. For dessert, I make my friend Jenifer's grandfather's schaum torte— piled high with whipped cream and strawberries.

When properly cooked, the roe should feel firm and have a hint of pink in the center. Be warned: Preparing this meal can be dangerous. When all that butter and all those eggs are cooked over a high heat, the sacs pop and spray. So stand back. It's definitely worth the risk.

✳ ALLISON-AND-LARRY SHAD ROE

Serves 4 really good friends

1 tablespoon butter	Heat the butter and the olive oil in a large, heavy frying pan until just smoking. (Cast iron is nice.)
1 tablespoon olive oil	
1 cup seasoned flour	
Salt, to taste	
Pepper, to taste	Season the flour to taste with salt and pepper. Dredge the roe through the mixture and lay gently in the hot pan. Keep the heat medium-high to high. Cook for 3 to 5 minutes per side, depending on size. The roe should be firm but pink in the middle.
4 sets shad roe	
2 tablespoons anchovy paste, or to taste	
½ cup (1 stick) softened butter, for anchovy butter	

While the roe is cooking, mix the anchovy paste to taste with the softened butter in a bowl.

Place each set of roe on a warmed plate. Place a dollop of anchovy butter on each set. It melts and puddles around the roe. Pass the rest of the anchovy butter.

✳ JENIFER'S GRANDFATHER'S SCHAUM TORTE

This is a perfect spring dessert. It's essentially a big meringue filled with whipped cream and fresh strawberries. It's very old-fashioned and looks beautiful.

Makes 6 servings

7 large egg whites
2 cups sugar (sifted 4 times or use superfine sugar)
1 tablespoon white vinegar
1 teaspoon vanilla extract
1 quart strawberries, hulled and cut in half (save a few whole, for garnish)
1 pint heavy cream

Preheat the oven to 275°F.
Grease a 10-inch springform pan.

Beat the egg whites on high until stiff. Add the sugar slowly. This will take 10 to 15 minutes. Add the vinegar and mix. Add the vanilla and mix. The mixture should be stiff and glossy.

Spread the mixture in the pan and bake for 1 hour. Turn off the oven, open the door, and leave for another hour.

Remove from the oven and when completely cool remove from the pan. Run a sharp knife around the sides to loosen the meringue. Pile the cut strawberries on top. Frost with whipped cream and decorate with whole strawberries.

SACRED COWS

✳ ✳ ✳

*Only a rank degenerate would drive 1,500 miles
across Texas without eating a chicken-fried steak.*
LARRY MCMURTRY

A CHICKEN-FRIED steak is not chicken and it is not steak. It is, essentially, a deep-fried hamburger. It is served with cream gravy that, in my experience, has the consistency and motility of library paste. The first time I ordered chicken-fried steak, it came with a small stainless-steel pitcher containing a grayish substance. Efforts to pour the mucilage proved futile. It didn't move. I was young. It was long ago. I am willing to listen to those who tell me much CFS—as it's sometimes called—comes with good cream gravy. I've just never been able to get the image of that first pitcherful out of my mind.

Texans love chicken-fried steak. And they need never be without it. It's available for breakfast with eggs and grits, and for lunch and dinner with mashed potatoes and vegetables steamed for several decades. It's usually made with an inexpensive, tough piece of meat, tenderized by pounding. It is breaded and fried, usually in a skillet, the way chicken is. Hence the name. In recent years, cooks have switched from lard to vegetable oil for health reasons.

CFS is probably the descendant of the weinerschnitzel brought by the many Germans who settled in Texas. Beef was substituted for the veal and frying replaced a quick sauté. Celebrity chefs have upgraded the dish to one using rib eye breaded in panko (Japanese bread crumbs) and served with a chipotle cream sauce. There is a lot of swanky cooking going on in Texas these days. Veal with roasted poblano sauce, tamales with crème fraîche, and jalapeño cheese grits are all sure signs of "New Texas Cuisine." Old Texas Cuisine is synonymous with *meat*. And meat in Texas is synonymous with *cow*.

In the late 1970s, my husband and I moved to College Station, Texas, to teach at Texas A&M University. A&M has a huge agriculture school that periodically slaughters its herds. Soon after we got there, we heard that lamb meat would be available. Yankees all over campus began lining up space in freezer lockers. Lamb, we quickly learned, was not the meat of choice in the state and that if we ate it we should keep it to ourselves. It was a reminder of old westerns with the sheep farmers and the cattle farmers always shooting at each other. We intended to chew on our chops quietly in the largest cattle-producing state in the country.

The holy trinity of Texas meat cooking is chicken-fried steak, barbecue, and chili. All are enjoyed with near religious fervor. Which does not, however, mean that everyone sings from the same hymnal.

Take barbecue. In a state that's bigger than France, it's hard to reach agreement on whether mesquite, hickory, or pecan wood work best or if it's preferable to cook the meat for ten hours or two days. (It's the heat and smoke, not the flame, that cook the meat.)

There is one thing on which all agree: Barbecue means brisket. Until we moved to Texas, I thought brisket was something you ate on Jewish holidays. Both Texas brisket and Jewish brisket require long cooking. That's about the only point of intersection. Brisket for barbecue is untrimmed, which means there's a lot of fat. Sausages and ribs are barbecued, too, but it's really all about the brisket.

Then there's the question of sauce. Texas barbecue is *never* cooked with the barbecue sauce. Some people use a "sop," a sauce made of some combination of beer, lemon juice, vinegar, and onion juice to baste the meat and keep it moist. This is thrown away after cooking. If you want to put a tomato-based sauce on afterward, that's okay.

Barbecue is served with beans, coleslaw, and/or potato salad, Texas toast (fat slices of toasted white bread), and jalapeños. Everything in Texas is served with a jalapeño, the state pepper.

You definitely need something to wash down this hot food with in what is usually hot weather. Texans drink three things with food: tea, beer, or Dr Pepper. Tea means sweet iced tea and is available anywhere at any time. If you ask for "tea" in Texas you'll get iced tea. You must specify "hot tea" for a cup of tea. This, however, doesn't always work. I was once in the town of Bastrop in the so-called Lost Pines of central Texas and went into a café and properly asked for a cup of "hot tea." The young waitress looked like a deer in the headlights. Ultimately, she put a teaspoon of instant sweet iced tea mix in a cup and poured boiling water over it. Don't try that at home.

The other nonalcoholic beverage of choice is Dr Pepper. Somewhat confusingly, it is subsumed under the generic category of "Coke." So a guest at our house once asked, "Do you have any Coke?" No, sorry. He then spotted a Dr Pepper. "Oh, see there, you have a Dr Pepper. That's my favorite Coke."

Lone Star is the national beer of Texans. It comes in a long-necked bottle and is, therefore, called a longneck. As in, "Hey, git me a longneck whahl yuhr up, willya?" Other acceptable beers are Shiner and Pearl, also from Texas. Some fancy folks drink Mexican beer. Beer, particularly, is the drink of choice with chili.

Before our Texas adventure, I would have sworn chili con carne (chili with meat) was a slightly soupy mixture of hamburger meat, green pepper, chili powder, onions, tomatoes, maybe a pinch of cloves and sugar, and, of course, kidney beans. That's what it is in the Midwest.

In Texas, however, I think you can get arrested if you put beans in your chili. It is the Texas state dish, so there is probably a law. You can serve beans on the side if you want them, but never, never

cook them in the chili. As a matter of fact, cook almost none of
the aforementioned ingredients in the chili.

In Texas, chili is this: meat and heat. Most serious chili cooks
also have a closely guarded secret ingredient. Mine is masa harina,
the corn flour used to make tortillas. It thickens the liquid and
gives the chili a subtle, smoky taste.

For meat, Texans use chili grind, coarsely chopped beef or
chuck. You may substitute rattlesnake, armadillo, or other road-
kill. It is preferable to sear the meat in lard or suet, but the faint of
heart may use vegetable oil. The heat comes from chili peppers,
chopped, diced, powdered, or liquefied. Different cooks use different chilies, depending on their heat tolerance. The chili powder
you have in your spice drawer won't cut it. The only other ingredient is a little beer or broth. This said, no two Texans make chili
alike, and each insists he or she knows the "right way" to do it.

The who-makes-the-best-chili wars went national in 1967 when
Wick Fowler, a Texas newspaperman, took umbrage at a story by
H. Allen Smith—a Yankee—titled "Nobody Knows More About
Chili Than I Do." Smith claimed that no one in Texas could make
a proper chili. His recipe included beans. Fowler and Smith agreed
to a culinary dual in Terlingua, Texas, a ghost town 11 miles west
of Study Butte, 7 miles east of Lajitas, and 279 miles from the near-
est airport. The contest ended in a tie when the judge declared that
his taste buds were "ruint." A bottle of buttermilk, by the way,
works as a fire extinguisher for the tongue. Every year since, thousands of chiliheads go to Terlingua for the International Chili
Cookoff.

The Republic of Texas Chilympiad is held annually in San Mar-
cos. The winner automatically goes to Terlingua, but some cooks
take more pride in making the best chili in Texas than the best chili
in the world. There is a movement for the adoption of chili as the
national food of the United States.

While Texans prefer meat, they do eat some fish. On the coast,
you'll find the same seafood you'd find anywhere on the Gulf

Coast: redfish, sea trout, oysters, and shrimp. But thirty miles inland, it's the heartland, and you'll find only fried catfish. I used to fish with my mother and grandmother with bamboo poles at the lake by our house in Minneapolis. If I caught a catfish they'd say in unison: "Cut your line." These bewhiskered, ugly fish that have to be *skinned* before they can be cooked were considered dirty, disgusting, bottom feeders. Then I moved to Texas and found them on the menu. After several false starts, I finally ordered, ate, and enjoyed fried catfish. Lots of beer helps.

Fish is just not a big part of inland Texas culture. When we moved to College Station from "back East" in the late 1970s, I wanted to make the French fish soup *bourride* for our first dinner party. I had just learned to make it from a friend in New York. I went to Skaggs-Albertson, the local big grocery store, and asked where the fish section was. There was none. I asked where I'd find frozen fish. There was none. I went to the information booth and told the guy there what I was trying to make and he suggested Mrs. Paul's fish sticks.

I realized I had to forget the past and open my mouth to new things. I traded in plain scrambled eggs for migas—scrambled eggs with chilies. I stuffed jalapeños with cream cheese as appetizers. I studied hot sauces and green and red salsas. I came to love the kolaches (fruit or sausage-stuffed yeast buns) we ate at the bakery in the town of Snook (real name), where the Czech cowboys hung out. I discovered that cactus can be pickled and eaten, that Texas ruby red grapefruit are the best, and that corn bread and beans make a complete meal. Fajitas, now common everywhere, were a Texas novelty at the time.

In the end, I learned to make a pretty good Texas chili and my husband mastered real Texas barbecue. When we moved away from Texas, however, we left the chicken-fried steak behind.

✳ REAL TEXAS CHILI

This is the kind of chili I learned to make in Texas. You end up with essence of meat. It's extremely rich. I put out bowls of Michael's cooked pinto beans, chopped green onions, grated Monterey Jack cheese, and sour cream on the side. Latino markets and some supermarkets have plain ground chili powder without other spices added.

Makes 10 servings (1 cup each)

½ cup masa harina
½ cup ground red chili powder
5 pounds lean beef chuck, cut into ¼-inch cubes or chili grind
¼ cup olive oil (feel free to use lard or suet)
2½ cups beer
2½ cups beef broth
3 cloves garlic, minced
2 teaspoons coriander
2 teaspoons cumin
2 teaspoons dried oregano
½ teaspoon salt

Combine the masa harina and chili powder in a large bowl. Add the beef and toss to coat.

Heat the oil in a large soup pot over medium heat. Add one-third of the beef and cook until browned on all sides, about 6 minutes. Transfer to another bowl and repeat the process with the remaining beef. Add all the beef to the pot, stir in the remaining ingredients, and reduce the heat to low. Cook, covered, until the meat is extremely tender, 3 to 4 hours, stirring often.

✳ REAL TEXAS BARBECUE

My husband spent seven years in Texas experimenting with barbecue. He ended up with a pretty straightforward approach. It's really, really good. He doesn't baste but is not philosophically opposed to basting. Be sure you get an untrimmed brisket. That means it will be covered in fat. A trimmed brisket cooked this way will end up as a strip of leather. He puts the prepared barbecue

sauce in a coffee can and sets it inside the barbecue to absorb some
of the smoky flavor.

Makes 10 to 12 servings

Salt and pepper
10- to 12-pound boneless
  whole beef brisket,
  untrimmed
2 to 3 tablespoons
  Worcestershire sauce
4 cloves garlic, thinly sliced

Salt and pepper the whole brisket and rub
with Worcestershire sauce. Turn fat side up,
make cuts all over the top with a sharp paring knife, and insert slivers of garlic.

Put a pan with a little water in the bottom center of the barbecue. This
catches the fat and adds a little steam.

Soak four handfuls of mesquite, pecan, or hickory wood chunks or chips.

Place 30 briquettes on each side of the barbecue and light. When the coals
are white-hot, lay a handful of soaked wood chips on each side and place
the meat, fat side up, in the middle of the rack above the fire. No flame
should touch the meat. The coals should always be on the sides of the grill.
Cover the grill.

After 1 hour, add 5 briquettes per side. An hour later, add 5 more to each
side. Add a handful of soaked wood each time you add briquettes.

Leave for another 4 hours to slow cook.

Remove the meat from the barbecue, trim the fat completely and cut
against the grain with a very sharp knife. Serve with barbecue sauce.

✳ BARBECUE SAUCE

Makes 2 cups

½ tablespoon vegetable oil
4 cloves garlic, minced

In a small saucepan, heat the oil and stir in
the garlic and onion. Cook until wilted.

½ medium onion, chopped
1½ cups ketchup
¼ cup yellow mustard
¾ cup white or cider vinegar
1 tablespoon
  Worcestershire sauce
2 teaspoons cumin
1 teaspoon celery seed
Tabasco or chipotle pepper
  sauce, to taste

In a separate bowl, combine the ketchup, mustard, vinegar, and Worcestershire sauce. Mix well. Add to the garlic-and-onion mixture and cook over low heat for 15 minutes. Add cumin and celery seed. Taste for seasoning. Simmer for 25 minutes. Add Tabasco or pepper sauce to taste. Simmer for 10 more minutes.

Put in an unbreakable container and place in the barbecue to absorb the smoke taste in the third hour of cooking the brisket. Leave for ½ hour. Remove and set aside. Reheat before serving.

✳ MICHAEL'S BEANS

Michael also learned to make real Texas beans to go with the real Texas barbecue. Like the meat, they cook for a long time.

Makes 10 to 12 servings

2 bags (16 ounces each)
  pinto beans
4 bay leaves
20 peppercorns tied in
  cheesecloth
¼ cup olive oil
2 teaspoons Mexican
  oregano
Salt, to taste

Pick over the beans, place them in a bowl, and cover with water. Soak the beans overnight.

Drain the beans, put them in a large saucepan, and cover with fresh water by an inch. Bring the beans to a boil. Add the bay leaves, peppercorns, and oil. Lower the burner temperature to simmer and cook for an hour, covered. Add the oregano and salt to taste and simmer, uncovered, for 2 more hours.

Remove 2 cups of beans and ½ cup liquid and puree in a food processor. Remove the liquid from the beans in the pot so there is just enough to cover the beans. Mix the puree into the beans and stir to blend. Simmer, covered, for 1 more hour. Watch the beans to be sure they don't burn.

MARKET PLEASURES

※　　※　　※

To market, to market, to buy a fat pig,
Home again, home again, jiggety jig;
To market, to market, to buy a fat hog;
Home again, home again, jiggety-jog;
To market, to market, to buy a plum bun,
Home again, home again, market is done.

NURSERY RHYME

EVERY SATURDAY morning at 8:30, Stephanie and I meet at the market. We have coffee and a bran muffin, talk about our children and other world events, and then begin our weekly ritual at Washington, D.C.'s Eastern Market.

We step into the market and out of the contemporary world. Eastern Market doesn't look much different inside today than it did when it opened in 1873 as part of the city's public market system. The lofty, one-story open market hall with stalls and ceiling fans badly needs renovation and cleaning but it remains the vibrant center of the community. It is where many of us shop every day, like European housewives, for fresh fish, meats, poultry, and bread. This is where we go for cold cuts and cheese, fresh pasta and sauces. If we wanted to, we could even buy pigs' feet. On Monday, the one day the market is closed, we suffer.

The block-long brick Italianate structure has been in continuous operation since the day it opened. It is the only remaining public fresh food market in town. There have been drives to tear it down and others to gentrify it, but the community and the vendors will not let it go. It is a shrine, a temple, a holy place.

Washington is a dog-eat-dog rather than a live-and-let-live kind of place. That's why the Capitol Hill neighborhood is so appealing. It's a small town—a village, really—in the middle of the big city. The Eastern Market is the village square—its heart and soul.

On Saturday, Stephanie and I start outside with the vendors from small farms. They often bring garden flowers and sell out early. At the end of April, we begin to look for the woman who brings little bouquets of lily of the valley and the farmers who bring bunches of fragrant lilacs. A few weeks later, we wait for the peonies. By midsummer, from one end to the other, the market looks like a field of Kansas sunflowers. In fall the mums move in.

You can watch the seasons change from the gentle green of spring asparagus to the bright yellow of summer corn and the deep orange of fall squash. In winter, there's nothing outdoors but the rows of Christmas trees that turn the outdoor farmers' line into a fragrant pine forest. An all-day watchman guards the trees, sleeps in a truck, and watches football on a small TV. In the more fecund seasons, farmers from Maryland, West Virginia, Pennsylvania, and Virginia set up their produce stands underneath the long shed roof outside.

Because we're serious marketgoers, Stephanie and I own equipment. We have carts on wheels and long-handled bags in canvas, oilcloth, and mesh in various shapes and sizes. We bring the carts when we're buying turkeys, more than a dozen ears of corn, or flats of seedlings. We bump into friends and neighbors with their arms and baskets loaded with fresh produce and seasonal flowers. We coo over babies in strollers. We ogle politicians. We talk to vendors indoors and out whom we've come to know over the years. A lot of neighborhood kids work for farmers on weekends. My son started hawking apples when he was ten and worked at three different stands throughout the years. More than a decade later, the same vendors still ask about him.

On Saturdays, we maneuver around the long line of people waiting to get in to Market Lunch, the eatery inside the market building. They come for blueberry buckwheat pancakes ("plate o' blues") or eggs and grits for breakfast or a good crab cake, incredible fried oysters, and soft-shell crabs for lunch. Orders are shouted down the counter and loitering is loudly discouraged.

In the mid-1990s, Market Lunch tried to go upscale with an espresso machine. You walked up to a window outside the building and ordered your half-caf, half-decaf skinny latte from Mary, a very large African American woman, who would look at you and roll her eyes. You could almost hear her thinking, These crazy yuppies—three dollars for a cup of coffee. Market Lunch is really not an espresso drink kind of place, and the service was discontinued after a brief run. When Mary died after twenty-four years at the market, half the neighborhood went to her funeral.

As if the Eastern Market weren't enough, there's an open-air fresh fish market on the Potomac River, not far from the Capitol. Crabs, oysters, clams, whole and filleted fish are sold under a highway overpass from floating barges, anchored to concrete banks, which go up and down with the tide. Unlike the Eastern Market, which is well known to tourists, Maine Avenue is for locals.

The wharf is one of the few places in Washington that feels like part of a real city. While it doesn't have the social aspect of a market in a residential neighborhood, the bustling, colorful scene is worth the trip. Vendors from each barge call out for customers who include diplomats and day laborers. The colors, sizes, shapes, and varieties of seafood are stunning. Oysters on the half shell, cooked crabs and shrimp, crab soup and chowder are sold to go, and go you must because there's no place to sit or even lean.

There are many other cities with old markets that have remained vital—Reading Terminal Market in Philadelphia, Pike Place Market in Seattle, West Side Market in Cleveland, Lexington Market in Baltimore. Instead of vestiges of the past, these markets are now beacons for the future.

Public markets have become fashionable. They had fallen out of favor with the advent of supermarkets and the year-round availabil-

ity of just about anything. But we're over that. After decades of eating apples in spring and asparagus in winter, we jumped on the local, seasonal farm wagon. Everything old is new again. A hundred
years ago, city dwellers had to shop at farmers' markets to get fresh
produce. We're back. Once again, we want farmhouse cheeses,
pasture-fed beef, and heirloom fruits and vegetables. We'll trade a
perfect, round, red apple that's had most of the flavor hybridized
out of it for one that looks funny but was grown on a small local
farm with seeds saved for generations and that tastes like the apples
of our childhoods. Ditto for tomatoes, beans, melons, and corn.

I remember going with my mother on Saturdays to the Minneapolis farmers' market where two hundred vendors had trucked
in produce from their farms. It was a magical place. It remains vibrant today and reflects the demographic changes in the state and
the country. Many of the vendors now are immigrants from
Southeast Asia and have introduced bitter melon and lemongrass
to midwestern tables.

Throughout the country, old markets are being revitalized and
new ones being built. Many of the new markets have revitalized
down-and-out neighborhoods as well as provided a source for organic buffalo meat.

There are also far more outdoor farmers' markets. The number in the United States has doubled in a decade. Now concrete-
bound New Yorkers buy Mr. Stripey tomatoes and fingerling
potatoes from family farmers who bring their goods to greenmar-
kets in the city. At the outdoor farmers' market in a park in the
middle of Portland, Oregon, you can sample fresh oysters. On the
tiny Hawaiian Island of Kauai, there's an outdoor market somewhere every day where you can stock up on passion fruit and taro.

California, of course, is farmers' market heaven. It's a reminder
that in addition to hot tubs and movie stars, the Golden State
grows forty crops not grown in any other state. Even Hollywood
has farmers' markets, the market at Third and Fairfax has been an
L.A. institution since the 1930s.

There are now four hundred certified farmers' markets (where farmers sell only what they've grown themselves) in California, up from just a handful in the late 1970s. One of them has become a major San Francisco destination.

In 1992, a farmers' market was set up as a onetime "harvest market" in front of the 1898 Ferry Building overlooking San Francisco Bay. It was such a hit that the market is now there twice a week year-round. Regional farmers and ranchers bring produce, meats, flowers, cheeses, breads, and jams. On Saturdays, fifteen thousand shoppers come to look, buy, watch cooking demonstrations, and chat with farmers. All by the San Francisco Bay.

Just three years before the market started, a two-tiered freeway ran along the Embarcadero roadway separating the city from the waterfront. The highway was so damaged in the Loma Prieta earthquake it was torn down. Its removal allowed for the redevelopment of the Ferry Building into a marketplace with shops, restaurants, and cafés and the farmers' market on the outdoor plaza.

Much of the world never gave up on its markets. They remain, like museums of food, for residents and travelers to enjoy. Of course, there are disappointments. On my first trip to Europe at age nineteen, I discovered that Les Halles—the legendary market of Paris—had closed and moved to the suburbs just before I got there.

Because I travel on my stomach, I plot my food adventures before I pack my bag. When we went to Provence, I organized our itinerary to coincide with the movement of the traveling markets. That way, we could always be sure of a supply of triple cream cheese, wild boar sausage, crusty bread, and local wine for or picnics on hills under olive trees.

In Barcelona, I wanted a hotel on the Ramblas, the city's lively, sleepless walking street, near La Boqueria, the biggest market in Europe. This is my idea of a good time. Piles of fresh, sometimes live, fish, mounds of the salt cod so important in Catalan cooking, sides of jamón ibérico (ham from pigs fed only acorns) hanging from iron hooks, baskets of truffles, colorful fruits and vegetables, fragrant herbs, dried fruits, Spanish almonds. There are also several small tapas bars with a few stools for in-market dining.

I went to London to see how the Borough Market had reinvented itself. This extraordinary food bazaar under the railroad tracks leading to the London Bridge is the descendant of a medieval market near the spot from which Chaucer's pilgrims started their trip. Today, producers from all over the United Kingdom come there to wander among the incredible displays of mushrooms, farmhouse cheeses, sausages, and pork pies.

In Israel we walked through the skinny, winding streets of Tel Aviv's Souk HaCarmel, a typical Middle Eastern street market. It is a colorful, noisy scene. Vendors yell at shoppers to buy clothes, cosmetics, and kitchen equipment as well as food. The stalls are filled with the exotic sweets, nuts, and other comestibles of this part of the world: pistachios, guavas, nuts, dates, crates of olives, and colorful spices spilling out of sacks. The fruits and vegetables of Israel are famously fresh and beautiful. While the souk is crowded every day, it is particularly bustling on Friday as shoppers rush to get what they need before the Sabbath begins at sundown.

You can learn the entire history of Mexico through its markets. The melding of Spanish and native cultures is on display in market stalls. Native to Mexico are tubs of beans in every color, corn as meal and tortillas, and an endless variety of chilies. The Spanish added sugar, cheese, and some domestic animals. Then there are all those glorious vegetables and fruits—strawberries, mangoes, papayas, avocados, tomatoes, and squash. And the herbs and spices— cinnamon, cumin, cilantro, and epazote. Indian women sit on the ground slicing nopales (prickly pear cactus). The air is full of the smell of pork rinds frying. Shoppers barter for clothing, batteries, and garden tools.

It's at a city's market that you come to understand the city. When you see how real people shop for food you begin to understand who they are and how they live. It's the "life" part of city life and the "heart" part of heart of town. If you're very lucky, you live nearby.

❋ OVEN-ROASTED RATATOUILLE

The end-of-summer market may be the most spectacular of the year. It's too hard to choose among the green and yellow squash, eggplant in every shade of purple, red and yellow tomatoes, peppers of every hue, mushrooms of many shapes. So just buy a few of everything and make ratatouille. I've been doing it all together in the oven—a lot less time and oil than the traditional way. The following is a general guide. Use whatever strikes your fancy at the market. (If you have time, salt the sliced eggplant and let sit in a colander for about ½ hour to eliminate some of the vegetable's water.)

Makes 10 servings

3 bell peppers in whatever colors you like, stemmed, seeded, and cut into thick strips

6 small eggplant, white and/or purple, stemmed and cut into 1-inch rounds

2 medium yellow squash (or 5 small), stemmed and cut into 1-inch rounds

2 medium zucchini (or 5 small), stemmed and cut into 1-inch rounds

½ pound green beans, halved (or haricots verts, trimmed)

2 cups shiitake or wild mushrooms, thickly sliced

2 medium red onions, cut into ½-inch rings

3 medium tomatoes (any kind), cut in wedges

Preheat the oven to 500°F.

Place all the ingredients except the tomatoes in a large roasting pan and toss with the garlic, olive oil, and salt and pepper. Strew sprigs of fresh herbs over the mixture.

Roast the vegetables until almost tender, about 30 minutes. Stir occasionally. Add the tomatoes and stir. Roast another 10 minutes or until the vegetables are fork tender. Sprinkle with extra chopped basil and toss to combine. Serve warm or at room temperature.

10 cloves garlic, peeled,
   halved, and germ
   removed
Olive oil
Salt and freshly ground
   black pepper to taste
Sprigs of fresh herbs
   (rosemary, thyme,
   marjoram, oregano, basil)
Basil, chopped

✳ ITALIAN PLUMS

Small, blue-skinned Italian prune plums are at the market at
the end of the plum season and stay only until early fall. I hoard
them and make as many things as I can.

✳ SIS'S PLUM CONSERVE

My mother's friend Sis got this recipe from her aunt Margaret
in New York. It is the best jam I have ever eaten.

Makes 15 to 20 half-pint jars

---

3 pounds blue Italian
   prune plums, pitted and
   cut up
3 pounds sugar
3 oranges with peel, cut up
   small
Juice of 2 lemons
½ pound raisins, any kind
½ pound walnuts

In a large saucepan, simmer the plums,
sugar, oranges, and lemon juice until almost gel stage. (I'm not a canner and didn't
know what this meant, so I called Sis. She
says it means the mixture is thickened and a
spreadable consistency. This takes a very
long time.) Add the raisins, then the walnuts, and cook another 10 minutes. Put in
sterilized jars and enjoy for months. (Sis
says if she doesn't have new jars she puts a
layer of paraffin over the top of the jar to
seal.)

❉ FERN'S RHUBARB CAKE

My mother made this cake in the spring with the first rhubarb.

Makes 6 to 8 servings

FOR THE CAKE

½ cup (1 stick) butter

1½ cups brown sugar

1 large egg

1 cup cream

1 teaspoon vanilla extract

1 teaspoon baking soda

Pinch of salt

2 scant cups flour

1½ cups rhubarb, finely diced

Preheat the oven to 350°F.

Butter a 9 × 9-inch baking pan.

In the bowl of an electric mixer, cream the butter and sugar. Add the egg, cream, and vanilla and mix. Add the baking soda, salt, and flour and blend. Stir in the rhubarb.

FOR THE TOPPING

½ cup sugar

2 tablespoon butter

1 teaspoon cinnamon

½ cup chopped walnuts or pecans

Pour the batter into the pan. Mix the topping ingredients and sprinkle over the cake. Bake for 45 minutes.

FRUITS OF THE SEA

※　※　※

In the light of what Proust wrote with so mild a stimulus, it is the world's loss that he did not have a heartier appetite. On a dozen Gardiner's Island oysters, a bowl of clam chowder, a peck of steamers, some bay scallops, three sautéed soft-shelled crabs, . . . a thin swordfish steak of generous area, a pair of lobsters, and a Long Island Duck, he might have written a masterpiece.

A. J. LIEBLING

I MET my first squid in Monterey, California, when I was in my thirties.

My mother had discouraged a relationship with the mollusk based on her own bad experience. As a young woman, she was in a downtown Minneapolis supermarket and saw a sign for squid, something she'd never heard of, seen, or eaten. So she bought one. She took it home and sautéed it in a little cast-iron frying pan. "I remember holding my nose and saying to your father, 'It doesn't smell very good,'" she says. Then all at once, the squid turned as black as the skillet. "We threw it in the incinerator," she says. Explanations about cleaning squid and being sure to remove the ink sac have still not convinced her to give it another try.

There are no squid in the freshwater lakes of the Upper Midwest, and before fish became frequent fliers the whole concept of seafood was pretty limited. The word *seafood* itself usually referred to shellfish. The word *fish* came from one of the ten thousand freshwater lakes the glaciers left behind.

There were small fish—crappies, sunfish, perch—that could be quickly cleaned and fried in a pan. And there were big fish— walleye and northern pike. They were scaled, gutted, and cut into fillets or baked in the oven with onions and tomato sauce. Fish and shellfish from the ocean came frozen.

In Monterey, we stayed with friends in a cottage by the wharf. Eva and Richard both grew up in California and knew their way around a squid. They taught me to clean this soft-bodied, ten-armed marine creature and I was so taken with the whole process we made an all-squid dinner. We had grilled squid, fried squid, and baked squid with squid stuffing.

It was an upper-level seminar in seafood education. From there, I went on for advanced degrees on both coasts.

We dug for clams with our toes in the low tide on Fire Island and made them into pasta sauce. We ate soft clam bellies at the legendary Gage and Tollner's in Brooklyn. We tucked into lobster at shacks on the Maine coast and ate plump rope-cultured mussels roasted and bathed in garlic-almond butter at Fore Street Restaurant in Portland, Maine. We ate tiny western oysters raw in Portland, Oregon, and grilled in Inverness, California.

I began hanging around fish markets, where I learned a couple of important things: Fish should be fresh and except for shrimp, shellfish should be alive. Fresh fish have clear, bright eyes and shiny skin. They don't smell fishy. Crustaceans should be moving and bivalves should be closed. Shrimp will have been frozen except for those locally caught. Scallops are usually sold shucked.

I timidly began to try these things at home. I learned to boil shrimp in a simple court bouillon (which I had never heard of before) and served it for dinner with cocktail sauce and a lot of napkins. I learned to make mussels steamed in a light tomato sauce. I broiled oysters. I made San Francisco–style cioppino. I looked for eel to put in "real" French bouillabaisse.

I know seafood farming and air travel mean everything is now available year-round. But I'm old-fashioned. I like things in their season. So I still prefer oysters in months containing the letter R. I eat crabs in the summer and mussels in the winter.

March is the moment for shad and its roe. Maryland has spring and fall rockfish seasons. May is the time to celebrate the existence of the Copper River salmon.

I started a relationship with ocean fish through fillets—which seemed manageable. Then I worked my way up to cooking a whole fish. Fillets are fine for a school night, but a whole fish is the perfect dinner party entrée. It meets all the requirements: delicious, dramatic, and dead simple.

My first effort was a whole poached salmon. I didn't have a fish poacher so I rigged up a vessel with an oblong copper casserole and a dish towel. It worked fine and the whole poaching thing was remarkably easy. I made a mayonnaise sauce to serve alongside the salmon. I decorated the fish with cucumber slices and lemon wedges. It was sensational.

From there I moved on to baking a whole stuffed fish. I started with rockfish, the Maryland state fish (called a striped bass outside the Chesapeake Bay area). Stuffing a fish is a twofer. You get a nicely seasoned fish as well as a starchy side dish. The only other thing you need to make a dinner party is a salad.

My standard welcome-to-the-area or sorry-you're-moving dinner is a whole rockfish stuffed with crab. It's easy, tasty, theatrical, and regional. I've also stuffed rockfish with shrimp and with oysters. It all works.

After mastering these two approaches I branched out.

I wanted to make something special for my mother-in-law's eightieth birthday. I saw a picture in a food magazine and knew what I had to do: Bake a ten-pound salmon in a salt crust. The salt seals in the moisture but doesn't leave the fish tasting salty.

Using this technique, the fish should be gutted and cleaned with the head and tail left on. You can bake a small fish or a huge fish. Some people insist it's better if the scales are left on. It doesn't really matter since they'll come off with the skin when the salt crust is removed.

To season the fish, just stuff it with a few handfuls of mixed fresh herbs and some lemon slices. You don't even have to close the cavity with skewers and string. Just make sure your stuffing fills the cavity and sticks out a little.

Find a rimmed baking sheet that's large enough to hold the fish, line it with aluminum foil, and cover it with about ½ inch of coarse (not ground) sea salt. (Note: You can mix the salt with a little water or egg white to make it easier to manipulate.) Put a few bay leaves on the salt.

Lay the fish on top of the salt and cover everything but the head and tail with another ½ inch of salt. Scrunch the foil around the fish and, if you haven't mixed the salt with some liquid, sprinkle a little water over the whole thing. Cook in the middle of a pre-heated 450°F oven for about 10 minutes a pound.

When it's done, the salt will have become a hard crust encasing the fish. After you take the fish out of the oven, let it rest for 15 to 20 minutes. Then crack the top of the salt crust with the back of a heavy knife or spoon. Gently break it away, taking care not to puncture the fish. Most of the skin will come away with the crust. What's left is an incredibly moist, flavorful fish, lightly seasoned with fresh herbs. It's a miracle.

The big fish was such a hit at the family party, I made it for a bridal luncheon. Then I cooked it for a friend's birthday dinner. It became part of my special-occasion repertoire.

One summer I was having ten people for dinner and it was 103 degrees outside. I didn't want to heat up the kitchen, which meant, of course, that my husband grilled. I had read about wrapping a whole fish in newspaper and grilling it. The time was right to try it.

Start with a big, cleaned fish. Season it inside and out with salt and pepper and stuff with herbs, onions, lemons, anything you like. Take two center pages of the newspaper (any section you want), lay it out flat, spread some herbs on the open pages, and place the fish on top of them. Drizzle it all with a little olive oil. Wrap the fish tightly and tie with a lot of kitchen string. Your hands will be black.

Then run the whole package under running water until it's

pretty damp, place on the barbecue rack, and cook for about a half hour on each side, or 15 minutes for each inch of thickness. The paper doesn't burn but does give the fish a nice smoky flavor. I don't know why.

I do know that all these techniques could be applied to the walleye. But I also know you can never go home again. I do, however, have new marine friends. I have not cooked squid since that night in Monterey, but I can go down to the wharf by my house any time I want to and get reacquainted. I also know that some things never change. My mother still won't eat it.

✳ ROCKFISH STUFFED WITH CRAB

The rockfish, sadly, is again in danger. After years of overfishing, regulated seasons returned wild rock to abundance. Now, they are suffering from polluted waters. There is a lot of farmed rockfish, but I really prefer wild rock (also called striped bass).

1 whole rockfish (4 to 5 pounds) with head and tail, cleaned
Salt, to taste
Pepper, to taste
1 tablespoon lemon juice
1 pound jumbo lump crabmeat
¼ cup (½ stick) melted butter
¼ cup chopped celery
¼ cup chopped parsley
Up to ½ cup fresh bread crumbs

Preheat the oven to 400°F.
Line a shallow baking pan with a double thickness of aluminum foil sprayed with cooking oil.

Sprinkle the fish inside and out with salt, pepper, and lemon juice. Place in the shallow baking pan. If the fish is too big to stretch out straight, curve it as if it were swimming.

Combine all the other ingredients, adding the bread crumbs incrementally until the stuffing has the consistency you like. Stuff the fish. Close with skewers and tie shut with kitchen string.

Bake uncovered until the fish flakes easily when tested with a fork, 30 to 40 minutes.

❊ EASY MUSSELS

The editorial page editor of the first newspaper I worked for and her husband were wonderful cooks. This is what they made us the first time they had us for dinner. I had never eaten mussels, and I've loved them ever since. I like a lot of garlic. Adapt to your taste. This can be served over pasta if you want to stretch the meal.

Makes 4 servings

4 pounds live mussels
3 tablespoons olive oil
4 teaspoons minced garlic
¼ cup chopped parsley
1 can (16 ounces) Italian
  plum tomatoes, drained
  and coarsely chopped
½ cup dry white wine

Scrub the mussels and gently pull off their stringy black beards. If an open mussel closes when you press the shells together, it's fine. Throw away any mussels that stay open.

In a heavy saucepan, heat the oil. Sauté the garlic, over medium-low heat, until it is lightly colored. Be careful not to burn. Stir in the parsley and the tomatoes. Simmer uncovered, until the oil and tomatoes separate, about 30 minutes. This can be done ahead of time and reheated when you're ready to add the mussels.

Put the mussels and wine in a pot, cover, and cook over high heat until they have all opened their shells. Discard any that aren't open.

Serve in bowls.

Maine. Globalization brought burritos to Iowa and sushi to Santa Fe. The cheesesteak, once as Philadelphian as the Liberty Bell, is now peddled by national cheesesteak chains.

There are exceptions. Egg creams—which contain neither eggs nor cream—have stayed in New York. The Amish still have the patent on whoopee pies (two pieces of moist cake with filling in the middle). Black-and-white boxes containing See's candy remind people of sweet times in California.

In 2005, New Orleans suffered terrible damage from two violent hurricanes. Amidst concerns about health and safety, one couldn't help but think about the region's food. New Orleans has always been a national culinary treasure. Popcorn shrimp and gumbo are served in plenty of places beyond the bayous, but it's a different experience to eat crawfish étouffée while listening to zydeco music in Lafayette, Louisiana, than it is in a strip mall off the Jersey Turnpike. And you really do have to go to the Central Grocery on Decatur Street in New Orleans to get a good muffuletta, a sandwich of olive salad, meats, and cheeses on round bread. My friend Marguerite is from New Orleans and is a legendary Washington hostess. If she's having a party, she orders crawfish, shrimp, crabs, and gumbo from New Orleans. For dessert she serves a typical New Orleans cake called a Doberge cake. Descended from a Viennese torte, it has eight to ten thin layers separated by icing. It looks just like a Smith Island cake.

✳ SMITH ISLAND TEN-LAYER CAKE

Frances Kitching was born on Smith Island and lived there all her life. She ran an inn on the island, and tourists came to eat her cooking for more than twenty years. Her recipe for Smith Island Ten-Layer Cake is used by permission from Tidewater Publishers, who published *Mrs. Kitching's Smith Island Cookbook*.

Makes 12 to 14 servings

2 cups sugar
1 cup (2 sticks) unsalted
  butter, cut into chunks
5 large eggs
3 cups all-purpose flour
¼ teaspoon salt
1 heaping teaspoon baking
  powder
1 cup evaporated milk
2 teaspoons vanilla extract
½ cup water
Chocolate Icing (recipe
  follows)

Preheat the oven to 350°F.
Lightly grease ten 9-inch pans

In the bowl of an electric mixer, cream together the sugar and butter. Add the eggs,
one at a time, and beat until smooth. Sift together the flour, salt, and baking powder.
Mix into the egg mixture, one cup at a time.
With the mixer running, slowly pour in the
evaporated milk, then the vanilla and water.
Mix just until incorporated.

Using a serving spoon, put 3 spoonfuls of batter into each of the ten pans,
using the back of the spoon to spread evenly. (Note: The layers cook so
quickly, I did this by rotating three pans.) Bake three layers at a time on the
middle rack of the oven for 8 minutes. You'll know a layer is done when
you hold it near your ear and you don't hear it sizzle.

Start making the icing when the first layers go in the oven. Put the cake together as the layers are finished. Let the layers cool a couple of minutes in
the pans. Run a spatula around the edge of the pan and ease the layer out of
the pan. Don't worry if it tears; no one will notice when the cake is finished. Use 2 or 3 spoonfuls of icing between each layer. Cover the top and
sides of the cake with the rest of the icing. Push the icing that runs onto the
plate back onto the cake.

CHOCOLATE ICING
2 cups sugar
1 cup evaporated milk
5 ounces unsweetened
  baking chocolate
½ cup (1 stick) unsalted
  butter
½ to 1 teaspoon vanilla
  extract

Put the sugar and evaporated milk in a
medium pan. Cook and stir over medium-
low heat until warm. Add the chocolate and
cook to melt. Add the butter and let it melt.
Cook over medium heat at a slow boil for
10 to 15 minutes. Stir occasionally. Add the
vanilla. The icing will be thin, but will thicken
as it cools.

✳ WILD RICE STUFFING

This is my son's favorite part of Thanksgiving. I usually double or triple the recipe so he has enough for days of leftovers.

Makes 8 servings

PART I

1½ cups uncooked wild rice	Place the rice in a colander and wash well under cold running water. Drain well.
1 cup finely minced onion	
½ cup (1 stick) butter	
1 tablespoon finely chopped parsley	In a large saucepan, cook the onions in the butter, stirring until wilted. Add the parsley and rice. Continue stirring and cooking for about 5 minutes, then add the broth and season with salt and pepper. Bring to a boil, cover, and simmer until the rice is tender, 30 to 40 minutes.
4 cups chicken broth	
Salt and freshly ground pepper, to taste	

PART II

¼ cup (½ stick) butter	Heat the butter in a large skillet. Add the celery and leaves and sliced mushrooms. Cook until soft.
1 cup diced celery and leaves	
1 cup thickly sliced mushrooms	
Cooked wild rice	Combine the cooked wild rice, celery and mushroom mixture, thyme, and almonds. Season to taste.
½ teaspoon thyme	
1 cup slivered almonds, sautéed in butter until lightly browned	
Salt and pepper, to taste	

Stuff inside the bird and/or place in a buttered casserole and bake, covered, at 350°F for 35 to 40 minutes. Remove the cover, baste with the turkey juices, and bake for another 15 minutes.

VEGETARIAN TIMES

※　※　※

*My hearse will be followed not by mourning coaches but by herds
of oxen, sheep, swine, flocks of poultry and a small traveling
aquarium of live fish, all wearing white scarves in honor of the man who
perished rather than eat his fellow creatures.*

GEORGE BERNARD SHAW

I N THE late 1980s, every third grader in America was intent on
preventing deforestation in Brazil. "Mommy, we must save the
rain forest," they would say at the dinner table. Their passion led
naturally to other weighty concerns about saving the planet.

I thought this was a good thing. But by the time my son was fifteen, his consciousness had evolved to the point where he found it
immoral to eat meat. We then faced the dinner dilemma of how to
feed two carnivores and a growing boy whose favorite vegetable
was the olive. We had traveled to unknown territory.

Apparently, I was lucky. When my son told me he was going
vegetarian he softened it by saying, "Don't worry Mom, I'm not
a vegan." Vegans eat no animal products or by-products. That
means no milk, no cheese, no eggs. Imagine my relief.

Of course, we should have been prepared. Lisa, Bart's sister
on *The Simpsons,* had already become a vegetarian, and American teenagers were increasingly abandoning their Big Macs and
Chicken McNuggets. Explanations varied: ethics, health, religion,
environment, animal rights, coolness, political correctness. They
tended to suppress another really good reason. It drove their parents crazy.

There are vegetarian rock bands and vegetarian celebrities. If

Madonna and Bruce Springsteen are going meatless, why shouldn't your teenage daughter or son be a vegetarian? If this doesn't impress some parents, teens can also mention that Socrates, Leonardo da Vinci, Benjamin Franklin, Albert Einstein, and Clara Barton were vegetarians.

There are many compelling arguments to be made for not eating meat. I thought about it in the 1970s while I walked around in earth shoes, ate granola, and proudly reminded people that Bob Dylan was from Minnesota. Along with 3 million other people, I read Frances Moore Lappe's *Diet for a Small Planet*. I learned that eating has social, environmental, and political consequences. I believed it all, but in the end tofu-nut loaf didn't seem a good trade for a hamburger. Then I got married and went through a meat-intensive decade or so. In the 1990s, I went to work for the U.S. Department of Agriculture. There I learned about the evils of fat, the dangers of pesticides, food tainted with *E. coli*, diseased chickens, and mad cows.

So when my son became a vegetarian, I was sympathetic. I think we should eat more bulgur. I seek out the eggs of the free-range chicken. I can see the inner beauty of a gnarled heirloom tomato.

It also was a lot easier to cook vegetarian than it was in my granola days. Some of the vegetarian evolution began in Ithaca, New York. The Moosewood Restaurant there grew from a small natural foods eatery into a big company with consulting services, T-shirts, salad dressings, and cookbooks. The first *Moosewood Cookbook* became one of the bestselling cookbooks of all time, introducing the world to sophisticated health food. The recipes were easy and good. You could now be politically correct without suffering. Other good vegetarian cookbooks followed, and in 1998, *Vegetarian Cooking for Everyone,* by Deborah Madison, won all the best-cookbook awards. Cooks began to take its message to heart: You don't have to be a vegetarian to eat like one.

I knew things had changed when a friend told me about going

to a fancy vegetarian wedding. The menu included: heirloom tomato and brioche salad with baby arugula, olio agrumato, and Pecorino panna cotta; slow-cooked romano beans with roasted baby beets, pearl couscous, Lucques olives, Marcona almonds, and sherry brown butter; tagine of chickpeas, shelling peas, cavolo nero, and new red and sweet potatoes. I recognize only every other word.

Ingredients for meat-free meals are now easily available. The tofu, bulk grains, and organic vegetables once only available in health food stores are now at Safeway. You can buy frozen vegetarian entrées and get a tofurkey for Thanksgiving. There are more Whole Foods stores than blades of organic grass. There's been universal buy-in: A plant-based diet is a healthy diet.

Here's the rub. The typical American teenager does not like whole grains or vegetables. When he gave up meat, my son would not eat any food that had ever touched tomatoes, spinach, or eggplant. He used to rule out peas, mushrooms, and zucchini, but got to a point where he said, "I can live with them in small quantities." Which meant he accepted them in a dish and then picked them out.

Sure, dark leafy greens are full of calcium. He wouldn't eat dark leafy greens. There's a lot of iron in blackstrap molasses. Right. "Yucky" kidney beans are a great source of zinc. "Gross" veggie burgers provide vitamin B_{12}.

For my son, this left the white diet—cheese, pasta, bread, ice cream, eggs, butter, and potatoes. To him, mac 'n' cheese was a balanced meal.

I tried to explain the needs of the growing body to him. I mentioned that protein, iron, calcium, and the other vitamins and minerals he needed were not available in a diet of pizza, nachos, and Coke. I was reminded, once again, that I know nothing. I took him to a nutritionist. It turned out she didn't know anything, either.

I was not upset that he was a vegetarian. I was upset that he would stop growing, compromise his immune system, and lose his teeth.

So I resorted to stealth feeding. I put little bags of cut-up watermelon (iron source) in the refrigerator on the assumption that if you make it easy enough, they'll eat it. I bought a lifetime supply of hummus to go with the carrots and celery, cut up in their own separate baggies. I did enough research for a dissertation on tasty bean dishes to bring some protein in under the radar. I slipped vegetables into stir-fries. I discovered that nuts contain not only protein but calcium as well, so I filled jars with almonds and peanuts. I pushed unbuttered, fiber-rich popcorn as a snack. I replaced ice cream with frozen fruit-juice bars (no sugar added). Tofu became my friend.

Finally, my husband invented two black bean dishes that our son actually liked. I came up with some black-eyed pea cakes that passed the test. Big chef salads with cheese, chickpeas, avocado, and preapproved vegetables were allowed. Sesame noodles (with a little broccoli) were a hit. I devised a pizza using whole-wheat pita bread, mozzarella, marinated artichoke hearts, onion, and peppers, which, with a small tossed salad, was an acceptable meal. I somehow managed four years' worth of meals without breaking the skin of a single tomato.

Then, on his first day of college, when his feeding was no longer my responsibility, when I couldn't even see what he was eating, my son started eating meat again. He said the cafeteria food was "disgusting" and he felt he wasn't getting enough protein. So he came full circle. We would take him to restaurants when we visited. He would always order the side of beef with bacon on top, pizza with sausage and pepperoni, a pork roast with a side of chicken. He still, however, will not eat a tomato.

❋ BLACK BEAN AND CORN CHILI

My husband came up with this vegetarian chili and our son liked it. I think the corn bread top was a big attraction.

Makes 6 to 8 servings

2 tablespoons vegetable oil
1 medium onion, chopped
1 bell pepper (any color),
  chopped
2 cloves garlic, minced
1 tablespoon ground cumin
2 teaspoons dried oregano
2 bay leaves
1 (4-ounce) can chopped
  mild green chilies
3 (15-ounce) cans black
  beans, drained and rinsed
1 cup vegetable broth
2 cups fresh, frozen, or
  canned corn kernels,
  drained
Salt and pepper, to taste
¼ cup fresh cilantro,
  chopped
Box (8½ ounces) of corn
  bread mix

Heat the oil in a large saucepan. Add the onion, pepper, and garlic and cook over medium-low heat, stirring occasionally, until the vegetables wilt, about 5 minutes. Add the cumin, oregano, bay leaves, and chilies and mix. Cook for 1 to 2 minutes. Add the black beans and broth and simmer for 20 minutes. Add the corn and cook for 10 minutes more. Season with salt and pepper. Pour the chili into an ovenproof casserole. Sprinkle with the cilantro.

Preheat the oven to 400°F.

Follow the directions on the corn bread package. Spread the batter over the chili and bake until the corn bread is cooked and golden brown, approximately 20 to 25 minutes.

VIVA MEXICO

✳︎ ✳︎ ✳︎

[Mexican food is] . . . earthy food, festive food,
happy food, celebration food.
CRAIG CLAIBORNE

I T TOOK a long time for gringos to see beyond the combination
platter. "Mexican food" was a taco, enchilada, tamale, and a side
of refried beans. We dismissed it as fast, greasy, undistinguished
food. Ay carumba, were we wrong.

Mexico is eight times the size of Great Britain, so it shouldn't
come as a huge surprise that its cooking traditions go beyond the
enchilada. This complex cuisine has ancient roots and reflects influences of the Aztecs and Mayans as well as the Spanish and
French. It's all more interesting than the boiled suppers we inher-
ited from New England.

The long border Mexico shares with California, Arizona, New
Mexico, and Texas has resulted in what is often generically called
Tex-Mex food and what many in the United States think of as
"Mexican food." For much of the last half century, that was about
all that was available in much of the United States. There were real
Mexican restaurants near the border, but few farther north.

Then food became fast. Handheld items such as tacos and burritos were naturals. The fast-food gods clearly saw the possibilities.
Glen Bell opened Bell's Drive-in (Taco Bell's precursor) about the
same time Dick and Mac McDonald opened their hamburger
stand in the same town of San Bernardino, California. Ronald Mc-
Donald and the talking Chihuahua were not far behind.

My avant-garde parents brought the inspiration to cook Mexican home with them from a trip to Acapulco and Mexico City. Be-

fore they left Mexico, they sent postcards of Diego Rivera murals
to their friends in Minneapolis inviting them to a Mexican dinner
party. In the 1950s, no one in Minnesota ate Mexican food since it
was not from Scandinavia. There was, however, a small Mexican
community in West St. Paul. My mother found a restaurant there
and bought bollitos (hard-crusted Mexican rolls) to serve with the
Mexican dishes from the Spanish-English cookbook she brought
home from Mexico. They hired music students from the University of Minnesota as mariachi players. It was such a success, they
had the same party two weeks later.

I didn't taste Mexican food that night or for many years after,
but my subconscious entered the data that it was worth exploration. My husband grew up in Baltimore, another Mexican
food–free zone. So the first time we had real Mexican food was
in Mexico. We got to Mexico City the day the peso was devalued
and were, therefore, able to eat far beyond our graduate-student,
newspaper-reporter means. Finding ourselves rich, at least for the
day, we looked up the most expensive restaurant in the guidebook.

La Hacienda de los Morales is a grand colonial sixteenth-
century hacienda with a beautiful garden and courtyard. We felt
like we'd wandered onto a movie set. We knew Mexicans ate late,
so we went at 8:30. The restaurant was empty. It remained empty
while we were eating our pork cooked in clay, whole fish covered
in pickled onions and peppers, and a corn fungus (also called corn
smut) considered a pest in the United States and a truffle in Mexico. At 10, people finally started arriving. Suddenly, everyone stood
up. The Mexican president had come for dinner. We figured that
meant we were eating real Mexican food.

The next day we went to the other side of town and the culinary spectrum. We were the only Anglos in a Yucatecan restaurant
in a poor part of the city. We had a memorable meal—spicy pickled carrots, chicken wrapped in banana leaves and cooked in an
underground charcoal pit, foods flavored with sour orange and
achiote, a paste made from ground annatto seeds. This is the food
of the Yucatán, of Cancún, the jungles, and the Mayans.

We discovered that while regional cuisines differ, they are all built on one foundation: corn. In addition to corn, we have the Mexicans to thank for beans, chilies, tomatoes, avocados, squash, vanilla, chocolate, and turkeys. Quite a contribution.

We returned from that first trip hooked on both Mexico and its food. As soon as we got back to New Jersey, I bought *Cuisines of Mexico* by Diana Kennedy, the high priestess of Mexican cooking. I decided to make pollo pibil, chicken cooked in a banana leaf. No banana leaves at the A&P. We had tickets to the Metropolitan Opera, so I figured we could go to East Harlem to La Marqueta del Barrio. Okay, my geography's not so good. We did get the banana leaves and still made the opening curtain of *La Bohème* on the other side of town. The only other elusive ingredient was Seville orange juice but Mrs. Kennedy said white vinegar would work. The bitter oranges are still hard to find, but banana leaves are available in Latino markets everywhere.

In the years since that first trip, we've been to Mexico many times. We've had Yucatecan food in Merida, Cozumel, and the Mayan ruins at Uxmal. We've eaten molé in Oaxaca and the many corn-based dishes of Michoacan. I had my first taste of raw fish not at a sushi bar but on a Mexican beach. In ceviche, the raw fish is actually "cooked" by lime juice.

Then we moved to Texas and had a lot of good and bad Tex-Mex and real-Mex food. There were plenty of processed-cheese nachos and bad margaritas advertised for "hungry hombres," but there were more authentic experiences, too. We ate wonderful Mexican-style breakfasts of migas—eggs scrambled with tortilla, diced onions, chilies, tomatoes, and cheese—or simple breakfast tacos filled with eggs, potatoes, and beans. We found a woman in the barrio of North Bryan who sold homemade tamales that we bought for New Year's Eve. On trips to San Antonio we ate queso fundido, Mexican cheese fondue with spicy chorizo, and cilantro cream enchiladas in cantinas with strolling mariachi players. In fancier restaurants we enjoyed pork tenderloin marinated in Mexican spices and ceviche made with yellowfin tuna.

By the time we moved to Washington, D.C., we would use any excuse for a Mexican meal. Pretexts are not hard to find. Fiestas are an essential part of Mexican culture and food is an essential part of the fiesta. So when I was in Mexico one October and saw sugar skulls for sale my first thought, like my parents before me, was . . . party time.

Every November 1 and 2, Mexicans celebrate death. On El Dia de los Muertos (Day of the Dead), Mexicans visit dead relatives and friends in the cemetery and welcome them back to their homes with feasts, flowers, candles, elaborate altars, and *pan de muerto* ("bread of the dead"), decorated with sugar bones. By mid-October, Mexican shops are filled with skull-shaped candy, intricately cutout tissue paper banners, papier-mâché and clay skeletons. I cleaned up. Instead of invitations featuring Diego Rivera murals, I sent postcards of dancing skeletons. I filled clay pots with colorful Mexican paper flowers, used the tissue paper cutouts as place mats, and put small clay skulls at each place. Dinner was molé poblano de guajolote (turkey molé), a traditional Mexican celebration food and Mexico's national dish.

When I first heard about molé I was skeptical. A sauce of peppers, spices, seeds, garlic, onions, almonds, and chocolate? Served over turkey? But it works. Think of it as a Mexican curry. Molé—which roughly translates as "a pepper concoction"—is a rough, velvety brownish-reddish mixture made of at least fifteen ingredients that all, somehow, come together to form a delicious, earthy sauce. The little bit of chocolate blends nicely with the spicy, nutty, fiery tastes of the other ingredients and adds richness.

There are a number of stories about the origins of molé poblano. The one I like best gives credit to the Dominican nuns at the convent of Santa Rosa in Puebla in the 1600s. The nuns were told at the last minute to prepare something for a visiting viceroy. So they threw the chilies and chocolate of Mexico in with the almonds and spices of Spain and served it over turkey, also native to Mexico.

While each region of Mexico has its own chili-based sauces, the molé capital of contemporary Mexico is Oaxaca. This far southern state with a huge indigenous population is called the land of seven molés for its versions that come in greens, yellows, and black.

A molé recipe can either be complicated or *very* complicated. It's a special sauce served on special occasions—fiesta food. Molés are Mexico—a dash of Spain, a pinch of France, and a healthy dose of Aztec and Mayan. It is a food emblematic of the country and its people.

Mexico is a poor country with a rich history and a hopeful heart. I once traveled by train through the Mexican countryside and saw people living in cast-off railroad cars. Outside each one were coffee cans planted with bright flowers. This undaunted spirit comes out at Mexico's fiestas, in village squares, colorful textiles, and certainly in the country's gastronomy. The food varies somewhat by region, but it's all Mexican—a cuisine that goes far beyond the combo plate.

✳ CEVICHE

Raw fish cooked in lime juice is a refreshing first course for any Mexican meal. I use bay scallops if I can get them since you don't even have to cut them up. Add or subtract ingredients to taste. Ceviche is made differently everywhere.

Makes 4 servings

1¼ pounds bay scallops or sea scallops cut into ½-inch pieces
Lime juice, to cover
2 pickled jalapeños
½ cup green olives stuffed with pimientos
1 small avocado, diced
2 shallots
¼ cup cilantro leaves, optional

In a nonreactive bowl, cover the scallops with lime juice. Refrigerate for 4 to 5 hours for well-done fish, 1 to 2 if you like it rawer. Stir occasionally. Pour off half the juice. Mix the ceviche with the rest of the ingredients. Serve in individual bowls sprinkled with cilantro if you like.

✳ MOLÉ POBLANO DE GUAJOLOTE (TURKEY MOLÉ)

I make this in a Rumertopf—a clay cooker that approximates a *cazuela,* the large earthenware pot used to make molé in Mexico. Much Mexican cooking is done in clay. I use only dark meat because I like the flavor better in the molé. You can certainly mix in white meat or use all white meat if you prefer. The first three ingredients are dried chilies available in some supermarkets and at Latino markets. The *ancho,* a ripened poblano chili, is the most common. It is a deep reddish brown. Search for the others, though. It makes a difference. The *pasilla* is a long, slender chili about 6 inches long. In some places it is called a *negro* chili. The *mulatto* looks a lot like the ancho but is tougher, less wrinkled, a little bigger, and has a sweeter taste.

Makes 8 to 10 servings

6 ancho chilies
5 pasilla chilies
8 mulatto chilies
¼ cup sesame seeds, toasted
½ teaspoon anise seeds, toasted
1 cup blanched almonds, toasted
½ teaspoon ground cloves
½ teaspoon ground cinnamon
½ teaspoon coriander
1 teaspoon Mexican oregano
1 teaspoon cumin

Remove the veins, stems, and seeds from the chilies and tear them roughly into 1- to 2-inch pieces. Place in a bowl and pour boiling water over them to cover. Soak for an hour. Drain, saving ½ cup of the soaking liquid. When they are cool enough to handle, put the chilies and the soaking liquid into a food processor with the sesame seeds, anise seeds, almonds, ground cloves, cinnamon, coriander, oregano, and cumin. Process into a chunky puree.

3 tablespoons lard (or canola oil)
1½ squares (1½ ounces) unsweetened chocolate
½ cup raisins

Heat the lard (or oil) in a medium saucepan and sauté the chili puree over medium heat for about 10 minutes, stirring constantly. Set aside to cool. When cool, mix in the chocolate and raisins.

6 pounds turkey thighs and
  drumsticks
1 pound (about 3 medium)
  tomatoes, chopped, about
  2½ cups
1 large onion, chopped
  (about 2 cups)
4 cloves garlic, minced
1 cup chicken broth
Salt
Freshly ground black
  pepper

Meanwhile, soak the top and bottom of a clay cooker, large enough to hold the turkey, in water to cover for 30 minutes. Drain.

In a food processor, chop together the tomatoes, onion, and garlic. Mix with the chicken broth.

Alternate layers of turkey pieces and chili mixture in the clay pot. Pour the tomato mixture over the top. Salt well, and add freshly ground pepper, to taste.

Place the pot in a cold oven. Turn the temperature to 425°F. Cook for about 3 hours or until the turkey is almost coming off the bone. Stir after 1 hour. Serve with rice.

PLAIN AND SIMPLE

✳   ✳   ✳

Take all you want, eat all you take.
AMISH SAYING

Y ou're feeling overwhelmed by the twenty-first century—too
many meetings, late nights, unreasonable bosses, demanding
clients, crying children. You'd like to check into a spa in the desert
and have someone put hot rocks on your back and massage your
feet. You need to get away from it all. Of course, you don't have
the time.

The solution? The Amish.

A few hours at an Amish market can give you the will to go on.
It is a trip to another time and another place that doesn't involve
standing in airport security lines or using up vacation days.

It took me fifteen years in Washington, D.C., to figure this out.
Don't wait that long. There are Amish communities in twenty-two
states (the largest are in Ohio and Pennsylvania) and they may
have markets near you.

The Amish markets of Maryland are close enough to Washington, D.C., for all the overworked, stressed-out, type-As to get a
quick hit of tranquillity. You couldn't be farther from the worst of
Washington if you were on Mars.

Every Thursday, Friday, and Saturday at 4:00 A.M. Amish and
Mennonite men and women leave the fertile fields of Lancaster
County, Pennsylvania, and climb into vans operated by "English," hired, non-Amish drivers who take them south. Because
the Amish eschew modern technology, they drive only horses

and buggies. They go home each night and come back the next day.

The Maryland markets stand empty the rest of the week, but for those three days they're filled with what the Amish call "wonderful good" products. There is garden-fresh produce, picture-perfect meats, seven varieties of sausage, succulent pork chops filled with bread stuffing, Lebanon bologna (a smoky dry sausage), liverwurst, dried chipped beef, and all kinds of jerky. Each market has a large area with commercial ovens, where much of the baking is done. Sweet and savory breads are piled next to fresh-baked pies, cakes, cookies, gooey sticky buns, and typical Pennsylvania Dutch treasures such as shoofly pie made with molasses and brown sugar. You could wrap yourself up in the warm smells that come from these ovens.

"Many people come here to unwind, to experience a different world, a different time," Aaron Beiler at the Annapolis market told Nancy and me when we took a tour of the nearby Amish markets.

People also come because of the freshness and quality of the products for sale. The produce, meats, poultry, baked goods, and canned goods all look like they were hired from a central casting for food. The chickens are plump and yellow, the meat is red and juicy, the carrots look like they've just been pulled from the garden. Probably because they have.

The Amish have been practicing sustainable agriculture since long before the phrase was invented. That is, they farm in a way that protects the environment, supports the community, and respects all persons and animals involved in raising food. You don't have to ask an Amish poultry farmer if his chickens are crowded into tiny cages.

The Amish firmly believe in waste not. Food is a gift not to be squandered, so they use every edible piece of meat. Their display cases hold souse (pickled pigs' feet), head cheese (sausage made from all the bits of meat off the head of a calf or pig, combined with a gelatinous meat broth and cooked in a mold), and the famous Pennsylvania Dutch scrapple. While large scraps of pork are made into sausage, the smallest bits are ground up and mixed with cornmeal, formed into a loaf, cut into slices, fried, and eaten for breakfast. Scrapple. Quite onomatopoeic.

Because their gardens and fields produce more than a family eats in season, a lot of canned goods and preserves come to market. These include jams, jellies, fruit butters, and fruits and vegetables. Big Bell jars filled with "yummy pickle" (sliced pickled cucumber topped with pickled cauliflower and carrots) and whole peaches fill the shelves. It looks like a grandmother's cellar. At the end of their canning, Amish women gather the leftover vegetables, cook them, and preserve them in a sweet-and-sour syrup to make their best-known relish—chow-chow.

The market "delis" sell potato salad, pepper cabbage, bread pudding, deviled eggs, cranberry relish, red beet eggs (hard-boiled eggs soaked in beet juice), and dried lima beans cooked in a brown sugar syrup with bits of ham. At one market, we met a woman who bakes twenty loaves of bread a day at home for the sandwiches she and her husband sell at the market.

The Amish value a life that is plain and simple. As they read it, the Bible tells them to live separate from the world. This can mean a life without electricity, telephones, or cars, and farming that relies on horses, not machinery. They dress, too, according to their interpretation of Scripture. Their clothing is plain and unadorned. Amish women wear modest, solid-colored, long-sleeved, long-hemmed dresses. Men wear deep-hued shirts, wide-brimmed straw or black hats, suspenders, and pants closed with buttons.

These people stick to their standards but accept some modernization. Aaron uses the phone and fax machine at the Annapolis market and is very interested in the Internet. But he has no misgivings about his commitment to the Amish traditions. "I like my life," he says. "We have no crime, no divorce. We don't worry about our children getting hurt." No wonder we find it comforting to visit this world.

Food, naturally, is an important part of a daily life in which families sit down together for meals and gather with their community for big events such as barn raisings and weddings. All the Amish we met at the markets talked about the wedding spreads. Weddings are held in the fall after the harvest and are the biggest feast days of the year. After the ceremony, four hundred or so people go to the bride's house for a midday dinner of "roast" (roast chicken with bread stuffing), mashed potatoes, creamed celery, bread and butter, tapioca pudding, and cherry pie. An evening supper is usually stewed chicken, macaroni and cheese, cold cuts. You cannot eat like this and then go back to your computer. If you're invited to an Amish wedding and are not going to set up for and clean up after four hundred guests, milk a barn full of cows, and help with the haying until sunset, show restraint.

Not that restraint is hard to demonstrate in some instances. At one market, Melvin Lapp told us that after church in his community it is common to have schnitz (dried apple) pie and bread with cheese spread or "church spread" made with a combination of corn syrup or molasses, peanut butter, and marshmallow cream. Okay, theirs is not a perfect world.

The Amish have developed and preserved a distinct regional cuisine. To them, however, it's just plain cooking for a plain lifestyle, hearty and filling food that supports the physical labor of people who rely on what they can grow for their daily meals.

The markets we visited all have restaurants serving Amish home-style fare. For breakfast, you can get eggs with scrapple and cornmeal mush (available only in the colder months) or creamed chipped beef on toast, followed by a hot apple dumpling with whipped cream, ice cream, or milk. Lunch could be homemade chicken pot pie (more like chicken and dumplings), grilled liver, and onions or sausages with mashed potatoes and sauerkraut.

Most cooking, they say, is done "by feel." Recipes are passed from mother to daughter orally or in handwritten notes.

I have to be honest. I don't do much Amish cooking. It's pretty heavy food for someone who lifts a bale of paper rather than hay. If I followed their diet I'd be as big as an Amish barn. Going to the markets, however, is a wonderful break from postmodern reality, and I love to pick up jars of apple butter, a container of chicken pot pie, a cheesy bread, and some of those beautiful meats to take home.

The appeal of the Amish approach to food and life was evident in the national media coverage of the death of Elizabeth Coblentz, a sixty-six-year-old Amish homemaker who chronicled the order's cooking traditions in a syndicated column read weekly by two million people in one hundred newspapers for more than a decade. She wrote in longhand by the light of a kerosene lamp. In addition to recipes and cooking, Mrs. Coblentz wrote about cornhusking bees, barn raisings, and life with her eight children and thirty-two grandchildren. "She was a calm voice in a chaotic world," her editor said after her death.

The Amish markets draw people of all ages, colors, and socioeconomic groups. They are not the trendy shoppers who go to hip urban markets carrying handwoven African baskets into which to put their artisanal goat cheese. They come, and come back again and again, because of the high-quality fresh food and the friendly, gentle people.

Walking out of our last market into a suburban parking lot with a dollar store, nail salon, and several chain restaurants, Nancy and I got into the car, put on our seat belts, and at that moment our cell phones rang simultaneously. Out of the calm, back to the chaos.

✳ VERNA'S WATERMELON PICKLES

Gayle's mother, Verna, grew up in a German community in North Dakota, where she learned to make many typical country dishes similar to those made in Amish homes. Gayle remembers fondly her mother's *kase knepfla* (dry curd cheese mixed with onion and egg yolks wrapped in dough, boiled, then fried) and *blatchinda* (pumpkin or apple pastry) as well as these pickled watermelon rinds.

Makes 1 quart

3 cups watermelon rinds (white part only with a bit of pink)
1 tablespoon Kosher salt
1 teaspoon mixed pickling spices
½ clove garlic
6 sprigs dill

Place one dill flower in the jar and then fill the jar with the rinds. Add the salt, pickling spices, garlic, and dill. Fill the jar with cold water. Cover and shake. Leave jar unrefrigerated for 4 to 5 days.

NOTE: She uses the same recipe for yellow wax beans she has parboiled. They're ready after 3 days.

EATING CHINESE

✳ ✳ ✳

Our lives are not in the lap of the gods, but in the lap of our cooks.
LIN YUTANG

BEFORE THERE was kung pao chicken or tea-smoked duck, there was Chinese. Not Hunan, Szechuan, or Fujian. Just Chinese. As in, "Do you want to go out for Chinese?"

This was before people went to restaurants nine times a week. When they did leave home, they often went out for Chinese at the neighborhood restaurant with the pagoda-shaped roof, paper lanterns, and Asian paintings. They chose one from column A and two from column B.

The meal probably started with spareribs, egg rolls, and wonton soup and ended with orange sherbet and fortune cookies. In between were chop suey, chow mein, egg foo yong, sweet-and-sour pork, and shrimp with lobster sauce.

In a meat-and-potatoes culture, it was our introduction to exotic foreign food. It also was as American as apple pie.

In the late 1800s, large numbers of Chinese laborers came to North America to work on the transcontinental railroads. Discrimination and prejudice kept many of them from good jobs. So they became tailors and laundrymen and cooks.

At first, they cooked only for other Chinese workers. As they had in China, they used all parts of the animal in cooking. When curious North Americans showed up to eat, the Chinese cooks knew the outlanders wouldn't be interested in dishes made with chicken feet, duck blood, pig's kidney, or marinated pig intestine. So they made adjustments. They made the exotic approachable.

They made chop suey.

While it is usually thought of as an American invention, there are several conflicting stories. One goes that a Chinese cook in California, asked to prepare food at an unreasonable hour, threw together whatever he could find and called it chop suey, based on a Chinese word for "leftovers." Another holds that a Chinese ambassador, arriving in New York in 1896, had his cooks invent something his American hosts would eat. Still others contend it is based on a dish from a rural area south of Canton, from which most of the Chinese had emigrated.

Whatever its origins, chop suey became an American dish made of bits of pork, chicken, or beef; bean sprouts; water chestnuts; bamboo shoots and celery all chopped up, simmered with a soy-based sauce, and served on rice. In other words, it can be anything you want it to be.

While they are similar, chop suey and chow mein are not the same thing. Chow mein is a noodle (mein) dish and is considered the more Chinese of the two. In China, the noodles are parboiled, then stir-fried in hot oil. In North America, the fried noodles usually come in a can. It is these crispy, canned noodles that many Americans remember so fondly when they remember their first Chinese meals.

I have vivid memories of those canned noodles on the kitchen shelf. We'd break into them and eat them as snacks. La Choy in 1920, and Chun King in 1946 started selling canned Chinese noodles, sauces, and vegetables. Americans could finally make Chinese food at home.

My friend Elizabeth was a foreign correspondent in Cambodia during the Vietnam War. But her first introduction to Asian food was when she was growing up in Dennison, Iowa. She says her mother did not believe in waste. "After Thanksgiving," she says, "we knew that Friday would be meatless, we'd have turkey sandwiches on Saturday, our regular Sunday dinner, and turkey chop suey Monday night."

By the early twentieth century, chow mein and chop suey

started showing up in American cookbooks. The 1930 edition of
the early-twentieth-century classic *The Settlement Cookbook* has a
recipe for chop suey using "Chinese sauce." It is served with "Chinese rice," a cup of rice cooked with water. In other words, plain
white rice. There is another recipe for "chicken chop suey for fifteen people," using chicken, veal, and pork. The recipe for Chinese
noodles (chow mein) looks more traditional than later versions. It
calls for water chestnuts (which had to be peeled) and fried, freshly
made noodles. The 1950 edition uses a can of fried noodles. The
1962 edition of *The Joy of Cooking* includes a recipe for "chop suey
or chow mein" and is accompanied by these comments:

> *These vaguely Chinese dishes, which can be made with cooked
> pork, chicken, or seafood, differ in that chop suey is served over
> steamed rice and chow mein over fried noodles. They resemble some
> Chinese porcelain patterns originally made strictly for export. To
> get the feeling of true Chinese food, read Mrs. Buwei Yang Chao's
> delightful* How to Cook and Eat in Chinese.

This book, now out of print, was written in the 1940s by a Chinese woman doctor in imperfect English. She adapted Chinese
home cooking for American cooks. It is a classic cookbook. In her
preface to the book, Pearl Buck writes:

> *As a Chinese, she knows exactly what Americans don't know. It is
> worth this book's weight in gold and diamonds if American
> women will learn how to cook vegetables as the Chinese cook
> them, quickly and lightly, without water and waste. It is worth
> jade and rubies if they will abandon the horrid American custom
> of putting cooked rice under the cold water faucet and washing
> out all its flavor. It is of inestimable value to the war effort and
> also to the economy of peace if they will learn to use meat for its
> taste in a dish of something else, instead of using it chiefly for its
> substance.*

My mother's favorite cookbook, *The New Antoinette Pope School Cookbook,* came out just after World War II with a whole section on Cantonese cooking. (Oddly, this section includes a recipe for the Japanese dish sukiyaki.) Many soldiers came back from the war in the Pacific with experience in Asian cuisine. Eating Chinese had become an American enthusiasm.

My mother remembers going to the Nankin Café in Minneapolis when she was a little girl in the 1920s. The Nankin was still serving chicken chow mein and egg foo yong when I was growing up thirty years later. I remember aquariums filled with goldfish and colorful paper lanterns. People still pine for the Nankin's chow mein.

While I was eating at the Nankin in the 1950s, my friend Irene was chasing after the Chow-Chow Cup truck on Long Island. It was like an ice cream truck that sold Chinese food, but its musical bells played an Asian-style melody rather than the Good Humor man theme. The Chow-Chow Cup sold hot, greasy egg rolls and chicken chow mein in a bowl made of Chinese noodles.

My mother's best friend in Minneapolis was from New York and took her family to John's Place with its huge lacquered tables topped with marble because she thought it was more authentic. John was Chinese and had Chinese waiters. The Nankin, on the other hand, was owned by Jews.

Which makes sense. Chinese food became a second cuisine for American Jews. Scholars have tried to figure out why, but it remains a mystery. Sunday night was Chinese, unusual for a religion with taboos against shellfish and pork.

My husband's grandmother was raised in a Reformed Jewish orphanage but kept a kosher home for her husband. Every now and then, she'd get a hankering for lobster Cantonese, call a cab, and go to Jimmy Woo's in downtown Baltimore. I had my first post-Nankin experience at Jimmy Woo's—young chow wonton soup, a big bowl of soup with noodles, chicken, leeks, shrimp, and dumplings. The scales fell from my eyes.

Not long after that meal, my husband and I took a three-week camping trip through western Canada. Every town we went through had a Chinese restaurant. Moose Jaw, Saskatchewan, founded as an Indian fur traders camp, had a Chinese restaurant. We stayed in Calgary, Alberta, a big city with a Wild West ambience in the foothills of the Rocky Mountains and had a transcendent culinary moment at a restaurant called the Silver Dragon. We were the only Caucasians in a room filled with Chinese families. No one spoke much English, so we pointed to the things we wanted as they passed by. We got four or five dishes and began to understand that we knew nothing about Chinese food.

China, it turns out, is a very big country. We only knew about the food of Canton, and we didn't know much about that. An exquisite cuisine, real Cantonese food was rare in early Chinese-American restaurants. American eaters began to see the big picture after immigration laws were loosened and new Chinese immigrants and new food arrived. Then Nixon went to China 1972, and everyone wanted "authentic" Chinese food.

Hunan and Szechuan restaurants opened in New York and California and the rest of the country followed. We began to order General Tso's chicken and crispy orange beef. No more chop suey. No more chow mein. But I did hang on to my mother's recipe for egg foo yong.

※ FERN'S EGG FOO YONG

I found this among my mother's recipes. We tried it and liked it. It's like a Chinese-style frittata.

Makes 4 servings

FOR THE PANCAKES
1 cup cooked meat or
   chicken

Mix all the ingredients together except the oil. Heat the oil in a large skillet and fry the

½ cup water chestnuts
1 cup bean sprouts
¼ cup chopped onions
¾ cup thinly sliced celery
6 large eggs
2 tablespoons soy sauce
Cooking oil

mixture on both sides until browned. Keep warm.

FOR THE SAUCE
1 tablespoon cornstarch
2 teaspoons cold water
1 cup chicken stock
2 tablespoons soy sauce

Mix the cornstarch and water in a saucepan. Add the chicken stock and soy sauce and cook until clear and thickened. Pour over the warm pancakes.

IT'S BAWLMER, HON

✻ ✻ ✻

Baltimore [is] where the art of cooking crabs reaches its highest perfection.
H. L. MENCKEN

THE SPACE shuttle should visit planet Baltimore (called Bawlmer by its inhabitants). This city's eccentric character and remarkable food traditions are unknown elsewhere in the solar system.

Baltimore's crab customs alone are worth anthropological study. There are rules, traditions, and accepted modes of behavior. There are strange hierarchies. There are special tools. This study would reveal an entire culture derived from Chesapeake Bay crustaceans. In this city, blue crabs from the Chesapeake Bay are a way of life.

In summer, steamed and spiced hard-shelled blue crabs provide hours of entertainment. The rest of the year, crabmeat is used in soufflés, fluffs, and dips. It is stuffed into fish and mushrooms, simmered in soup, and, most important, made into crab cakes.

My husband, a Baltimore native, remembers walking through neighborhoods of row houses in the summer and hearing the Orioles game on transistor radios coming from the tiny backyards where people would sit all Sunday afternoon cracking crabs, drinking National Bohemian beer, and listening to the game. He says he would walk for blocks and never miss a pitch.

I ate my first crab with a large group of Baltimoreans when I was in college. I was way out of my league. We went to one of the big Baltimore crab houses. These cathedrals of crab all have the same furnishings and linens—long tables covered in brown butcher paper. There are no eating utensils and piles of paper napkins. The waitress appeared and said to the person at the table who looked like the leader, "What can I getcha, hon?" "Hon" is an all-purpose greeting. "Hey, hon," in Bawlmerese means, "Hello." We ordered dozens of crabs and a pitcher of beer. This is the basic crab feast menu. If you want to get fancy, you can order coleslaw and corn on the cob. If you don't want to talk to anyone, the Orioles game is always on TV.

The waitress brought a plastic tray heaped with spicy, steamed crabs that she dumped in the middle of the table. Wooden mallets and paring knives were piled near the crabs. The group set upon the crabs, ripping them apart with their hands, and sucking the meat out with their teeth. I knew I wasn't in Kansas anymore.

I had a vague idea how to get into a lobster, but crabs are smaller and more intricate. I started beating on them with a wooden mallet. "That's how tourists eat crabs," I was told. "Just pull off the legs and claws, tear the apron off the stomach, break the shell in half and pull the meat out." After mangling a few, I finally got the hang of it. It's okay to use the little knives to get meat out of the claws and you can even use the hammers if you have an unusually hard shell. You just have to tap lightly and use sparingly. Otherwise, you will be mocked.

Eating crabs is a commitment. It's slow, labor intensive, messy, and somewhat violent. It takes a long time to get to the good part. It can also hurt. Bandage any paper cuts, scrapes, or scratches to keep the lethal crab spices from your wound. Sound horrible? I had so much fun, I married the alien who introduced me to the ways of the crab people.

We were out of crab country for a few years, but when we moved to Washington, D.C., we were back in business. In September, when the crabs are really good, there was an annual block party crab feast in the alley. We borrowed tables from a church, used newspaper end rolls as tablecloths, and got a keg of beer. There were balloons. We moved a block away and now hold backyard crab feasts throughout the summer. Large groups meet at crab houses all over Maryland to eat crabs and drink beer. Sometimes these gatherings are on the water; other times they are at shacks off the highway.

If the hard-shell crab is king of Baltimore foods, the crab cake is queen. Crab cakes are taken so seriously that there are three different kinds sold at Camden Yards, where the Orioles play baseball. One version was made to the secret specifications of owner Peter Angelos.

My friend Scott remembers his admissions interview at Johns Hopkins: "I kept trying to figure out why the admissions guy kept talking about 'drinking beer and eating crapcakes.' I didn't understand the local religion."

Everyone in Baltimore knows where to get "the best" crab cakes. And it is astonishing how many crab joints have won awards for having "the best crab cakes in Baltimore." My husband swears by Angelina's, where they have been serving crab cakes for fifty years. Angelina's is appealing not only because it makes such a good crab cake but also because it is such a cool place—an Italian restaurant over an Irish pub. How can you beat Guinness and crab cakes?

My favorite "award-winning" crab cakes are made at Faidley's Seafood, which dominates one end of downtown Baltimore's Lexington Market, the world's largest, continuously running public market. At Faidley's, top-of-the-line lump crabmeat is ever so lightly bound and gently broiled under the guidance of the aptly named Nancy Faidley Devine, whose grandfather founded the seafood market in 1886. Faidley's is surrounded by stalls selling fresh fish and regional delicacies such as marsh rabbit, aka muskrat, one of the scariest things I've ever seen.

While you can still shoot oysters at Faidley's raw bar, Maryland's robust oyster industry is a wistful memory. There was a time when oysters were so plentiful that Baltimore's streets were paved with their shells. In their backyards, people kept barrels of oysters they'd dip into throughout the winter. In the early seventeenth century, there were so many oyster beds in the Chesapeake bay the waters were hazardous to ships. Crabs were the food of summer and oysters were the sustenance of winter. Oysters are still served all over town—raw, fried, stewed—but the industry, sadly, is down to about 1 percent of its historic level.

Faidley's also may be one of the last places in Baltimore and, therefore, on earth to still sell coddies. Russian Jewish immigrants began peddling coddies in the early 1900s. Flaked codfish was mixed with mashed potatoes, crushed crackers, salt and pepper, formed into little cakes, fried and served with yellow mustard between two saltine crackers. They were available everywhere— drugstores, corner stores, bars, delis. When my mother-in-law walked home from P.S. 61 in the 1930s, she stopped at a little candy store across the street for a coddie for two cents. My husband also went to P.S. 61, but got his coddies—up to a nickel by this time—at a corner drugstore on the way home. He washed it down with Almond Smash, an amaretto-tasting soda made by a Baltimore soda company.

The Lexington Market is two stories high and fills two city blocks. It could serve as the city's culinary visitors' center. Inside at the more than one hundred stalls are examples of other Baltimore foods as well as fare representing the city's many strong ethnic groups. The politically incorrectly named Polock Johnny's has been serving plump Polish sausages with sauerkraut and brown mustard since 1921. The 175-year-old Berger's Bakery is the home of the Berger cookie, one of the best mass-produced cookies ever made. The cakelike cookie is topped with a small mountain of fudge. You can get cavities by just looking at a Berger cookie. I saw them mentioned on a French food blog and they were referred to as "chocolate crèmes." A Baltimore reader wrote: "They're not chocolate crèmes. They're just Berger cookies." Mary Mervis Delicatessen has been in Lexington Market since 1913, Woodrow Wilson's first year in the White House. People stand in line at lunchtime for shrimp salad and brisket sandwiches.

Lexington Market also has vendors who sell Baltimore's other culinary gift—the snowball. You might think a snowball is the same as a snow cone, but you would be wrong. In a snowball, the ice is coarser and the syrup is thicker. And with a dollop of ice cream or marshmallow it is pure Baltimore summertime.

In the 1930s, my father-in-law would play tennis until midnight at the only downtown Baltimore park with lights. In those days before air-conditioning, some families slept outdoors in the parks to escape the suffocating heat and humidity that made their homes feel unbearably close. A little night air and a snowball provided relief.

After his tennis game, my father-in-law had a two-mile walk home. On his way, he now tells his grandchildren, he would stop at least twice for snowballs at makeshift stands in row house cellars. The sidewalk-level windows were open, and he could see someone's hand shaving a huge block of ice covered in a piece of cloth to keep it cold. He would order a basic snowball for two cents. For another penny you could add marshmallow and for a nickel more, ice cream.

Nowadays, the snowball season opens a few weeks after the Orioles throw out the first ball. Drugstores that still have soda fountains—a few, naturally, still exist in Baltimore—bring their snowball machines out of storage. Makeshift stands appear in parking lots and at the side of the road.

My brother-in-law Eddie goes to a place in a shopping center parking lot that's owned by the nephew of my father-in-law's barber. That's so Baltimore. Everyone knows who's related to everyone else and how. When two Baltimoreans meet, the first question is, "Where did you go to high school?" That places you in the Baltimore pantheon.

My brother-in-law Stevan goes to JT's Market and Deli in the working-class neighborhood of Hampden at least twice a week for his cherry snowball. They have the classics—cherry, chocolate, root beer, and egg custard. But they also have a new line of funky flavors like skylight (it's blue) and syrups named after superheroes and cartoon characters like Spider-Man and Sponge Bob Squarepants. Once they had Britney Spears syrup but it wasn't too popular. Anyone from Baltimore could have predicted that.

I've had snowballs with shaved ice, ice cream, and exotic fruit flavorings in Hawaii, where they put condensed milk on top. We stopped at a similar snowball stand in the mountains of North Carolina. And I hear that New Orleans has a similar concoction. But only in Baltimore is the snowball a cultural icon.

While the city's food scene is colorful and unusual it is also traditional. Things don't change much in Charm City. Baltimoreans are parochial and proud of it. Everyone's searching for the "authentic" these days. Baltimore's never lost it. So if the astronauts don't get there for another few centuries, they'll probably still be able to follow their crab cakes with a cherry snowball.

❄ CRAB CAKES

I use only lump crabmeat for crab cakes. This is the crème de la crab—big, white lumps of sweet crabmeat. I also sauté or broil but never deep fry. All these things, of course, are a matter of personal preference. I try to use as little of the binding ingredients as possible so you taste mostly crab. You have to do it by feel. After you form the cakes, put them on wax paper in a pie plate or cookie sheet and refrigerate for an hour or so; they hold their shape better when cooked. Pick over the crab carefully looking for bits of shell. Be careful not to tear apart the lumps.

Makes 4 servings

1 pound lump crabmeat
1 large egg
1 to 2 tablespoons
  mayonnaise
1 teaspoon dry yellow
  mustard
1 teaspoon Worcestershire
  sauce
Dash of Tabasco or other
  hot sauce
1 tablespoon chopped fresh
  parsley
2 tablespoons to ¼ cup fine
  dry bread crumbs
1½ tablespoon butter
1½ tablespoon olive oil

Put the crabmeat in a bowl and pick over, looking for shell.

In a small bowl, mix the egg, 1 tablespoon of the mayonnaise, mustard, Worcestershire sauce, Tabasco sauce, and parsley. Add more mayonnaise if absolutely necessary.

Sprinkle some of the bread crumbs over the crab and add the egg mixture. Use only as much of the bread crumbs as you need to bind the mixture together. Mix the ingredients gently so you don't break up the lumps of crab. If it doesn't seem firm enough, add a few more bread crumbs. Form into 4 loose patties that can hold their shape. Place on waxed paper and refrigerate for an hour or more.

In a large skillet, melt the butter and olive oil and gently sauté the patties until golden brown on each side.

INDEX

✳   ✳   ✳

Entries in small capitals indicate recipes.